Canarsie

Canarsie

The Jews
and Italians
of Brooklyn
against Liberalism

JONATHAN RIEDER

Harvard University Press • Cambridge, Massachusetts
and London, England 1985

Library of Congress Cataloging in Publication Data

Rieder, Jonathan.
    Canarsie : the Jews and Italians of Brooklyn against liberalism.

    Bibliography: p.
    Includes index.
    1. Canarsie (New York, N.Y.)—Politics and government.
2. Jews—New York (N.Y.)—Politics and government.
3. Jews—New York (N.Y.)—Attitudes.
4. Italian Americans—New York (N.Y.)—Politics and government.
5. Italian Americans—New York (N.Y.)—Attitudes.
6. New York (N.Y.)—Politics and government—1951–
7. Liberalism—New York (N.Y.)—Case studies.   I. Title.
F128.68.C36R54   1985   974.7′23   84-15660
ISBN 0-674-09360-7 (alk. paper)

Designed by Gwen Frankfeldt

For Catherine

Acknowledgments

I have accumulated many debts while working on this book. Kai Erikson watched the manuscript grow and change, often in response to his deft editorial intercessions. I am grateful as well for all his less tangible contributions. I thank David Apter, Peter Gay, Nathan Glazer, Rem Rieder, Alexander Ross, Edmund Schlain, Gladys Topkis, and R. Stephen Warner for their invaluable comments. Eric Rieder not only scrutinized the book for lapses of style and logic but also spent a day helping me haul old *Canarsie Couriers* out of a dank basement, a true test of brotherly loyalty. It gives me special pleasure that Laurence M. Levin, a good friend since seventh grade, took the fine photographs that appear in this book. William Warner stole time from his studies of literary theory to help me interview voters during the 1976 presidential election. Mendel Gurfein, a man of rare intellect, attended meetings and tracked down important data for me.

The book was in good hands at Harvard University Press. I always left my talks with William Goodman, the editor in the earliest phases of the project, with a feeling of creative renewal. Peg Anderson did a splendid job of copy editing. Michael Aronson, my editor, unfailingly provided suggestions and exhortation. Above all, he helped me find the right blend of theory and narrative.

Hundreds of Canarsians made this project possible and enjoyable. I will not compromise their privacy by naming them, except for two public figures whose generosity demands acknowledgment: Anthony Genovesi of the Thomas Jefferson Democratic Club, a district leader of the 39th Assembly District, and Alan Erlichman, who, during most of my research, was chairman of the Concerned Citizens of Canarsie. They both taught me much about Canarsie politics, aided the research in countless ways, and were good friends to me when I was in the field.

I inherited my commitment to a practical liberalism from my parents, Dolly Rieder and Rick Rieder. They read drafts of the book, forced me to refine my argument, caught mistakes of grammar. What *didn't* they do? As always, they were a boundless source of emotional and intellectual sustenance. Mainly, I thank them for being who they are.

Catherine J. Ross made this a better book in ways too numerous to list here. One measure of her heroism is that she lived with *Canarsie* during the entire period of its writing. As a confirmed West Side chauvinist, she never imagined she would come to spend so much time, at least vicariously, in the great borough of Brooklyn. I am glad she journeyed there with me. I dedicate this book to her.

Contents

Canarsie

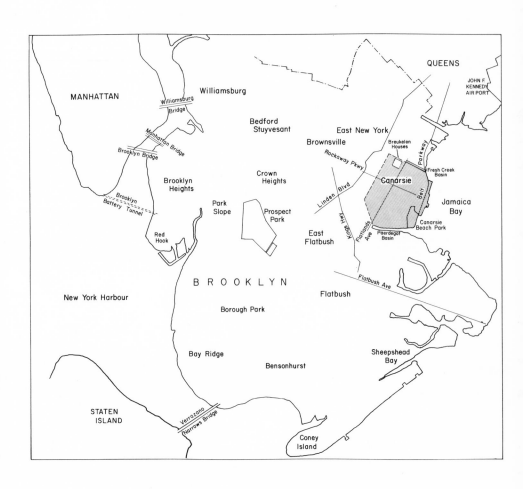

MANHATTAN

Williamsburg

Williamsburg
Bridge

Bedford
Stuyvesant

QUEENS

JOHN F
KENNEDY
AIR PORT

East New York

Brownsville

Breukelen
Houses

Manhattan Bridge

Brooklyn Bridge

Crown
Heights

Rockaway Pkwy

Parkway

Fresh Creek
Basin

Canarsie

Belt

Brooklyn
Heights

Linden Blvd

Jamaica
Bay

Brooklyn
Battery Tunnel

Park
Slope

Prospect
Park

Canarsie
Beach Park

Red
Hook

East
Flatbush

Kings Hwy

Flatlands Ave

Paerdegat
Basin

B R O O K L Y N

New York Harbour

Borough Park

Flatbush

Flatbush Ave

Bay Ridge

Bensonhurst

Sheepshead
Bay

STATEN
ISLAND

Verrazano
Narrows Bridge

Coney
Island

introduction
Danger and Dispossession

Perched along Jamaica Bay on filled marshland in a corner of southeast Brooklyn, Canarsie is a houseproud neighborhood of about 70,000 people, mainly middle-income Jews and Italians. A haven in a seamy metropolis, the community exudes an air of shabby but respectable domesticity. Two-family brick row houses line the compulsive grid of streets or, in the older Italian section, squeeze into the vacant spaces next to bungalows built earlier in the century. The residents see themselves as the plain, doughty backbone of America — cabbies and teachers, merchants and craftsmen, salesmen and police — who stoically bear their burdens, raise their families, and serve the country.

They are mostly children and grandchildren of immigrants, and some are immigrants themselves. They have come a long way from the shtetls of eastern Europe and the sultry towns of Sicily and southern Italy. But they have not traveled so far that they don't nervously glance back, just a mile or two, to the grimy ghettos of Brownsville and East New York where many of them spent their youth, ghettos that have since become hopeless reservations of the black and Hispanic poor. Like many other Americans who have struggled to attain a modestly blessed position in life, the people of Canarsie feel that America has been good to them. Yet between 1960 and 1980 it was becoming increasingly hard to sustain that faith, as ominously, inexplicably, things began to go awry. Canarsians experienced those years as a time of danger and dispossession — culturally and internationally, but especially racially. A mood of outrage and betrayal succeeded self-congratulatory optimism. Out of that discontent arose new political and cultural temptations and dangers.

That period of frantic change forced Canarsians to explain misfortune, to resolve conflicts, and to protect their interests. They had to summon all of their moral and political strength to assimilate or fend off the new realities. The sweeping away of brittle defenses permitted a glimpse into the deep structures of belief, of action, and of sentiment, which are hidden by everyday routine. What is it precisely that I was privileged to witness, beyond the vaporous generalities of change? The answer is: the travails of liberalism. This book will not delve into the structural causes of those trials, which would require another sort of analysis, but will examine the crisis as it was lived by ordinary people in Brooklyn.

In the fall of 1972, after an integration-minded school board ordered Canarsie to take into its schools a few dozen black children from Brownsville, the residents moved quickly to secure the borders and repulse the strangers. A white boycott of the schools kept ten thousand children from their lessons for a week. A few housewives, liberated for the moment from the bonds of domesticity, lobbed rocks at school buses. Marchers raised banners that read, "Canarsie Schools for Canarsie Children."

Pointing to the unsavory acts of a few protesters, some pundit coined the epithet "Canarsieism," staining the community with the memory of a brawling avenger, Senator Joe McCarthy. In its editorials the *New York Times* concluded, "The shameful situation in Canarsie illustrates the forces of unreason sweeping over the city and nation," and hoped that "the arrival of new [black] pupils can be turned into a friendly occasion rather than a shameful blocking of the schoolhouse door à la Little Rock."[1] Presumably, the associations came quickly to *Times* readers: Canarsie, backlash country, racist thuggery.

At a meeting to sustain the tempo of the boycott, one of Canarsie's few black residents shuddered. " 'My God,' I thought, 'This is madness! What can be wrong with my neighbors?' " His face was grim as he remembered. "It was neighbor against neighbor. I sat there in that meeting with five other blacks, we were the only ones there, and it was frightening. All that cheering and jeering: we could have been in Columbia, South Carolina, or Selma, Alabama!" Sickened by the spectacle of whites hurling spittle and invective at black schoolchildren, Wilfred Cartey, a black poet, turned to verse: "They rend the silence / the silent majority / screeching white-powdered / hatred / on the backs of little / black children."[2]

In the crowd in front of Wilson Junior High, two women fumed. "Our families voted liberal all their life and look where it got us," one of them said. She turned to her friend, pointing a finger. "You know, you're Jewish and I'm Jewish and you know as well as I know that the only place to buy a home in this city is in an Italian neighborhood, because the Italians have more guts than the Jews."[3] What did this commotion hold for the future of liberalism? Some of the insurgents parading in the streets were the people and the children of the people who were the New Deal's source of élan, provided its ballast, and gave it their votes. Without the loyalty of people like these, the old liberalism must surely collapse.

Scholars have probed the fury that erupted in the 1960s and 1970s in lower-middle-class communities. And like the label "Canarsieism," their formulations have helped to replace the sloppiness of reality with a misleading metaphoric neatness. To make sense of middle-class discontent, writers have invoked white racism, "embourgeoisement," labor market rivalry, apple-pie authoritarianism, Lockean individualism, neopopulist retaliation, right-wing protectionism, postindustrial society, and political ethnicity.[4] If each of these concepts explains a piece of the puzzle, the danger is that the pattern of the whole may vanish.

Middle America was not a hard geographic place delimited by a political jurisdiction. Nor was it a *cri de coeur* of a middle class nervous about its fading privileges. It was more than a vague spot on the social pyramid or a flight by Luddites into a clarifying past or a fixation on the virtues of bootstrapping. Middle America was not even just the backward-turning movement of a vengeful hinterland. The middle classes had many complaints, their discontent had many sources. No single factor accounts for it.

Economic need and psychic strain inclined the middle classes toward a certain fractiousness, but these alone did not prod them to action. Middle America arose from a conjunction of internal wants and historical events that bedeviled them: the civil rights revolution, the problems of the cities, black power, the war in Vietnam, the disaffection of the young, stagflation, the revolution in morals. All these played havoc with the normal routines of politics, cleaving the country in two and fragmenting the Democratic Party. As the British journalist Godfrey Hodgson described it, "The schism went deeper than mere political disagreement. It was as if, from 1967 on, for several years, two different tribes of Americans experienced the same outward events but experienced them as two quite different realities."[5]

Middle America felt molested by formidable powers: blacks and liberals and bureaucrats. Reaction to these forces gave middle-class politics its distinctive imagery of danger and dispossession. The middle classes never lost this wish to preserve, although the various factions never agreed precisely on what was to be saved or how the task was to be accomplished. Though convinced of their righteousness, they felt helpless to enforce their authority, at least for a time. In the early 1960s the intellegentsia had claimed alienation as their private affliction; by the end of the decade the white middle classes had also succumbed to that malaise. They went on to withdraw their pledges of trust from a liberal state depleted of credibility. Unwilling to give the government a blank check, the middle classes delivered their votes on a straight quid pro quo basis: stop the change.

Middle America felt itself a victim, the object of others' will. Later it took the initiative, becoming a preacher, often a punisher. The resentment of the white middle classes gave conservatives a chance to ply the politics of revenge. Liberals became the targets of demagogues who incited audiences with righteous appeals to silent, forgotten average Americans. To the men in Nixon's White House, wrote Jonathan Schell, "The time seemed ripe for an 'offensive' against the opposition which would outdo in uncontrolled vehemence and intensity anything they had attempted so far. Attorney General [John] Mitchell said to a reporter, 'This country is going so far right you are not even going to recognize it.' They believed that, as one White House aide put it, they 'had the liberal Establishment in total rout.' "[6] The parties of order tried to reclaim an America purged of the frenzies of a decade.

There were many Middle Americas. In the Deep South reaction was tinged with the mania of good old boys and more than a residue of Jim Crow. Marshall Frady observed of his native South, "Life is simply more glandular than it is in the rest of the nation. Southerners tend to belong and believe through blood and weather and common earth and common enemy and common travail, rather than belonging, believing, cerebrally. The tribal instinct is what they answer to." Some observers saw in the discontent of the sunbelt the fast-draw nationalism and contempt for eastern money changers that Vachel Lindsay had caricatured in his satire of William Jennings Bryan, that "prairie avenger, mountain lion ... smashing Plymouth Rock with his boulders from the West."[7] In Canarsie, middle-class upset was entangled in the quest of Brooklyn immigrants for respectability, in the mysteries of Italian-American provincialism, in the ambivalent emotions of Jewish liberalism.

As either the demon of the left or the hope of right-wing vision-

Introduction 5

aries, Middle America remained a false union. Nixon's southern strategy hastened the breakup of a liberal majority already buckling under the pressure of internal contradictions, yet it failed to join sagebrush rebels, Old South diehards, and Catholic workers in perfect communion. Middle America was a mixture of discrete forces, with points of tension as well as of affinity. Conflicts between plebeians and patricians, regions of economic growth and of decline, Protestants and Catholics, made it difficult to develop a collegial spirit. Discontent gave conservatives an opening, but the old majority first had to fail or abdicate for the new one to coalesce. Savvy leaders would have to devise persuasive policy and compelling rhetoric to convert discontent into something that was more than fleeting protest or passing fancy.

The making of Middle America in a remote corner of Brooklyn tells a great deal about the fate of contemporary reform. At first glance, the thinking of the people of Canarsie appears to have changed a good deal in a generation. The hard luck of Democrat Jimmy Carter in 1980 hints at the seismic changes that have altered Brooklyn politics over the past half century. Between 1920 and 1932 Canarsians moved from a mixture of Democratic, Republican, and Socialist sympathies into the Democratic camp. Italian Republicans and Jewish Socialists virtually slid off the pages of the 1932 Kings County enrollment books, swelling Democratic registration tallies and piling up support for Franklin Roosevelt. Forty-eight years later a sunbelt Protestant Republican corralled a majority of Jewish and Italian votes in Canarsie. That Ronald Reagan swept the Italian lunchpail precincts is not entirely surprising, nor that he earned accolades from recent émigré Russian Jews with little fondness for détente. But Reagan also ran well in precincts full of Jewish teachers, the kind of people who had chosen Adlai Stevenson, John Kennedy, and Lyndon Johnson by margins of eight to one.

An Italian man, whose father had followed with relish the *Brooklyn Tablet*'s approving coverage of Joseph McCarthy's witch hunts, said in 1977 that he was more conservative than he used to be. But the daughter of socialist garment workers who read the *Jewish Daily Forward,* a paper whose masthead urged the workers of the world to unite, volunteered that she too felt less liberal than previously, although her fleeting grimace betrayed a trace of ambivalence. At times equivocally, but almost unanimously, the residents described themselves as "more conservative." The significance of these shifts in self-labeling is not immediately evident. The import

and nuances of such changes do not lie scattered about on the surface of things, transparently accessible to all. Labels may reflect primal impulses; they are freighted with complex and ambivalent
associations that remain opaque to strangers. Or they may be the
prosaic stuff of habit, absorbed with little heed from the background
noise of society's pedestrian conversations.

An even more pressing problem of understanding lies in the many
meanings of the word *liberalism:* a doctrine of political rights, the
free market economy of classical individualism, moderation of the
excesses of the business cycle, to name just a few. Canarsians, however, did not have such rarified ideas in mind when they complained
about liberalism. For them the word had a variety of earthier meanings that did not always cohere logically. Since 1960 the Jews and
Italians of Canarsie have embellished and modified the meaning of
liberalism, associating it with profligacy, spinelessness, malevolence,
masochism, elitism, fantasy, anarchy, idealism, softness, irresponsibility, and sanctimoniousness. The term *conservative* acquired
connotations of pragmatism, character, reciprocity, truthfulness,
stoicism, manliness, realism, hardness, vengeance, strictness, and responsibility. This book explores the process by which that change in
meaning was accomplished.

In order to chart the political odyssey of Canarsians, I adopted the
stance of the ethnographer, trying to dwell long enough in a single
place to find the larger truth in all its subtlety. Because I wanted to
understand how the crisis of liberalism impinged on people's intimate life, I relied on intensive personal interviews. Almost all the
events described in this book I observed at first hand between 1975
and 1977, and for eighteen of those twenty-four months—from January 1976 to July 1977—I lived in Brooklyn a few miles from Canarsie. I spent most of my waking hours there developing confidants,
endlessly talking, and taking part in the life of political and civic
groups. Over the next two years I returned to the community inter-
mittently for brief stays and then again in 1980 for a two-week visit,
the midpoint of which was the presidential election. The reader
should keep in mind that most of the interviews took place in 1976
and 1977, years when the issues of black nationalism, the Vietnam
war, and Watergate were alive in Canarsians' consciousness, although declining in relevance.

The time I spent in deep conversation gave Canarsians the chance
to test me and, eventually, to vouch for me. Early in my stay, in a
community nervous about racial encroachment, I asked a fumbling

question about busing. Less than an hour later, when I entered the headquarters of the Jefferson Democratic Club, a political leader barked at me, "Hey, what do you think you're doing, spreading rumors about blacks coming into the schools?" I explained that I had simply asked a woman a question about the desirability of integration. The leader retorted in a self-parody of Brooklynese, "I know, I told her you're okay. But remember, you're a Yankee in a small southern town and the folks are *noivous.*"

All but a few of the quotations here were said to me by Canarsians and recorded on tape or, when they preferred, in writing at the time. I have removed all the names, I have changed a few details that might otherwise permit attribution, and in some places I have resorted to an inelegant but anonymous vagueness: "As one civic leader said," "A Jewish activist thought," "An Italian traditionalist felt." I have made these modest alterations to abide by the ethical imperatives of confidentiality, but especially to respect the privacy that Canarsians relinquished when they took me into their world.

I could not have written this kind of book without the cooperation of the people of Canarsie. The success of this brand of sociology is always an act of collusion, unwitting or designed, between the interviewer and subjects who refuse to act the part of witless puppets. Canarsians were a candid and courageous lot. Some saw the chance to indulge in puffery, but for the most part they braved the risks that come into play when individuals reveal themselves to a stranger. Canarsians gave me a precious part of themselves. I regret that I could not repay all the friendship, time, argument, trust, Kosher deli, sarcasm, coffee, kvetching, Italian pastry, and shots of whiskey they shared with me.

During my stay in Brooklyn, the initial suspicion of a stranger lingered for months, then yielded in a ritual induction. I had traveled with a band of right-wing activists across Brooklyn to a convocation of white backlash groups. My companions included some boosters of George Wallace and Spiro Agnew who suspected that my politics might not be theirs. One woman said to me as we stood in the vast cavern of an Italian catering hall, "You know, Jon, you've become like our adopted son. But remember, when it comes time for you to write this up, make sure you don't stick it to us."

Something characteristically Italian clung to her plainspoken words: unpretentious warmth, evoking a world divided neatly between loyal kin and perfidious strangers, with an implicit threat of swift reprisal for betrayal. I took her warning to heart as a principle of fidelity but also as a popular version of enlightenment: stay close to the truth. Democratic boss Meade Esposito seconded her thoughts in his inimitable way. "Hey Yale kid, you know who writes books? Liars and squealers. Throw the books out the window, get out on the streets and learn something!" I did not try to stick it to anyone, I did get out on the streets a bit, but I *have* written a book.

Some people in Brooklyn may be pained by some of what I have written. Still, I have tried to tell the truth about Canarsians, in their vicious moments as well as their moments of grace. There were plenty of both. The request most often made of me was fairness, which I have honored by showing the humor of the residents along with the vengefulness, the generosity as well as the racism. The last thing most Canarsians would respect is an academic gone native, sentimentalizing their nasty side and getting trapped in a folk romance. These folks are not romantic. Naturalism, not romanticism, is the appropriate aesthetic for capturing the culture of Brooklyn white ethnicity. The odd mixed truth of the American middle-income classes lies somewhere between the caricature of rabid hardhats and the false populist worship of "real" Americans.

A cautionary word may help the reader keep that ambiguous truth in mind. Because of my interest in organized forms of white reaction, parts of the book record the activities of the most activist and defensive cadres in Canarsie. While I duly note the more generous and progressive strains in the community, it does bear warning here that in a few chapters conservative activists and organizations assume a prominence that does not truly reflect the range of Canarsie opinion.

The book has another kind of emphasis. Above all, it highlights the uniqueness of Canarsians' experience of the world. The people of Canarsie are a vivid lot. They can be engaging, high-flown, poignant, racist, sarcastic, bawdy. The narrative style I have chosen enhances that impression of their distinctiveness; I have let them tell much of the story in their own words, and I have kept my own theoretical preoccupations in the background. As a result, it is important to affirm that essential axiom of comparative sociology: people's grievances are reflections of general laws as well as unrepeatable expressions of their own singularity.

The point of view has a more fundamental consequence. Only rarely do blacks interrupt the flow of white narrative to judge, to reflect, to impugn; only rarely do I abandon scholarly detachment, place myself at the center of the action, and offer a personal verdict.

I tell the story of the crisis of liberalism overwhelmingly from Canarsians' vantage point because I am convinced that such a focus best highlights the social forces that shape white definitions of reality. That choice carries with it a certain danger. The ceaseless drumbeat of white complaint may leave a few readers with the mistaken impression that all worthy claims to sympathy lie with the white lower middle classes. It might suggest to some that the exclamations of white outrage represent my own considered opinion. Neither of these presumptions is correct. My aim is not to engage in special pleading, to blame or acclaim, but to explain sociologically how Canarsians came to feel certain powerful feelings that have had immense political consequences. If in the course of this account of the complexity of white reaction Canarsians become explicable or even draw the reader's sympathy, I am confident that such understanding will ultimately benefit black and white Americans alike.

The point is not to take sides. There can be no question about whether blacks or whites are the greater victims. The complaints of Canarsians about ghetto culture and reverse discrimination pale before the historic brutalization of black Americans, but that truth would be cold comfort to Canarsians. Few of us, the privileged along with the vulnerable, find consolation in such abstract, historic truths. The very posing of the question in that fashion, setting up a situation in which black or white interests can be satisfied only at the expense of the other party, symbolizes much of the recent failure of liberalism.

The lessons of Canarsie are critical ingredients for a revitalized liberalism that does not wish to be consigned to irrelevance. Canarsie suggests the direction to be taken by future forces that wish the privilege of ruling without sacrificing the worthy goal of justice. Any coalition that fails to understand the grievances that collected in places like Canarsie all across America in the past two decades will achieve neither justice nor incumbency.

part one

History

1. The Fenced Land

Sanctuary

*"Most of us who live in Canarsie came from
ghettos. But once we made it to Canarsie, we
finally had a little piece of the country. It was like
we had moved to a little shtetl."*

Canarsie owes its name to the Algonquian word for fort, fenced land,
or palisade. The proud Canarsie Indians played a momentous role in
the founding of Manhattan. Grand Sachem Penhawitz and a band of
braves had ranged far from their Brooklyn homeland and were en-
camped on the isle of Manhattan when Peter Minuit stumbled upon
them. Minuit cut a deal with the Indians and bought the island for
the legendary twenty-four dollars, a hefty portion of it doled out in
wampum. The paltry sum might easily be taken as another instance
of unequal exchange between white imperialists and people of color,
but appearances deceive: the Indians did the fleecing. Like the
blockbuster who spins a duplicitous yarn, Penhawitz was not above
resorting to a little chicanery. In fact, the land did not belong to the
Canarsie tribe.[1] In 1976 a burly Canarsie hardhat, pondering the
welfare burden and liquidity crunch that then afflicted the city, reflected on history with retrospective sarcasm. The Indians, he offered, had simply dumped a property of dubious long-term value
that was vulnerable to an influx of "the lower element." Perhaps, the
man thought, the chief had mused to himself before selling, "There
goes the neighborhood."

When the smell of brine wafts off Jamaica Bay, one can imagine
Canarsie as a sleepy fishing and farming village in the 1800s. The
place endured as a bucolic hamlet late into this century. At Golden
Gate Amusement Park, which opened in 1907, the beery dance halls

and pugilistic displays by the sea lured day trippers from all across Brooklyn. The population then consisted of 3,000 Germans, Dutch, Scottish, and Irish, plus Italian fishermen who mined the rich beds of oysters in Jamaica Bay. During the 1920s the handful of Italian masons and Jewish tailors became a swarm, foreshadowing Canarsie's present ethnic makeup. The pollution of the bay killed off the fishing industry, and the Depression left its grim legacy in the 1940s: 20 percent of the work force unemployed or sustained by public works projects. Most residents then were unlettered blue-collar workers. Close to half of the adults were foreign born, most of them eastern European Jews or southern Italians.

Aesthetically, Canarsie was a swampy netherworld. The authors of the Works Progress Administration described it in 1939 as "a sparsely settled community laid out in dispiriting flatlands, smoked over by the perpetual reek of fires in the vast refuse dump at its western end. Its residential section of one- and two-family houses and shacks (most of which resemble those in Charles Burchfield's paintings) is broken by weedy lots and small truck farms cultivated by Italians."[2]

The area was the object of cruel barbs. "There were stock jokes about Canarsie as a 'Three M' village—mud, mortgages and malaria."[3] When Alfred Kazin returned in the 1940s to his childhood haunts in the Brownsville section of Brooklyn, he remembered "a place so celebrated in New York vaudeville houses for its squalor that the very sound of the word was always good for a laugh. CAN-NARR-SIE! They fell into the aisles."[4] On "The Honeymooners" Ralph Kramden and Ed Norton learn that their Raccoon Lodge of Bensonhurst is going to bowl Canarsie; the expressions on their faces tell the audience that Canarsie must be the end of the world. In the movie *Trouble along the Way,* John Wayne plays a hardnosed coach who returns to his parish school on the Lower East Side of Manhattan. As he watches a feckless quarterback in action, he growls, "Kid, your passing's from Canarsie."

Canarsie entered the imagination of the literati as well. On an expedition to America in the late 1940s, Simone de Beauvoir asked her guide, William Phillips, a founder of *Partisan Review,* how to get to Canarsie. "I could not understand why a French writer on a first visit had to rush out to Canarsie as soon as she got off the boat. Only later, when I became aware of what she was looking for, did it occur to me that she probably had heard that Canarsie was a 'workers' district,' in the European sense. Then came all the other stock questions: how could she see the Negro section? She did not say 'down-trodden,' but the intonation was there."[5]

Today the frame bungalows with baroque statuary saints on the lawn evoke an earlier time. Old Canarsie hands like to recall the intimate feeling of community: little Italian ladies cutting dandelions for homemade wine, the vegetable gardens with their gnarled growth, hunts for rabbits in the marsh grass. One journalist recorded the sentiments of those for whom "Canarsie was a special place of homeyness and friendliness. *Fraindlichkeit* is the way Yiddish-speaking residents described it. *Amicizia* is the Italian word for the same thing. It was Brooklyn of an earlier century, and little Old New York in its most idyllic form."[6]

Developers gave Canarsie a sleek new look in the 1950s. Visions of the vacant swampland on the edge of the city, Brooklyn's last patch of frontier, caught the eye of real estate promoters. They anticipated the bullish demand for land by those still pent up in the old immigrant quarters, where younger residents, second-generation Jews and Italians living with small children in walkup apartments, had been lifted to modest prosperity by postwar affluence. The state eased the flow of credit, subsidizing middle-class debt with Federal Housing Administration loans and veterans' mortgage guarantees. Two builders, Harry and Sidney Waxman, turned the possibilities into a brisk trade in private homes. They covered the two hundred acres of Seaview Village with forty blocks of modest Cape Cod, ranch style, split level, and attached brick row houses. The first two-bedroom model, squeezed onto its 42-by-100-foot plot, sold for $13,-750 in 1956. Other builders imitated the Waxman lead in the following decade, and nondescript multifamily brick row homes soon filled the vast tracts west of Rockaway Parkway.

The new residents encircled the Old Canarsie core, occupied its eastern and western flanks, and changed the complexion of the neighborhood. In 1960 Old Canarsie was a sleepy, mainly Italian community, with a remnant of the original Irish, German, and British inhabitants, and some Russian and Polish Jews. Two-thirds of the men were blue-collar workers, many of them operators of machinery or skilled craftsmen. Fewer than 25 percent had graduated from high school. Family income averaged $6,000.

The newcomers, mainly Jewish but also Italian, were more affluent and educated than the resident Italians. There were many young couples at the peak of their child-bearing years and even some upper-middle-class families in a few of the earliest tracts. In the toniest area of single-family, quasi-suburban homes in Seaview Village, the median income in 1960 was $11,000. Many of the early settlers soon traded up and moved on to more affluent suburbs. As one resident recalled, "There was a vast resale on this block and the blocks around here in the early 1960s. They were going on to more expensive homes out on Long Island. And later, after the 1968 school strike, a lot of the more wealthy left, because they were afraid of what situations their children would encounter in the public schools."

The more typical, Jewish tracts of New Canarsie, west of Rockaway Parkway, and the less prestigious parts of Seaview Village had a lower social standing. Half to three-quarters of the New Canarsians were white-collar workers, including a large number of salesmen, schoolteachers, and clerical workers. In the Jewish enclaves that were heavily blue-collar, the proportion of those with high school diplomas, 50 percent, was double that in Italian Old Canarsie, but few of the Jews had attended college.

Communal tensions inevitably marked the transition from bucolic village to tractland suburbia. The entrenched Italians, who occasionally muttered "Mezzochristi" (Christ killers), under their breath, did not always extend Christian charity to the droves of Jewish invaders. One of the few Anglo-Saxons remaining in Canarsie in the 1970s, a self-professed member of a "dying breed," told a story of the Italians grumbling, " 'We don't want them Jews coming in here.' The Jews were moving in here fast and furious, and the Italians were stubborn. So I told them, 'The Jews want education bad, so let's work together for better schools. You can't stop the tide.' I was labeled a Jew-lover by those ignorant Italian ladies at P.S. 114. They resented the Jews. They didn't like the end of the empty lots and the hordes of people."

The population of Canarsie soared from 30,000 in 1950 to 50,000 in 1960 to 80,000 in 1970, when it began a gradual decline. Lots marketed at $400 in 1950 went for twenty times that amount fifteen years later. Whites from racially transitional neighborhoods replenished the buying and rental markets through the 1960s and 1970s. In the latter half of the 1970s, Israelis, Russian émigré Jews, mobile Chinese and other Asian Americans, and Orthodox Jews filled some of the vacancies. Middle-class black buyers finally began to crack the racial barrier in Canarsie's northern quadrant during the late 1970s.

For the migrants of the 1960s, at least those attracted by the lure of a new neighborhood rather than reeling from racial change in the old one, moving to Canarsie had simple and complex meanings. The care they invested in the neighborhood reflected their joy at living in a safe place, with good schools and amenities. Homeowners' solicitousness for their properties expressed the sacrifice obliged by mortgage payments and the freshness for many of the experience of ownership. The pride in place also came from a less tangible accomplishment, not the jackpot pledged in some versions of the American mobility creed, but the chance to provide for family, to enjoy simple pleasures, and to live a life no longer pinched by privation.

A Jewish woman who had come to Canarsie from a city project in Brownsville remembered the Depression. "We were so poor in those days, you see, we didn't have very much. We think back to those days a lot. Our children have no idea of what it was like. We didn't need much to make do. There was stoopball and checkers and hopscotch. The ice would melt on the ice wagon, and we'd watch it melt down and change shapes. The kids today would laugh at us." Twenty years passed before she truly believed that the economic ground would not suddenly slide out from under her. The odyssey to Canarsie helped redeem the sacrifices of the 1930s. "Most of us who live in Canarsie came from ghettos. But once we made it to Canarsie, we finally had a little piece of the country. It was like we had moved to a little shtetl," she concluded, using the Yiddish word for village.

An Italian dockworker left the Italian ghetto of Red Hook, Brooklyn. The son of "hot-blooded Calabrians," he fondly described a youth spent hanging out, playing ball, and fighting the Irish gangs in South Brooklyn. He had known the desperate, endless search for work during the Depression, and he tenaciously held to his identity as "a working man." As he approached retirement, he sometimes yielded to a melancholy born of unfulfilled dreams. "I realize that my situation is my own doing. It's up to me to go get it. If I wanted more, I could have gone for trade school, but I didn't have the ambition. You see, in America, the intelligent man feels superior to a guy who works with his hands. Maybe it has to be like that, you need to give more respect to creative and intelligent people."

His wife, a booster of Ronald Reagan, told of the hard times with an impish grin. "You won't believe this about me, but I was a Communist when I was seventeen. But communism wasn't like it is today. We weren't out to overthrow the government. I remember joining a sit-down strike when I was a member of the Candle Makers Union. We were part of John L. Lewis's mine workers."

They both felt they had made impressive gains. The husband was grateful to the Longshoreman's Union which, despite the pension fund shysters, the coming of containerized cargo, and the kickbacks, secured his tenure in an $18,000-a-year job. His house in many ways embodied that process of betterment. He harked back to his thinking in the first flush of the move to Canarsie in the mid-1950s. "I wanted something better for my kids, and for myself." He moved to Canarsie on the strength of a $980 down payment required by the G.I. loan. "It was exhilarating to own my own home. I felt like I had finally achieved something."

Canarsie's rise out of the marshlands of Jamaica Bay symbolized the transformation of the middle classes in the years after World War II. Samuel Lubell penned the classical rendition of that "climbing of Jacob's ladder" by the children of the Depression and the passion for respectability that inspired it. "What makes them so significant politically is that having come to this country in roughly the same period, the so-called 'new' immigrants and their offspring shared common experiences in this country. All have been part of one of the epic population movements in history—of the upsurging out of the slums toward the middle class which has swept our major cities since the turn of the century and which is still going on." Lubell's portrait of the trip from Manhattan's Lower East Side to Forest Hills in Queens holds equally true for the move from Brownsville to Canarsie. "The spanning of that distance was a social revolution . . . If land hunger was the propelling force behind the agrarian frontier, the drive behind the urban frontier has been the hunger for social status."[7]

A stroll on a summer evening in 1976 suggested the supreme ordinariness of life in Canarsie. Blue skies, hazed over by smog during the day, were shading into the grayish pink pastels of dusk. The Belt Parkway was a sinuous curve between shore and land, humming with commuters heading for Long Island or the outer reaches of Queens and Brooklyn. Earlier that day, out on Canarsie pier, huddles of men in Bermuda shorts sat in beach chairs and kibitzed over cards, the quiet rhythmically broken by the roar of jets landing and taking off at Kennedy Airport a few miles east. Across the parkway in Seaview Village, Orthodox Jews in skullcaps headed for Sabbath services. Grabstein's Deli on Rockaway Parkway, with the neon-orange Hebrew lettering on the window, was crammed with families feasting on blintzes, corned beef, and knishes. Around the corner on Avenue L, stores emblazoned with the red, green, and white of the Italian flag exuded the odors of mortadella and prosciutto. Now teenagers claimed the strip, listening to the pounding beat of disco, as macho boys hustled young girls in halter tops and tight shorts. A mile away, in the heart of Old Canarsie, elderly Italians sat outside their bungalows, enjoying the after-dinner calm. In the receding light, Canarsie fell into a trance. The groups of people seemed suspended for a moment between the abrasions of the work week and the approaching weekend with its promise of small pleasures.

Canarsie is a haven, but the gift of immunity is not given freely. To keep their illusion of refuge the residents sealed out alien races, suspicious people, disturbing forces. They made their community into a fortress, a fenced land. With the exception of two public projects on the edge of Canarsie and three census tracts with two or three dozen blacks, none of the remaining twenty-eight tracts had more than ten blacks out of populations ranging from one thousand to four thousand people. Most blocks were entirely white. Nonetheless, Canarsians felt vulnerable to encroachment from the black communities that form an arc stretching from East Flatbush to the northwest, through Brownsville due north, to East New York in the northeast. Barriers of nature—Jamaica Bay to the south, Paerdegat Basin on the western flank, and Fresh Creek on the eastern flank—protect Canarsie, but those same boundaries limit the residents' options of flight and expansion.

The low-income Breukelen Homes project, a reservation of the black and Hispanic poor, stands in Canarsie's northeastern quadrant. A Canarsie black man fumed, "Breukelen Projects is like a concentration camp, it's Canarsie's Auschwitz. In effect they are telling blacks, 'Stay inside your Warsaw Ghetto!'" In 1970 the project was a perfect balance of whites and blacks. Ten years later 90 percent of its 5,265 residents were black, and the white 10 percent was predominantly Puerto Rican. Half of the families were headed by women, and half depended for their sustenance on public assistance. In the project young men sipped wine from bottles wrapped in paper bags and lounged on the corner near a thin strip of seamy storefronts. As two policemen drove along the edges of the project at dusk, they spotted a prostitute in iridescent, skintight pants. The officers hailed her, "Cleola, honey, what are you doing soliciting out here on the corner?" With cool defiance, she replied, "You can't do nothing 'bout it, 'cause the captain says I can stay out here as long as I keep a low profile."

One scholar of Mediterranean cultures has written, "Beyond the community lies the outside world which is generally regarded as hostile, from which come strangers, that is, unknown persons who, unlike the fellow-members of the community with whom relations are habitual and clearly structured, remain mysterious, their nature and their power in doubt."[8] The strangers of the ghetto, the blacks and Hispanics of Brownsville and East New York, excited white Canarsie's anxieties and fantasies. The community's penetrability and its adjacentcy to the underclasses vitiated the residents' freedom to think about race, poverty, and crime as abstractions. As a result, they felt a need to guard against the impurities of the world beyond their borders. One man captured this feeling neatly. "Who are the Canarsie people?" he asked rhetorically. "They came from places that expired. They're not rich. They bought a home in a sanctuary, and they're afraid they are going to lose it. They are saying, 'Don't tread on me.' They want to protect their turf."

After 1970 the people of Canarsie had to expend more and more energy to maintain the purity of their preserve. Still, the longing for invulnerability could not be satisfied. Try as they might, Canarsians discovered they could not stave off the city that surrounded them. Then they lost more than their spatial immunity. They lost the illusion of a self-sufficient life.

Flight to Canarsie

"You can't walk down Pitkin Avenue today . . .
It's not history, it's the way they live. They live like
animals."

The slums of East New York and Brownsville, which touch Canarsie's northern perimeter at Linden Boulevard, loom as a symbol of the dashed hopes and promises New York City dealt a generation of southern black and Puerto Rican immigrants. "Into Brooklyn in the late 1940s they started to come," Jimmy Breslin wrote of that first wave, "men with cotton-baling hooks in their pockets, and sad-faced women with arms leaden from hours spent jiggling small children in buses and railroad coach cars from Greenville in South Carolina and Waycross in Georgia and Jacksonville in Florida." A second wave came, "this one by plane. The late nights at old Idlewild Airport became filled with the poor arriving on cheap flights from Puerto Rico. Summer people in winter clothes, Jimmy Cannon called them."[9]

As the minorities pushed out from neighborhood to neighborhood, they spurred the flight of whites from Crown Heights, East New York, Brownsville, Bedford-Stuyvesant, Bushwick, and Williamsburg. In some places white flight was gradual, responsive to the relentless pressures of trickle-down and trade-up created by markets of credit and housing. Elsewhere the transition was a stampede incited by the ploys of fast-buck speculators.

That the minorities "aroused ferocious race and class hatreds" is undeniable,[10] but the statement obscures the range of emotions experienced by whites, which ran the gamut from fear to vengefulness to melancholy. Many fled because they believed the shifting racial composition of the neighborhood threatened their homes, schools, and children. Often racism and less than perfect information inflated nervousness into hysteria. But often the nervousness was reasonably attuned to reality. The end result—flight—was the same in either case.

Whites trickled into Canarsie from all across Brooklyn. An Italian dockworker left South Brooklyn in the late 1950s when a Puerto Rican family took up residence on the block. "The mother told her kid to use a jagged can opener to slash some kids. I wasn't going for that nonsense. It was unheard of, an adult telling kids to act like that!" A refugee from Nazi Germany told of a second escape, this time from Crown Heights, as a compulsion, not a choice. "I was pushed out. After my daughter was attacked in Lincoln Terrace Park, I decided it was time to get out."

The blockbusting of East Flatbush in the late 1960s and early 1970s created another rush to Canarsie. A Jewish election district captain in the Jefferson Democratic Club seethed with anger over the decline of white control of space. He described "the garbage" who moved into East Flatbush after the "hard-working blacks arrived. And then came the nigger kids, hanging out and playing those transistor radios, the rowdies, and they all got this walk they walk, which is kind of arrogant."

The earliest and largest streams of white migrants to Canarsie came from Brownsville and East New York, which once had been vibrant immigrant ghettos teaming with respectable Jewish and Italian families—poor and not-so-poor. An old Jewish garment worker declared with visible pride, "We lived in a ghetto maybe, but it wasn't such a slum!" The older generation told of Sunday pasta dinners and candy store hangouts, the excitement of stoop ball and the warmth of Passover dinner.

Much of Brownsville and East New York is now a desolate place. Junkies nod, social clubs blare soul and salsa, hookers preen for tricks at stoplights, rococo storefront tabernacles ring with the sound of tambourines, and decrepit tenements create a surrealist's landscape. When a police car cruised down one street on a sultry summer evening in 1976, milling blacks glowered at the white intruders. A man reputed to be a cannibal symbolized the seemingly alien lifestyles that rankled the white residents a mile away in Canarsie. Eat Em Up, as the cops referred to him affectionately, lived with his dogs in a wine-drunk stupor. The cops queried a little boy. "Hey boy, Eat Em Up gonna eat you up?" The boy shot back, "Nope, Eat Em Up's my friend." The cops laughed. "That Eat Em Up is funny as hell. You never heard expressions like he's got. On check day, when the welfare comes and he's been drinking, he'll come out waving his prick in the air and howling like one of his dogs."

Many Jews in Brownsville reacted to racial incursion simply by fleeing. An Italian Republican leader found an explanation for this in the Jews' age-old adjustment to persecution. "It goes back to their tradition: the Jews are wanderers. They always kept a suitcase packed and close to hand. The wandering Jews were pushed from here to there." A Jewish attorney told of the loss of quiet and custom that caused him to leave East New York. His family had lived on a block of four-story walk-up apartments that changed from Jewish to Hispanic in a convulsive few years in the early 1960s. The man recalled the arrival of the Puerto Ricans, who sat outdoors all summer playing dominoes, strumming guitars, drinking beer. "The Jews were shocked by it. And then there was a robbery of a delicatessen at Dumont and Alabama streets. My family began to feel unsettled by the men hanging around during the day, and the crime and the drugs." At first imperceptibly, but then with inescapable finality, the familiar backdrop of everyday life changed. "The Puerto Ricans came in, and the cockroaches came in. East New York used to be quiet on the High Holidays, but suddenly there was noise and gangs and bodegas. We no longer felt comfortable sleeping outside on mattresses on the fire escape on hot summer nights."

The forfeit of the fire escapes meant the receding of control over the world close at hand, an intrusion of danger into family life. When Alfred Kazin returned to Brownsville, a Proustian figure caught in the fugue of involuntary memory, the fire escapes were suddenly reborn in his mind. He described them so vividly that one smells and touches and sweats with him:

All along the block children are sleeping on the fire escapes. It is as hot tonight as it was this morning: first scorched, then damp. The thickness of the summer night weighs on us like wet wool. It is hard to breathe, to move. The old folks sit on their kitchen chairs in weary silence, cooling themselves with palmetto fans ... It is near midnight, but no one can bear to go to bed. The rooms smell like burning sulphur. The heat stored up inside all through the day now oozes from the walls and blows its gritty breath on the faces of the sleepless people along the pavement.[11]

One Jewish veteran of reform politics resisted moving out as her Brownsville project turned black and poor and tough. By osmosis she had absorbed the lessons of concern from her family. "The whole family read the *Jewish Daily Forward*. And we read books in Yiddish on Eugene Debs. My brothers worked to help the Scottsboro Boys, and Sacco-Vanzetti, now that was an important name in our family!" She remembered her brothers' byword, "Blacks are the last hired and the first fired." But one day in the laundry room of the project, a black girl slammed her hands across this woman's ears, leaving her stunned and wounded. She finally heeded her husband's plea to join the exodus.

The minorities were used as a scapegoat by a younger generation ready to cut its ties to the past and by an older generation suffering from the betrayals of aging. "The second generation," said a Jewish attorney, "was already leaving Brownsville. There was nothing to hold them in East New York. They were naturally going to places like Valley Stream out on Long Island to buy their own home. Sometimes they used the race thing as a justification to leave the family. In the old days, everybody couldn't get into the kitchen during Passover, there were so many people. But then the grandparents died, and the ties to ethnicity were lessened. When the grandparents died, there was a breakdown in patriarchal and matriarchal feelings. The old people sometimes blamed the blacks for all these things."

In the Italian section of East New York youths resisted black advances with fists and lug wrenches as well as with grumbling and witchcraft. In the mid-1960s blacks, Italians, and Hispanics jostled for primacy at the intersection of New Lots Avenue and Livonia and Ashford streets. A band of local teens—the Society for the Prevention of Niggers from Getting Everything (SPONGE)—picketed across from the black enclave. Mothers pushing baby strollers urged on the young guardians, whose signs declared, "Go Back to Africa,

Niggers." In one of the first ordeals of his administration, young mayor John Lindsay asked his staff why some corner of Brooklyn far from Manhattan's East Side had erupted. A staff member recalled, "We hardly knew where East New York was."

The distance was more than geographic. When Lindsay descended into the streets, he was greeted by shouts of "Go back to Africa with the niggers." In retrospect one can see that the encounter of a Yankee mayor and his liberal Jewish emissaries with young Italian toughs presaged the emerging cultural war between patrician conscience and plebeian rancor. Learning quickly, the Lindsay people contacted Joey Gallo, the factotum of a local Mafia clan. A story was circulating that Gallo had overheard some youths boasting they were going to "knock off some of those fucking niggers." Gallo had told them, "Don't talk that way. You cool it, or we'll have even more cops in this neighborhood. And from now on, you call those people colored people." The punk supposedly said under his breath, "All right, but I still think they're fucking niggers!" Gallo, it was reported, "picked him up and slammed him against the wall. He left him unconscious on the floor. 'I said they are *colored people*,' he said, and walked out of the bar. After word of that incident got around, tempers calmed considerably."[12]

Racial transition had traumatic effects even on those who had enjoyed friendship with blacks. One Italian man who had attended school in East New York during the turbulent years of changeover had painful memories. "The neighborhood was totally destroyed as soon as the blacks moved in. Buildings started burning down, and we had more crime. My sister and two of my little cousins went trick or treating one night, and about six or seven niggers ripped them off." He hesitated to brand an entire race. "I'm not saying it's all blacks. It's just that some people have blacks living right next to them, and sure, they're nice people. In my old neighborhood we used to have blacks who were nice people and we were friends and everything." But as numbers grew, and proportions altered, some mysterious threshold was crossed, and racial antagonism began to snowball:

As soon as enough of them move in, forget about it, the friendship is over. There was my black friend, a kid I used to come home with, I used to bring him home every day. We'd party together, have fun. I mean, we used to throw our racial slurs at each other, but that was because we liked each other, we were friends, and if I got into a fight, he stuck up for me, if he got into a fight, I stuck up for him. But after enough of them moved in, it didn't work out that way. They start taking sides, and that was the end of it. The only thing we could think of was to fight back.

Pitkin Avenue became a symbolic reproach for all the changes that had transformed Brooklyn. This artery that coursed through Brownsville once pulsated with the beat of immigrant trade, drive, politics, sarcasm, chutzpah, deli, recreation, dialectic. "Pitkin Avenue weighs on me," Kazin eulogized. "As you go up from Belmont, the neon glare suddenly lights up all the self-conscious confusion of Brownsville's show street ... except for Brownsville's ancestral stress on the food, the Yiddish theater, the left wing–right wing arguments around the tables in Hoffman's Cafeteria, the Zionist appeals along the route, it might be Main Street in any moderately large town ... No other Brownsville street brings home to me so many of the external things I once lived with. Pitkin Avenue is what Brownsville is most proud of, for walking down it on a Saturday night, when all the lights are ablaze."[13]

"I used to go up on Pitkin Avenue when it was all Jewish," an Italian plumber said with spirited Brooklyn chauvinism. "Pitkin Avenue was the best shopping street you could go to in the whole world. It was be-eee-you-ti-ful!" The son of a Brownsville bagel baker dissolved in visible delight, savoring the memory of nighttime family strolls along the avenue and one resplendent feast of honey cakes and tea at Dubin's Cafeteria. A furrier's son told of the Jewish socialists arguing in fine Talmudic fashion up and down the street. "My father would take me up on Pitkin Avenue on Sunday morning. By ten A.M., the sidewalks were jammed with people having political discussions. A liberal Democrat was about as right as you got."

The life of Pitkin Avenue did not withstand the destruction that swept across northern and central Brooklyn. "I remember a vital, active community of small shopkeepers and garment workers," said one man with sad bewilderment. "Of course, there was Murder Incorporated, but they stayed in their own poolroom, and we weren't too aware of them. But now you drive down Pitkin Avenue at five o'clock and there are iron shutters on the stores and the police have to walk in groups of three and four. It's terrible. I am amazed what happened to Brownsville. It's like it was bombed out. It looks like Dresden after the war."

Bafflement spilled over into diatribes against the people who presumably had ruined Brooklyn. A few Canarsians saw the ghetto as a jungle infested with dark-skinned "animals" whose wild sexuality and broken families defied all ideas of civilized conduct. An Italian utility worker wailed, "But you can't walk down Pitkin Avenue today, or anywhere in Brownsville. It's because these people don't know how to live. They steal, they got no values. They say it's history, but that's bullshit. It's not history, it's the way they live. They live like animals."

The man's work regularly took him north across Linden Boulevard into the ghetto. One night as he peered out of his manhole, he told how "I seen these niggers taking this woman and throwing her into the hallway. I seen 'em, kids, thirteen or fourteen, there were six or seven of them that done it. They ripped off all her clothes and did the whole job on her!" Riveted to the scene, he acted on the raw data of his senses to form his opinions, moving from the incident to generalizations without inhibition. "These people are always raping or killing someone, and it's always the same people that are doing it! It's always a minority, it's never a majority. I can't communicate with them. I don't have no pity for them. We don't want them animals here."

The ghetto remained opaque to this man, an evil to flee rather than an object of compassion or analysis. Some might see his anger as blaming the victim, but that judgment fails to grasp the intricate cultural rules that regulate the way groups allocate blame, explain misfortune, and decipher enigmas. Everything in the world of Canarsie impelled the residents to rail against people rather than slavery, labor markets, or similarly arcane forces. From where they stood, the people of Canarsie believed *they* were the victims.

The issues of race frightened them too immediately to permit the grace of compassion. They viewed the shifts in Brooklyn's racial complexion as an invasion by a hostile army. The military imagery rightly suggests the importance of the taking and ceding of territory and the power of numbers in shaping urban race relations.

Scores of residents had moved twice, first from Brownsville to the northern tip of eastern Flatbush, then south into Canarsie. But in 1972, finally settled in Canarsie, they faced the specter of Brownsville children being bused into Canarsie schools. Afraid that the cycle of racial change might begin again, a Jewish community leader offered the image of menaced Israel and vowed, "We ran once, but we've nowhere else to go. We're surrounded. The water is at our backs." To quiet a rising fear of Diaspora, he prescribed a solution in the Italian mode: "We must stand fast."

2. Ethnic Traditions

Ghetto People

"We Italians and Jews are all the same ...
We all like to play mahjong in Canarsie."

The coincidence of living in the same place conferred on the Jews and Italians of Canarsie the same risks, needs, and destiny. But the two peoples did not react to racial pressures in the same fashion. In the local wisdom that Jews run while Italians stand fast, there was a larger truth about each group's distinct style of dealing with threat. A variety of differences, both in politics and culture, accompanied that different capacity for stubbornness and pacifism. Historically, the Italians had epitomized the values of particularism, represented by loyalty to family, reliance on personal networks, and private settlement of disputes. In contrast, the Jews reflected the mode of universalism, represented by their idiom of humanism, allegiance to cosmopolitan ideals, and faith in the democratic state. The shift of a portion of Brooklyn Jewry from optimistic universalism to nervous provincialism symbolized the vulnerability of Jewish tradition, and of liberalism more generally, under conditions of urban racial strife.[1]

Canarsians professed a great respect for the American dream. They trusted the verdict of economic competition in which attainment of rewards depends on the talent or moxie of the individual, perhaps leavened by a splash of luck or connections. Even when the residents honored them more in the breach than in deed, they repeated the pieties of bootstrapping. The thought of welfare cheats rankled one woman, the daughter of Jewish garment workers. "My grandparents were like Russian serfs, but we climbed our way out of poverty, we worked our way up. We were poor when we were growing up, but we were never on home relief, and our family still had closeness and warmth!"

Her indignation seems full of a timeless American belief in self-reliance, the vestiges of a Puritan work ethic, it would seem. Yet to invoke the Protestant spirit to explain the resentments of sardonic Jews and cynical Italians surely retrieves the wrong tradition. An Italian unionist learned his thrift not from *McGuffey's Readers* or Chautauqua preachers, but from a rabbi who instructed him in the rudiments of accumulation. "He would tell me, 'Eugene, Eugene, can't I teach you anything? Any fool can spend, but it takes a wise man to save!' "

The people of Canarsie moved in circles that did not overlap with Protestant cliques. A PTA leader, munching on an Italian pastry, chatted with her Jewish and Italian girlfriends around a dinette table. "They are all WASPs at the presidential level," she lamented. "We need somebody from the Big Apple to understand our problems. We Italians and Jews are all the same, we have real good relations, but I'd be uncomfortable in a Protestant community. We all like to play mahjong in Canarsie." Leaning against the bar at the Knights of Columbus lodge, an Italian clerk fumbled for a second as he tried to characterize Protestants. "I don't know, I mean, I really haven't met too many of them. I don't know what kind of people they're like." A Jewish housewife put it this way. "It's good to meet all types of people, I guess, but I'm a ghetto person. In the summer I go to a bungalow colony in the Catskills where the people are just like me."

The immigrants and their offspring acquired the trappings of American kinship, language, and ideology, but they did not absorb Americanism wholesale. Selectively borrowing from the materials at hand, they built their own variants of American culture. Yiddish and Italian phrases crept naturally into the conversations of people with names like Vinnie and Irving, Speraccio and Berkowitz. A leader in the Italian-American Civil Rights League in Canarsie used the contemptuous Sicilian term for a rough punk, gorilla, or a brutish peasant. "The Italian used to be stereotyped as a *gavon,* as a man of no culture, like years ago when they showed Negroes spitting out watermelon seeds." The Jews often referred to the ideal of the decent, ethical man, a *mensch.*

The elegies recited in homage to the ancestors also kept the past alive. A Jewish woman told how her people were delivered from the

Diaspora. Her father was born in Kiev in the Ukraine, emigrated to Israel, then sailed for New York. Her mother grew up in Bessarabia. "The whole town escaped the draft in 1905 and bought land in Turkey. Then, after World War I, they lost the land, so they came to New York. Why, the whole town just picked up and left! Now you think it's a big deal to move to Long Island."

Canarsians paid a great deal of attention to ethnicity. That people were members of communal groups as much as they were singular personalities was an article of faith that silently shaped their perceptions of the world. At times the residents became extreme in their penchant for sorting, endlessly dividing the flow of life into obsessively refined categories. A synagogue of Sephardic Jews took that sectioning impulse to the outer edges of parody. As one congregant explained:

> We're the only Sephardic temple in the Canarsie/East Flatbush area with Spanish-Turkish ritual. We specialize in Cubans. The Cuban burial society is here. Those of Turkish ancestry know Ladino, though not the Cubans. Now our emphasis is on Castillian. The Cuban Sephardim and the non-Cuban Sephardim have their problems. The non-Cubans complain that the Cubans don't do work in support of the congregation. We had to form an affirmative action program to get Cubans on every committee. The Cubans have more closeness. At the Cuban burial society, they sing "HaTikva" [the Israeli national anthem], the "Star Spangled Banner," and the Cuban national anthem. But we Sephardim have to stick together. We are the last of the Mohicans.

Canarsians presumed that animosity between communal strangers was as inborn as the camaraderie of ethnic confrères. A Jewish artist reflected philosophically, "I have a hangup about intermarriage between Jews and non-Jews. I was brought up in a Jewish household and that's where I learned my traditions." He struck a melancholy note: "The human species is a weird creature. Everybody is afraid of things which are too different from them. It's a shame. If whites were pink, we'd throw whitey out the window."

In contrast, an Italian woman epitomized the quirky suspicions bred by provincialism. "I'm glad Mayor Beame is Jewish and not Italian," she said at the height of the New York City fiscal crisis of

1975, "so it's not one of our own people, our own kind, that gets the blame for it." Her preference for the familiar led to an odd alliance: "I went to integrated schools with blacks. I'm not prejudiced. I'd rather be with them than with Puerto Ricans. It's Puerto Ricans I don't like. They're sneaky."

The attractions of ethnicity have not prevented the gradual emptying out of the specific contents of Jewish and Italian heritage. Compared to their Old World parents, second- and third-generation Canarsians seemed refined and American. Rival influences of education, cultural change, and popular entertainment have spread through the community at uneven rates and in a variety of patterns.

The shedding of the past sometimes left a feeling of irretrievable loss. "We used to have the old Italian weddings," one second-generation Italian woman said. "We called them football weddings. Someone would yell, 'Hey, who wants the root beer?' and they'd throw out the root beer; 'Hey, who wants a sandwich?' and they'd throw the sandwich through the air. It was uncouth, it had no class, but it was lots of fun. Not like those fancy things you go to today where you have to look at the other guy to figure out which of the eighteen forks you're supposed to eat with."

Undoubtedly, some Canarsians have turned success into vulgar grasping or compulsive quest, and ceremonial events like weddings, bar mitzvahs, and sweet sixteen parties into occasions of sumptuous display. Arbiters of chic might look down on the decor of many Canarsie living rooms, with crimson velour flock on the walls, lush avocado rugs, and vinyl-covered sofas, as the clutter of kitsch. The ornate chandeliers and gilded mirrors of Italian catering halls could be seen as pretentions of the parvenu. Two Italian women with many Jewish friends decried the way the ostentatious show of status debased the meaning of genuine tradition. "These fancy weddings and bar mitzvahs are disgusting," they complained. "None of that has anything to do with the tradition. It's better to spend the money to go to Israel. It's showing off, keeping up with the Joneses. There's a 'Can you top this?' attitude. It's all show. The tradition doesn't mean anything with all those trappings."

One must be wary of projecting a fancier meaning onto Canarsians' pride and polish than the facts warrant; one should not view them only as avaricious, one-dimensional, or racist vulgarians. To take the part for the whole, molding the people into symbols, is to commit a companion form of one-dimensional thinking. Reductionism promotes a studied inattention to the qualities that the clichés of Middle America do not capture: loyalty, compassion, bawdiness, courage, directness. Concepts like materialism and narcissism do not do justice to the diversity of Canarsians, who ranged across the spectrum of patriotic gullibility, unregenerate individualism, and ethnicity manqué.

The residents varied in their liberation from ethnic traditions, in their devotion to socializing with those of like kind, in the amount of their contact with diverse lifestyles. Many of the working-class Italians were shielded from unfamiliar messages, while educated Jews were more often exposed to varied styles of living. Some Italians decried the Italian-American Civil Rights League, proudly insisting they were "Americans first," while others took great pride in their ethnic heritage. Many Orthodox Jews socialized primarily with other Orthodox Jews; some secular Jews socialized only with other secular Jews. Who were the less tribal? For many, the intensity and the form of their feelings of ethnicity fluctuated over time. "I kept a kosher home out of respect for my grandparents, but we eat non-kosher outside the home now. I want the children to know who they are, to know they are religious, to know their heritage. Once, we ate the [Passover] Seder in the kitchen and my kid asked, 'Aren't we Jewish anymore?'"

Ethnicity continued to shape Canarsie sensibilities and acquaintanceships. Defying those theorists who direly predict the atomization of American life, countless Americans remain joined to one another by bracing ties of kinship, ethnicity, territory, religion, and status. Informal, sentimental, and communal ties endure in the most advanced enclaves of modern society. Although these ties have declined in intensity or altered in function, few areas of life so aptly show the vitality of ethnicity as politics.[2]

Because communal traditions framed the way Canarsie Jews and Italians responded to threat in recent years, an exploration of their political subcultures must supplement my impressionistic vignettes. The archetypes of idealistic Jews and wily Italians point to aspects of their respective political tempers. A young Italian man whose wife was Jewish put it this way: "The Jews are weak, they are wishy-washy. But the Italians take a rock-hard, hard-nosed approach to things." Jewish sentimentality and Italian toughness reflect historic patterns of social organization that continued to play on the people of Canarsie in the 1970s.

Italian Tradition

*"Being an Italian, you love the family right or
wrong, you back it and stand fast."*

During the 1960s and 1970s Italians figured prominently in clashes
between blacks and whites throughout the Northeast and produced
white-hope saviors like Frank Rizzo in Philadelphia, Tough Tony
Imperiale in Newark, and Mario Procaccino in New York City. It is a
minor irony of American ethnic history that their Saracen blood
gave the southern Italians a dark complexion that sometimes resembles African more than Caucasian hues. Early Italian immigrants were victims in a number of infamous lynching episodes in the
American South. Historian John Higham has described the plight of
the Italians, whom southern whites considered anomalies that upset
the neat logic of their racial taxonomy. "Sections deeply sensitive to
complexion and cast of features readily detected a swarthy face. In
the South, the [Italian] newcomers' 'in-betweenness' seemed a double threat. He might endanger not only the purity of the white race
but also its solidarity."[3]

Most of the Italians in Canarsie traced their genealogy to the
peasants who came to New York City at the turn of the century to
escape agrarian misfortune in southern Italy and Sicily. They established cloistered urban villages whose members were tied by kinship,
dialect, and region, replicating the culture and social structure of the
old country. The arrival of the Italians in Canarsie expressed the
move some immigrants made from the urban core to the farmlands
of outlying Queens and the North Bronx. "Italians went to the end of
the subway lines and beyond, seeking cheap land on which to build
houses and raise vegetables and goats."[4]

The fruit trees tended so carefully by Canarsie Italians earlier in
the century attested to that nostalgia for agrarian simplicity. Truck
farms and jerry-built bungalows dotted the landscape of Canarsie in
the 1930s, often financed without mortgages from a great capacity
for labor and frugality. A construction worker remembered a family
tradition of home owning that the Depression halted only temporar-
ily. "My family always liked to own their own home. We only lost
our home once, when we had to go on relief during the Depression.
You see, if you pay for a home, and you work to improve it with your
own hands, let's say you build your own patio or barbecue brick by
brick, then you have memories of it with your family for a long time

to come." Love of home explains much of the grace of Italian neighborhoods that have survived, now surrounded by squalor.

The old neighborhoods were founded on strong personal ties and mistrust of formal agents of help such as experts, government, and law. Canarsie Italians today laud the benefits of sticking with "one's own kind" against strangers. An Italian man recalled the disbursement of credit as a sign of membership in a community of intimates; lending was dictated by the duty to help friends and repay obligations, not by frigid criteria of least risk and best return. "When I was a kid, I'd go to the corner store and get credit because the owner was a friend who knew me and my family. If you needed a quart of milk, you'd get it. But it's all commercial now."

The cult of the personal embodied a sensibility at odds with that of the marketplace, formal law, and meritocracy, which failed to distinguish between the treatment of insiders and of outsiders. By affirming the natural comforts of living in a familiar community of the like-minded, it justified closed neighborhoods, employment markets, and unions. As an Old Canarsie civic leader expressed it, "I believe that people should live among their own kind. The Italians always migrated to an Italian area, the Jews to a Jewish area, the Norwegians to a Norwegian area. That's the way it should be. There was always a Jewish part of East New York and an Italian part of East New York."[5]

The mystique of personal relations had its drawbacks. In the old country and America, Italians never achieved the leverage that comes from belonging to organizations that recruit members on other than personal criteria. While Canarsie Jews fluently cited aspects of a formal high culture or the fear of persecution that unites all Jews in perpetual vigilance, a high official in the national Italian-American Civil Rights League was capable of retorting, "I don't identify with anything in Italy except the family."[6]

The Italians survived the betrayals of history and nature by vesting all trust in the most personal of institutions. The Italian family, Luigi Barzini has written, "is a stronghold in a hostile land: within its walls and among its members, the individual finds consolation, help, advice, provisions, loans, weapons, allies and accomplices to aid him in his pursuits." Beyond its practical functions, the family was "invincible because it was the sacred ark in which Italians deposited and preserved against alien influences all their ancient ideals." That loyalty to the close-knit family constituted their only patriotism; "the law, the State and society function only if they do not directly interfere with the family's supreme interests."[7] Although praise of an ancient ideal could not hide increasing departures from its observance, a virtually religious veneration of the family ran through Italian Old Canarsie. Said a salesman, "Being an Italian, you love the family right or wrong, you back it and stand fast. It's the same thing with the country. I can say I don't like what's going on, but I won't tolerate others saying it."

The views of Old Canarsie Italians on the proper way to raise children epitomized the tension between modern culture and familism. Among the most cosmopolitan Jews, parenting was sometimes seen as a self-conscious task with an ultimate aim, and children as bundles of possibility who required an unhampering environment to flourish as individuals. Provincial Italians, by contrast, stressed the timelessness of human nature and the corollary need to hedge in that restive individuality with a web of communal rules. They often claimed that all desirable traits in children stemmed from a single source, respect for and obedience to parents.[8] "The first thing you want in a child," one man insisted, "is respect for parents. From that comes all the other things you want. Once you respect your parents, then you learn everything from them." Typically, a dockworker saw strictness as a remedy for the dangerously curious, antisocial impulses of children. "You must obey the family rules and have strict discipline, because human nature is strange. If kids can take an inch, they'll take a foot."

Resignation to the "facts of life" made Italians mistrust sanctimonious moralizers who appealed to the ethical side of human nature. An Italian policeman's analysis of ethnocentrism embodied that naturalistic spirit.[9] "Who isn't prejudiced? I see a guy walking around with a bone in the nose, I'm prejudiced because I don't like that bone in the nose, because he's different. Anyone who's different, who doesn't fit my thing, I'm prejudiced against him. I don't like him. This is a fact of life."

The inflections of realism are reminiscent of deep strains in southern Italian culture. If the Jews endured the millenia as a chosen people awaiting the advent of a Messiah, the Italians were too cynical to accept that optimistic theodicy. In contrast to the hopeful strain in American Protestantism that underlies revivalistic crusades against sin, no faith in the perfectability of mankind tempered Italian skepticism about projects of reform or disinterested benevolence. One famous homily warned, "Whoever forsakes the old ways for the new knows what he is losing, but not what he will find."

The Italians call southern Italy, the Mezzogiorno, "the land that time forgot," evoking the tragic implacability of existence. An alert moral community might regulate human nature through shame and surveillance, but neither inner conscience nor rational mastery could vanquish its primitive force. Imprisoned in the past, even the vernacular was "geared to the expression of ideas that were ancient, almost changeless, and highly restricted . . . Little wonder that even today the future tense among the Southern Italian peasantry is virtually unknown."[10]

New York's subways, skyscrapers, and bridges were built on the backs of Italian immigrants. Most Italians in Canarsie had a relative who had worked with a shovel, journeyed to distant cities in search of work, burrowed deep into the ground. A proud clerk who earned $13,000 a year in 1976 viewed his father's climb out of poverty to the modest comfort of a sanitation man as the model by which all minorities should improve themselves. "My father came from Palermo and went to work in the subways. He dug tunnels like all the other slobs did in his day to earn a living. And the man, by his own will, managed to improve his way of life. He brought us to Canarsie, with all the barriers to overcome, he learned to speak English and made a tremendous success out of himself." Less typically, a young construction worker with a militant analysis of the exploitation of white ethnics demanded, "Do you call it living when your grandfather had to dig a tunnel from morning until night? They made *us* dig the tunnels. When the earth caved in, it was always one of the Italians who died, nobody of consequence! We were slaves."

The children of the immigrants saw their forebears' labor as a payment of ethnic dues, to be indemnified by the success of later generations. The need to redeem the ancestral sacrifice fortified the belief that all ethnic groups had to put in their time, wait their turn, and sweat blood. That veneration of stoical endurance is not explained by a process of Americanization that subjected the fatalistic ethos of peasants to an alien individualism. Italian-American values were a successive recombination of aspects of American privatism and Italian familism. In southern Italy individualism was a badge of a man's ability to take care of his family. Conversely, dependency on the state confessed to a humiliating inability to realize the basic requirement of manly honor. "South Italians had a cultural bias against accepting public welfare . . . peasants considered reliance upon charity even more disgraceful than destitution."[11]

The residue of traditional lore imparted a conception of education that was at odds with the Jewish worship of schooling. Historically, Italian Americans have mistrusted the public schools as a potential rival to the influence of the family. *Ben educato* meant "raised with the core of one's personality woven of those values and attitudes, habits and skills that perpetuated l'ordine della famiglia."[12] One woman, typical of the new breed of upwardly mobile, cosmopolitan Italians in Canarsie, had won a victory for female autonomy when she insisted, against her family's wishes, on attending Brooklyn College. She captured the different approaches of Italian and Jewish households in Canarsie, as well as a beginning split between provincial and cosmopolitan Italians. "The Jews in Canarsie push their kids to excel in school. They really pressure their children. They won't see past 'My kid will be a doctor.' That's happening a little more now with the Italians, but we mainly say we want our kids to have a good job and to provide for the family." In Italian Old Canarsie, less than 50 percent of the adults in 1980 had graduated from high school, and just a shade more than 5 percent had completed college.

The Italians in Old Canarsie had made strides beyond their ancestors' station in life, mainly by moving into skilled blue-collar and lower white-collar positions. In 1980 half the work force labored in manual jobs, but only about 10 percent were professional or managerial workers. Most of the white-collar jobs were performed by women, many of whom were typists, secretaries, and bookkeepers. The majority of the men worked at blue-collar occupations, more of them as operators of machinery and laborers than as skilled craftsmen, precision production workers, and repairmen. In 1970 the number of Italian policemen, of construction craftsmen, of repairmen and mechanics, and of truckers each surpassed the number of schoolteachers. The paychecks of working wives helped raise median family income in 1980 to between $12,000 and $18,000. Less than one-fourth of the households had incomes above $25,000, and most of those did not reach the $35,000 mark.

The hard facts of income, occupation, and education remind us that Canarsie Italians were not simply the fleshly embodiment of traditional Italian values. If many of them seemed coarse in manners, laden with superstition, and blatantly ethnocentric, that was in large measure because these qualities tend to be shared by those who lack schooling, power, and income. Italians settled disputes, perceived minorities, and responded to politics in ways that derived significantly from their social standing. Canarsie Italians often wrongfully chalked up aspects of ghetto life to race; it would be equally misleading to attribute the parochialism of working-class life just to Italian culture.[13]

One consequence of the Italians' social position was the precariousness of their hold on middle-class life. The persistence of an identity as "little people," which mixed envy of and anger at fancy people of substance, testified to Italian vulnerability. "I'd say we're down-to-earth people in Canarsie, not the high-rise kind of person who thinks they can look down on others 'cause they're making more money than us," said an Italian clerk. Italian Conservative and Republican leaders in Canarsie did not defend the prerogatives of the country club set or corporate business. A Conservative Party activist who revered Joseph McCarthy and George Wallace complained, "It's unfair. The rich get richer, that's a fact. Take these New York City bonds. We can't buy $20,000 bonds and get the interest. It's for the people in the money class, not for people like us."

The Italians' social position also had cultural consequences. By regulating the worker's exposure to subversive and conventional truths, life on the job reinforces, undermines, or qualifies his culture.[14] The blue-collar work milieu provides a breathing space in which workers can express the vulgar and provincial qualities of plebeian life and flout middle-class ideals of gentility. Truckers, longshoremen, and hardhats perform the complex of patriarchal rites that include rowdy nose thumbing at polite society, contempt for feminized respectability, and reverence for physical courage. As one worker said, "I'm a rough tough guy and I don't back down from nobody!"

The code of respect for men who look after their own affairs diminished the scruples that working-class Italian men had about using force to settle a grudge. A white Protestant policeman from the South, who patrolled the streets of Canarsie, laughed at the differences he observed of Jews and Italians under arrest and in court. "I'm telling you," he drawled, "the difference is amazing. The Jews just won't fight like the Italians. The Italians will go to court, they're not afraid of retaliation, but the Jews are scared. You can't get them to press charges or to testify. But the Italians, they like to show off they're tough. If they can't fight their girlfriends or the police, then they'll fight the blacks." Later this policeman was killed by a local Italian youth.

Political leaders with a penchant for action drew the admiration of Italian men. General Douglas MacArthur and Senator Joseph McCarthy were remembered by many as firm men who "took no

crap from anybody." While Jews often cited Adlai Stevenson's elo-
quence, Italian workers preferred men who talked straight: plainly
rather than eloquently. Too much fancy talk might drain the resolve
to act.

Canarsie Italians were relatively casual about remote political
events and affected indifference to public affairs. Family, neighborhood, and jobs defined the horizons of their attention and knowledge.[15] One conservative activist despaired of catalyzing his
neighbors. He saw their immersion in family life as a formidable impediment to turning their resentments into leverage proportional to
their numbers. "We Italians are a backwards, ignorant people. The
only thing we care about is our home and our family. We're a conservative people, because we worked hard for what we got, and we
don't like to see others sitting about and collecting checks. But we
don't vote. It's incredible. We complain, but we just don't vote."

Hazy knowledge and inexperience added to an intuition that politics was manipulated by mysterious forces. Suspicion was often
transmitted down through the generations by adages like "All politicians are thieves," "The squeaky wheel gets the grease," and "One
hand washes the other." The penchant for projective thinking was
evident in the fluency with which Italian Americans resorted to conspiracy as a means of explaining events. A leader in the Italian-
American Civil Rights League offered a grandiose version. "There's
a conspiracy against Italian Americans, because we really are a majority of Americans. There are thirty-three million of us, although
the census is afraid to admit it. That is why the CIA shot Robert
Kennedy, Martin Luther King, and Joe Columbo. It was because
Columbo was trying to unite the have-nots against the haves. The
CIA did it because Joe Columbo would have upset the two-party
system."

Suspicion was more than a symptom of a paranoid personality: it
reflected the alienation of provincial Italians from the political system. Many of them felt that they were the objects rather than the
initiators of influence. However much Italian values instilled faith in
self-help, powerlessness also reinforced a willingness to rely on unofficial channels to gain a hearing.[16]

Mistrust of strangers, whether of local or global unknowns, encouraged a shrewd approach to political life that shaped the limits of
a leader's discretion. Canarsie Italians liked resolute leaders who
were not squeamish about their methods in defending their followers. Occasionally Mussolini was cited as a paragon of effective per-

formance. One leader in the Italian-American Civil Rights League argued, "I am an American, and naturally I believe in complete freedom. But, if you remember the time of Mussolini when the Fascists were in power, he was the only one who got things done, he was the only one who built roads and brought employment to starving people. If the Communists in Italy are now following what Mussolini did, then I say great, why not?"

One can detect an analogy between the benevolent patron who takes care of business without fastidious observance of the law and the Italian patriarch. Richard Gambino has depicted the traditional Italian father as a minister of the family's foreign affairs who promotes its security "in this microcosm of the world of sovereign states." Like a good Machiavellian, the father acts as "a true monarch for the good of his endangered kingdom, according to the severe rules of *realpolitik*."[17] In recent decades, blacks who encroached upon Italian kingdoms of home, family, and neighborhood discovered the truth of Gambino's depiction.

Pragmatism easily shaded into a tolerance for breaches of democracy. A Republican Italian leader evoked the tension between legalism and realism, often rendered as a conflict between ethnic foxiness and Jewish humanism or perfectionist Yankee zeal. "We're not lilywhite! We should lay aside the Constitution when we must. We did it with the Japanese during World War II, we put them in camps and plenty of them were innocent. But don't say it's wrong because it doesn't conform to our moral principles."

The electoral repercussions of these diverse forces were that ethics and ideology did not play an important role in fashioning political choices. Italian Americans were not tightly bound to a political party by the ties of loyalty. Their diffuse populist resentment of high-rise people did not translate into a broader social vision. The basic affinity of Italian Americans lay with conservative Democrats, rock-ribbed Republicans who abjured the lofty rhetoric of Yankee mugwumps, and nonideological local politicians who spoke to the needs of family and community.[18]

In 1920 the few dozen Canarsie Italians who were registered to vote demonstrated an unmistakable Republicanism. Virtually every citizen with an Italian surname in the twenty-sixth and twenty-seventh election districts of the old Second Assembly District, Grobanni Alissandro, Luigi Giacabone, and Vincenzo Luciano, enlisted in the Grand Old Party. Nationally, Italians adhered to "an almost literal faith in the McKinley slogan of the 'full dinner pail,' the belief that prosperity and the Republican Party went together. As long as jobs were available, the bulk of immigrants were content to follow the suggestions of their *padroni* on how to vote."[19]

The Depression challenged the credibility of that slogan, and Brooklyn Italians, along with the rest of ethnic New York, swarmed to Franklin Roosevelt in 1932. But later those Italians recollected Roosevelt in lukewarm tones, in sharp contrast to the vivid memories and effusive emotions of Canarsie Jews. The Italians displayed little enthusiasm for Roosevelt's transcendent purpose. An Italian white-collar worker spoke of New Deal attitudes as anachronistic, remote in time and urgency. "The reason why the Italians in Canarsie vote Republican is not that we are affluent. You see, during the Roosevelt era, the Democrats were for the poor, and they gave us programs which helped get us out of the Depression. At that time the New Deal was the only route to go. The Works Progress Administration and the Civilian Conservation Corps were good things. Even though they were socialistic, they were necessary because of what was happening."

Precepts of one-sided exchange like turning the other cheek, the Roman vision of clemency, or the feudal conception of noblesse oblige may slow the rush to vengeance. Charitable ideals allow grace time to an institution that has betrayed expectations of a just return.[20] But southern Italian culture never taught such merciful exemptions, and Italian Americans struck back hard when the Democrats violated Italian honor and interest.

Roosevelt's plummeting strength after 1932 prefigured the fickleness of the Catholic portion of the New Deal coalition. His condemnation of Mussolini's attack on France—"The hand that held the dagger has plunged it into the back of its neighbor"—stirred public outcry in Canarsie's Little Italy. One source of disenchantment with the Democratic party lay in the anti-Fascist foreign policy that led to war with Italy. As one Canarsie political leader said, "People were brainwashed into thinking the Republicans were the party of the rich and the Democrats were the party of the people. But I can't forget that Roosevelt sucked us into World War II. We never should have been in that war." Even more than the Anglophobic Irish, "Italian-Americans became probably the most anti-Roosevelt of all low-income groups. In 1944 he got only 41 percent of the vote in Italian districts in the city, while getting 61 percent in the city as a whole."[21]

The cold war fired Catholic anxieties about communism, intensified disaffection with the national Democratic party, and widened the political wedge between Jews and Catholics. "Alienated by the liberal internationalism which had plunged one generation of Americans into two wars and imposed a considerable strain on the psyches (although not the loyalty) of several major ethnic groups," the Italians joined other Catholics who had opposed Roosevelt in embracing the nationalist views of the Republican party. Surprising numbers of Italians in the 1970s volunteered favorable opinions about Joseph McCarthy, whom they saw as an unveiler of plots hatched by enemies rather than as a mean gutter fighter. An Italian Republican official argued, "Joe McCarthy was a good thing for America. If people have nothing to hide, why do they make all the fuss about rights? McCarthy performed a valuable service. He brought things to the light." In the 1952 Roper poll, more Italians approved of McCarthy than reviled him, by a hefty margin of 16 percent.[22]

Their approval does not tell us whether popular McCarthyism was a populist wish for revenge against patricians or "an anti-Communism relatively less restrained [by concern for] McCarthy's crudities."[23] But one Canarsie Italian leader remembered taking part in a vendetta against the local Red Menace. "I had a professor who was expelled from City College in the 1950s for taking the Fifth Amendment at a loyalty hearing. In 1953 five of my friends and I got a pro-McCarthy petition against him. We wanted to get rid of the Communists. Communists shouldn't be allowed to be teachers." Respectable leaders of civic, religious, and political life in Catholic Brooklyn also endorsed McCarthy. A shadow movement of right-wing nationalists predated and survived the "modern Republican" betrayal of the old-time religion. The events of the 1960s animated a combat-ready network of grassroots conservatives.

Disagreement between Jews and Italians over McCarthyism repeated a telling division between the Catholic reproach of Jewish leftist leanings and the Jewish fear of a Catholic bent for authoritarianism. Although muted by the passage of time, the ethnic recriminations were expressed in oblique ways. An Italian man active in the Knights of Columbus hinted at the cowardice of the Jews and the potential treachery of dual loyalties. "All Americans should know their heritage, but we are Americans first. That's what annoys me when Jews rally for Israel, but they wouldn't even do it for the Korean war, and they tried to keep their kids out of Vietnam. I'm Sicilian, but if Sicily went to war, I wouldn't think of sending trees there!

Jews claim they never had a country. Then why do they rally to another country?" A Jewish baker returned the ethnic suspicion
through his contempt for "ignorant" Catholics who remained in the
dark about the progressive strands of their own traditions. "I'm sur-
prised that the Italians are so conservative in Canarsie, what with
their radical tradition. But don't tell that to them or they'll get mad
as hell! It's like the Irish who don't even know that their 1916 revolution was a socialist revolution."

Adlai Stevenson's poor showing among Canarsie Italians in the
1950s signaled their receptivity to Republican presidential candidates. The Italians rallied to Dwight Eisenhower. The popularity of
a military hero cannot entirely explain that Republican success, for
the solid Democratic registration of 1932 had given way by 1952 to a
mixed pattern of party identification among the Italians in Canarsie,
in contrast to unflagging Jewish loyalty to the Democrats. The wid-
est breach between the two was in 1956 when Eisenhower received
more than 70 percent of Little Italy's vote, while in Jewish precincts
he ran 70 percent behind Stevenson, who took 85 percent of the vote
on the Democratic and Liberal lines. Nor did the modest Catholic
return to the Democrats in 1960 disguise the true direction of the
Italian vote. Among Kennedy's fellow Catholics in Italian Old Canarsie, Nixon may have come close to eking out a victory. As Keven
Phillips observed, Kennedy's pickup over Stevenson among New
York Catholics "boosted Democratic Catholic levels to only about
60 percent. And the large Catholic middle class of New York City
seems to have given Nixon a clear majority."[24]

The Italians resisted cultural, political, and racial change. And
when not entirely backward-glancing, they ignored revisions of culture and politics that did not touch the family or neighborhood.
Familism was thus paradoxical. It spurred Italians to action in public
affairs while giving them a private refuge from its intrusions. Italians
stood fast against black challenge, fiscal extravagance, and cultural
decadence. They embodied the hard, rowdy side of backlash because
history gave them resources of symbolic and physical toughness, because their social standing left them vulnerable to competition from
minorities, and because their values bred hostility to the permissive
currents of modern culture.

At the same time, Canarsie saw the birth of a gentler, softer brand
of backlash, practiced chiefly by Jews. Yet that generality must be
qualified as soon as it is uttered. Too many supremely decent Italians and too many Jews twisted with resentment disprove the sug-

gestion that all Jews were temperate *menschen,* all Italians racist *gavons.*

Jewish Tradition

*"My father was a man of his generation, a radical
who read Karl Marx like the Talmud."*

Commentators have often remarked on the kinship between Jews and Italians, but my analysis of the Jewish tradition highlights the points of divergence, with the accent on the destiny of Jewish liberalism. Canarsie's Jews could not decide whether that tradition was a curse or a blessing, and to resolve the conundrum, they had to undergo a painful ordeal of cultural questioning.

Their confusion resulted in part from a taboo on vengeance. The Talmud forbids returning evil for evil. Retribution is not the Law of the Book; it represents the blood lust of Gentiles. "He who avenges himself, or bears a grudge, acts as one who has had one hand cut by a knife, and now sticks it into the other hand for revenge." As black and Jewish interests collided in recent years, the heritage of meekness kept the Jews from striking back as swiftly as did their Italian neighbors. But gradually Canarsie Jews came to see the prohibition of vengeance as a slavishness which, as Walter Kaufmann restated Nietzsche, "would like nothing better than revenge." Slave morality means being "kindly when one is merely too weak and timid to act otherwise."[25] Such passivity in the face of threat creates from the despised fate of powerlessness an illusion of noble choosing.

Jews and Italians in Canarsie both claim to be family people, and they like to contrast their strong kinship ties with the fragile families of the black ghetto. Nathan Glazer wrote, "The Italian family resembles in some ways the Jewish one, in its strength, its heightened and uninhibited emotional quality, and even in some of its inner alliances. Thus, there is a strong tie between mother and son." In Jewish culture, however, the family has never had as strong a hold as in the Italian culture. The distinction between porous and impermeable family boundaries matches the historic differences between the two peoples. Italians rely on the family to settle grudges; Jews accept the state's monopoly on violence. Earthbound Italians are home owners; wandering Jews are apartment dwellers. Italian dialect was imprisoned in the past; Yiddish borrowed from many European languages. Irving Howe has noted, "Neither set nor formalized, always in rapid process of growth and dissolution, Yiddish was a language intimately reflecting the travail of wandering, exile, dispersion."[26]

Canarsians made their own observations about the difference. One evening, a group of Jewish and Italian men joshed together. A Jewish man told an ethnic joke. "Why," he asked, "do Italian men leave their fly open?" After an effective pause, he headed for the punchline. "To help them count to eleven." An Italian salesman recalled his father, who brooked no sass from his children. "My old man punched my brother and broke his eardrum." His Jewish buddy grinned. "I am telling you, the Jewish way is better than the Italian. Guilt is much more effective."

Even though the Jews and Italians arrived in America during roughly the same period, the economic disparity between them remains telling, both in Canarsie and across the nation. Compared to Italian Americans, the Jews have accumulated greater economic and cultural capital. Their future orientation has broadened their horizons in education, residence, and occupation beyond the ambit of Italian provincialism. "Do not make your son better than you are," Italian folklore warned parents. But "the culture of the [Jewish] East Side became a culture utterly devoted to its sons. Onto their backs it lowered all its aspirations and delusions, expecting that the children of the new world would reach the goals their fathers could not reach themselves."[27]

A pharmacist whose parents were garment workers exclaimed with exuberance, "I started off with nothing twenty years ago. I'm a poor little Jewish guy who made good. It's the Jewish dream, to give your kids all the things in life you don't have. It's a wife with her own car driving the kids to the orthodontist." He led a tour of his house, which contained six televisions for a five-member family. "I had a dream. I didn't want to be content and stand still and stay living in a slum in Brownsville."

The clothing industry first gave Brooklyn Jews a niche in the economy. Tailors, furriers, seamstresses, remnant dealers, haberdashers, and small manufacturers populated the biographies of Jewish Canarsians. Having built their base in the garment trades, the Jews began a steady movement out of the working class. The wife of a clerk in a small retail store did not forget the commandments of her father, a tailor in Brownsville: "We were always told, 'Get an education, go to work! We are a book people, a learned people, we're different from other ethnic groups.' The Italians in Canarsie say, 'Okay, get a job, just be a truck driver,' but we always heard, 'Do better, there's more to life than just getting by, do for yourself! Don't rely on others.' "

The tailor's exhortations disclosed the intimate link that was seen between education and success. If Americans have made education into a secular religion, the Jews have given the search for credentials a special adoration, and their strides relative to other ethnic groups have only confirmed the worthiness of the love object.[28] In Canarsie the median level of education in Jewish areas was between twelve and thirteen years in 1970, two years higher than in Italian Old Canarsie. In 1980 less than half the Italians had graduated from high school, while 67 to 87 percent of the residents in heavily Jewish areas had high school diplomas. And the Jews went on to jobs in education. In one Seaview Village census tract in 1970, teachers—109 of them—represented twelve percent of the work force, not including paraprofessionals and school principals. In another departure from the Italian pattern in Old Canarsie, the proportion of workers in education was generally double the proportion in the building trades. Anything that touched the schools or the United Federation of Teachers—and many things did as the pace of the civil rights movement quickened—touched Jewish interests.

If one path out of the working class led to teaching, another led to business enterprise, with its requirements of chutzpah and hustle. The owner of a small factory defined the voluntaristic ethic that spurred effort. "The Jewish people weren't treated equally, but we progressed. But we didn't progress because we were Jewish, but because we were a driving, pushing people. The story of America is a man gets a pushcart and sells apples, and buys a factory and manufactures apples. Take the story of Harry Henry. He sold linoleum on Rivington Street and now he owns Western Carpets. That's the American Dream."

Canarsie Jews had greater resources than the Italians. In the heavily Jewish areas the median annual income of families in 1980 was $20,000, and between a third and a half of them earned more than $25,000. Many more of the Jews—two-thirds to three-quarters—performed white-collar jobs. While the vast majority of white-collar Italians were clerical workers and salespersons, in the Jewish areas fully one-fifth to one-third of the work force was employed in managerial and professional occupations.

Like the Italians, the Jews were not defined by their ethnicity alone. If they seemed more genteel, it was because Italian workers happened to be workers, not because they happened to be Italians. Jewish worldliness was the result not only of the force of Jewish culture, but of the education and occupations of the Jews. When a Jewish attorney in Canarsie complained of the rudeness of Canarsie Jews, comparing them unfavorably to the "better class of Jews" across Ralph Avenue in Midwood and Mill Basin, he was giving voice to the obvious: Jews vary in social standing. Richard Hamilton may be right in observing that the upper middle class ranks high in tolerance in part because it is disproportionately Jewish. Yet it is also true that Jews rank high in tolerance because they inhabit the professional ranks of society.

The complexity does not end there. German, Eastern European, and Mediterranean Jews from the same class background do not embrace identical values. Among the mainly eastern European Jews of Canarsie, the lifestyles of residents from left-wing backgrounds, of pious Orthodox Jews, and of devotees of consumer culture were hardly the same. Indeed, in contrast to Borough Park, Crown Heights, and Williamsburg, Canarsie had never been home to large numbers of the scrupulously Orthodox, and that fact had a decisive effect on it politics and culture. The problem is comparing people who vary simultaneously on a number of variables.[29]

If Canarsie Jews enjoyed an edge over the Italians in education and income, the superiority was only relative within the borders of the middle-income classes. Out of thirty-some census tracts, the four with a median family income above $22,000 were all in Jewish sections, but in the majority of Jewish tracts, the median income ranged between $17,000 and $22,000. Although many Jewish families had annual incomes of better than $25,000, this usually represented the work of two wage earners, and most of them earned less than $35,000. Less than 20 percent of the Jewish adults had college diplomas.

Canarsians did not identify with the Olympian heights of the professional upper middle classes. The owner of a small factory strained "to work hard, so I can afford piano lessons for my daughter. I want to give her a little class." Like many of his Italian working-class neighbors, the man resented "these lawyers and college grads and do-gooders in Scarsdale. But they don't know anything about doing good." The greater reach of many Jews' contacts with affluent relatives bridged the distance between worlds and transmitted invidious judgments back to the community. One Canarsie woman separated herself from her neighbors, defensively insisting, "I would say I'm middle and not lower middle class. I'm different because I'm educated. I'd say the middle class is more snobbish. Take my brother. He lives in Great Neck, and he looks down on Canarsie, because the people are lower middle class and uneducated." For the bulk of Jews in Canarsie, abundance remained elusive. A rabbi summarized, "Simple survival, economic survival, is their main goal. They work hard just to make ends meet, but it's a constant struggle, and they are tired."

The Jews had a pronounced feeling of ethnic honor, another sign of their willingness to invest in loyalties beyond the nuclear family. The articulateness of the Jewish identity, and the capacity for immersion in the collective experience of Jewish suffering, ran contrary to the muteness of Canarsie Italians about their ethnicity. "The Jews have been through traumas," a Democratic politician explained. "But we have always survived. We are a separate and destined people. I have no illusion that the U.S. is paradise. America is Babylon. We must ask the question, 'Do we want death by assimilation? Do we want death by intermarriage? Or do we want to preserve our traditions?' "

Perhaps a greater spur to ethnic identity was the fear of external dangers. The presence of Holocaust survivors stoked ancient anxieties about persecution. One kindly man, his voice quavering with emotion, chronicled the lessons he had learned from suffering. "I am not in favor of restrictions on people because I have been restricted. I spent six good years of my life in Nazi concentration camps, and the Germans told me what to do, when to do it, and how to do it. I am the only one left alive from my entire family. I lost my mother, my sister, my brother, and my father. I am the only one left!" Few Canarsie Jews could afford to be unmindful of the sorry record of Jewish history, with its clear and silent admonitions. "Enlightened" Jews might chance that break with the past, might even urge Israel to move beyond the exaggerated fears sparked by some Masada complex. But for virtually all the Jews in Canarsie, the observant and the faithless, Zionism was inseparable from the issue of communal survival.

Jewish history advised a perpetual watchfulness for the eruption of anti-Semitism, as well as any populist movements that might focus on a vulnerable remnant. "There is much anti-Semitism in America," said a businessman. "But it's hidden, so you can't measure it. It's better that way. If it's brought to the surface, it only generates more anti-Semitism. If 40,000 people march down the street shouting 'Kill the Jews,' my neighbors might join them."

The lack of a tradition of violent self-help reinforced the Jewish dependence on the formal procedures of law. Their pacifism meant that they did not have the resources of toughness accumulated by the Italians. Jewish "suspicion of the physical" limited the taste for and skill in fighting. As one writer recalled from his childhood, "Intellectual and spiritual independence came easily to the Brownsville child . . . but the right to breathe freely, to use one's arms and legs and voice forcibly . . . these privileges had to be conquered inch by inch."[30] A woman who worked in Canarsie High School contrasted the Jewish fear of vigilantism with the Italian taste for action. "The Jews in Canarsie teach their kids 'Turn and run away, don't join in gang violence.' But the Italian boys like to show their muscles. They don't like to show they're afraid."

Jewish political culture contained a vigorous strain of universalism. Compare the southern Italians' injunction, "Distrust all strangers," with the Biblical command on the duties of Jews to the stranger or resident alien. "Ye shall have one manner of law; the stranger shall be as one of your own country; for I am the Lord your God." Leo Baeck observed, "The injustice done to [the stranger] who can appeal only to the rights of man is an injustice done to all humanity."[31]

Many older Jews still spoke in the tone, cadence, and inflection of idealism. The *lets* and *shoulds* of a Jewish widow, bitterly estranged from a city she hardly recognized any more, revealed the lingering power of her humanism. "I don't care if you worship a dog. You're a human being. No one should be an object of hatred and of people saying, 'My religion is better than yours.' You're entitled to respect! Let people live in harmony!"

The origins of Jewish tolerance have been traced to the precepts of high culture and to the positive law of the Talmud. A schoolteacher had worked as a volunteer in the civil rights movement, but even before that, "I wrote a high-flown letter in 1948 to the *New York Post* condemning prejudice. I saw the unfairness to the Jews and extended it. If people treated me unfairly because of what I was born, why was it right to treat others bad?" Her extension suggests that Jewish liberalism can also be seen as a self-protective device of a minority caught in a hostile plural society. Milton Himmelfarb has described this logic as "that Jewish particularism which likes to regard itelf as universalism."[32]

Progressive sympathies gave Jewish immigrant politics their special cachet. The Jews' idealistic streak was at odds with the Italian spirit of *furberia,* or cunning, or the Irish ethos of favor-trading.[33] A Jewish brand of socialism emerged out of that history. One Canarsie unionist described his father, "a man of his generation, a radical who read Karl Marx like the Talmud. In fact, which he read depended on how he felt that evening. I've seen him read religious tracts that would cross a rabbi's eyes, so deep were they with Talmudic law, as well as Lenin's *State and Revolution*." He ribbed his father for a great sectarianism. "You know the *Jewish Daily Forward*? They had 'Workers of the World Unite' on their masthead. Well my father called the editor, Abe Cahan, 'the betrayer of the working class.' He loved Ben Gold, the man who founded the furriers' union. To my father, Gold was the Moses who led the furriers out of Egypt."

Radicalism was a specialized passion, not to be confused with liberal tolerance. The Jewish faith in pluralism simply affirmed procedural safeguards for deviant opinions, as well as protections against popular movements that sought to override the law. Hawkish Orthodox Jews, Labor Zionist Democrats, and apolitical refugees from European fascism feared the iron fist, whether swung by Ukrainian Cossacks, Southern racists, or radical blacks.[34]

The union tradition remained lively among Canarsie Jews, especially the older generation. Unionism had its voluble proponents: bombastic pamphleteers, founders of locals, organizers who knew how to swim in the shark-infested waters of the garment district. They played an active pedagogic role for the rank and file, raising consciousness, framing demands, and transmitting beliefs about inequality counter to those circulating in the mainstream culture. A middle-aged Jewish man recalled that adversary lifestyle, and the special preoccupations it imposed on his family. "My mother used to worry when my father went out on strike. Would he come home from the strike in one piece? They were militants and had to arm themselves with knives to fight off the goons. As a child, Joe Hill was my hero. I remember singing 'I Dreamed I Saw Joe Hill.' My father always used to say, 'Don't waste your time singing, organize!' "

Over the years socialism faded from Jewish politics. The obsessions of Yiddishkeit gave way to normal party politics, and the Jews moved wholesale into the Democratic party. The voting changes in a district of garment workers spanning the East New York/Canarsie border marked the shift in Jewish sympathies. In 1920, 533 voters cast ballots for president: 313 (59 percent) for Socialist Eugene Debs,

174 (33 percent) for Republican Warren Harding, and a paltry 17 (3 percent) for Democrat James Davis. In 1928, however, the established allegiances were smashed as Al Smith—urban, wet, and Catholic—took 323 votes on the Democratic line, Hoover 78 Republican votes, and the total for all parties of the left—Socialist, Social Labor, and Workers—plummeted to 71 votes. Roosevelt's landslide in 1932 seemed almost anticlimactic after the Smith breakthrough.

The memory of Roosevelt as savior lasted for generations. "My parents are still Democrats all the way," one Canarsie woman began. "They held FDR as God. When he died, we all cried, we loved him so. He got us out of the Depression, and my parents thought Social Security was marvelous. We were very poor then." Nostalgia for the Brahmin *mensch* added to the visceral political identification. "We thought of Roosevelt in glowing terms. He saved the country, and we were all heartbroken when he died. My parents considered him Jewish. He was kindly and liberal and good. 'He should be a Jew,' they thought. 'He must be a Jew!' "

Roosevelt's image was tarnished only in retrospect, by allegations that he had refused to aid European Jews during World War II. A pharmacist's feeling of betrayal attests to the original intensity of his adoration. "My family thought FDR was the greatest thing in the world. We had his picture from *Life* magazine hung over the crack in the wall. But now I know about the Holocaust and I feel disenchanted. It's like finding out Babe Ruth was a drunk and John Kennedy had hookers in the White House. My hero did nothing for my people, he did nothing for the Jews."

Even progressive Jews could not help but be affected by the cold war. The waning of the wartime Russian-American entente, and Soviet anti-Semitism, inspired a vigorous anticommunism among Brooklyn Jews. Still, the fear of popular crusading diluted its virulence. In contrast to Old Canarsie Italians, many Jews continued to use "McCarthyite" and "fascist" as interchangeable epithets to symbolically ward off all threats to constitutional rights. "No protest is unpatriotic," one schoolteacher declared. "The right to protest is guaranteed in a democracy, and those who feel it is unpatriotic are holdovers from the McCarthy era." While pro-McCarthy respondents outnumbered those against him among Irish and Italian Americans in 1954, Jews overwhelmingly condemned McCarthy.[35]

The same reverence for rights was evident in the Jews' support for the civil rights movement in the South. While the provincialism of Italians shielded them from emotional investment in the plight of

southern blacks, the Jewish tradition blurred the boundaries of the
self and made it easy for Jews to imagine the persecution of others as
their own. "I never really knew any blacks when I was growing up,"
an elected official in the Jefferson Democratic Club recalled. "There
were only thirty blacks in my East New York high school of six hundred kids. But I supported the civil rights acts because segregation
was wrong per se. What happened to blacks in the South is what
happened to the Jews in Europe."[36]

Neither the cold war not the economic uplift of the 1950s altered
the compulsive Democratic loyalty of Brooklyn Jews; they simply
brought their political inheritance with them into an altered social
environment. As immigrant radicalism waned, Jewish allegiance to
the Democratic party congealed into a political *idée fixe,* even when
it lacked liberal content. Pulling the Democratic lever was second
nature, which only the turmoil of the late 1960s would seriously test.
Partisanship continued to flow down the great chain of family influence and pedagogy. "Being a Democrat," one Jewish businessman
recollected, "has been handed down from generation to generation.
We were always told, 'The Democrats are for the working man.' "[37]
The 1960 election repeated the established convention. The Jews in
Canarsie and Brownsville gave Catholic Kennedy a far greater proportion of their votes than did the Italian Catholics. In the areas of
New Canarsie where Jews had first moved in, Kennedy received at
least 85 percent of the vote, about 15 percent from Liberal party
voters.

The local ruling powers exemplified the resiliency of Jewish Democratic fidelity. The Jefferson Democratic Club is a veritable dynasty whose patronage power reaches into all corners of city and
state government. But the club is no exclusive organ of Jewish sep-
aratism; it is the home base of Meade Esposito, long-time boss of the
Brooklyn Democratic organization until 1984 and one of the last
grand potentates capable of pushing the politics of spoils in an era of
partisan decline, civil service reform, and independent voting. Anthony Genovesi's forceful presence as district leader of the 39th Assembly District has earned him the nickname AyaTony, a Brooklyn
variant of Ayatollah. Despite the leavening of Italian names, the of-
ficeholders and precinct captains are overwhelmingly Jewish, including in 1984 Councilman Herbert Berman, State Senator Howard
Babbush, and Assemblyman Stanley Fink.

A model of machine politics, the club handles the problems of its
constituents on biweekly club nights, uses the power of patronage to

extract favors from its standing army of precinct captains, and culti-
vates influence through interlocking positions on the boards of syno-
gogues and civic groups and the local school board. Above all, it
mobilizes a tightly controlled electorate of 3,000 dues-paying members. Every once in a while a good-government or right-wing backlash candidate dares to challenge the Jefferson Club. Then the club
calls in its markers and activates its boroughwide contacts in the
county organization or in connected labor unions and produces a
fleet of workers from all across Brooklyn who ferry people to the
polls on election day.

Despite the backroom bosses and the shysters chasing business,
the Jefferson is a political club with a difference. Stanley Fink, the
speaker of the New York State Assembly, has been a principled
guardian of civil liberties. A number of club officials and high-rank-
ing members came to political maturity through the inspiration of
Adlai Stevenson or of Brownsville progressivism.

The club's fusion of ethnic traditions parodies the contrast between canny Italians and lofty-minded Jews; the club also embodies
the rift between avarice and idealism in Jewish middle-class life. The
idealism, by far the less dominant strain, goes back to the Jewish reform movements of Brownsville in the 1950s. The Jefferson Club
grew out of the 5th Assembly District Independent Democrats,
founded by progressives who participated in the unions, the Liberal
party, and Brownsville tenants' groups. One early member recalled
their weekly meetings. "We were very idealistic then. We talked a lot
about 'popular democracy.' The point is we weren't only concerned
with our community. We had a broader vision." Another founder
reminisced, "We felt we were different. We were created along the
lines of a civic organization, and decisions were made by the participants. We were a mass organization, we weren't run by elites. Meade
Esposito reorganized all that later on, but he accepted it until he
could manipulate it as his political structure."

A quirk of history joined those Jewish visionaries to Esposito. A
somewhat shady-looking character from the Italian neighborhood of
Ocean Hill, Meade had been the target in the mid-1950s of a scurri-
lous slur by an Irish ward heeler named Harry Mohr, the district
leader of the 5th A.D. regular Democrats. Mohr made the fatal mistake of boasting to Esposito, "You can buy an Italian vote for a
nickel beer." Meade decided to unseat Mohr, and he sought out the
5th A.D. Independent Democrats to help him. A reformer present
that day worried aloud that Meade's style did not quite jibe with her

own. Was he a Communist perhaps? Her friend was better attuned to Meade's dress and bearing. "No, I don't think so. He looks more like a race track kind of guy to me." On that note the unlikely union was consummated, and it endured and prospered when the Jefferson Democratic Club followed the rest of white Brownsville to Canarsie in the mid-1960s.

The design of local politics had momentous implications for the course of white backlash in Canarsie. First, ethnic splits between Jews and Italians tended to overlap with ideological splits between liberals and conservatives and partisan splits between Democrats and Republicans. Second, many Italian Republicans and Conservatives were eager to serve as agents of racial combat, but the smaller number of Italian voters in Canarsie and the superior organization of the Democratic machine meant that Italian backlash candidates could not win elections. Third, any backlash sentiment generated in the Jewish grassroots met institutional obstacles that kept it from achieving public expression. The Jefferson Democrats worked to contain reactionary leanings.

For a time in the 1970s political events threatened the club's ability to suppress those issues. The local party system could not be immunized against the passions of urban crisis, the civil rights movement, and the Vietnam war, which inflamed the national Democratic party. In 1972 the busing crisis found the Jefferson Democrats caught between pressures from angry Jewish and Italian residents and their own commitment to law, to survival, and to respectability. Challenges from local right-wing Jews, as well as feuding between Italian conservatives and Jewish liberals, undermined the Jefferson Club's uncontested primacy.

A paradox emerges from the political paths taken by Italians and Jews. Progressive Jews looked backward to the archaic customs of the New Deal. Hidebound Italians looked forward to the rising influence of sunbelt-style Republicanism. One small sign of this shift was the steady decline of the Liberal party in Canarsie. A generation of voters not steeped in the old battles was coming of age, as was a new generation of issues for which the New Deal provided no clear guide. The Conservative party preempted third-party momentum on the issues of race, crime, welfare, Vietnam, and abortion.

Although the racial crisis strained traditional Jewish loyalties, certain regularities persisted. Some Jews attempted to wiggle out of the confines of their liberal and Democratic traditions, but were constrained by the very bonds they sought to loosen. The tortured ambivalence created by the tugs of tradition and self-interest was a signature of the Jewish experience. Italian conservatives in Canarsie complained bitterly of the Jewish fidelity to a party. How different that was from loyalty to one's kin, to home, to the neighborhood! Italians were natural conservatives: they had no effete pity or old rhetoric of class to deter them from the task of racial self-protection. But the Jews, they grumbled, "would vote for Adolf Eichmann if he was on the Democratic line." In reality, the relationship between social threat and ethnic values was a good deal more complex than the opposition of liberal Democratic Jews and conservative Republican Italians admits.

Jamaica Bay from Canarsie Pier

Seaview Village, Canarsie

Old Canarsie

Former synagogue, East New York, a mile from Canarsie

Brownsville, a mile from Canarsie

Bayview Homes, middle-income city housing

part two

Territorial, Social, and Cultural Threats

3. Vulnerable Places

Images of the Ghetto

"Flashy cars, booze, and broads is all they care about. They don't even want to get ahead for their families!"

To the residents of Canarsie, New York City in the 1970s had come to feel like an alien place. Their perception of the physical environment as dangerous and unpredictable was grounded in a set of undeniable realities—the proximity of large numbers of lower-class ghetto dwellers, the eruption of conflicts in the 1960s between blacks and whites at all class levels, and the breakdown of old patterns of racial dominance and deference. These factors shaped the way Canarsians experienced material and symbolic space.

Busing edicts and racial tipping undermined the faith of whites in the stability of their neighborhoods. What Canarsians took to be the menacing street style of black men appeared to violate the proprieties that make it possible to treat public encounters with strangers as routine happenings. Street crime diminished feelings of personal security and limited people's freedom to move through the city. Broad forces of economics and politics established the context of these abrasions, but rather more modest forces of space, numbers, and contact determined their precise impact on the people of Canarsie.

The immediacy of the dangers of place was ominous for the vitality of the New Deal coalition. Even where the new obsessions did not undermine liberal economic beliefs, closeness to the ghetto created new concerns which overshadowed the old ones or made them seem dreamily remote. One left-wing Canarsie man, who despaired over the rightward movement of many of his neighbors, understood the significance of closness to the ghetto. "When the people of Canarsie ran from East New York and Brownsville, they ran from their New Deal concepts of integration. They accepted the concept of civil rights, liberty for all, and freedom of expression until it impinged on them and their basic right to maintain the kind of society which doesn't threaten them. The basic fear of the minority community is participating with them where they live."[1]

Canarsians observing the unfamiliar folkways of the ghetto lacked the detachment of the anthropologist. They did not have the luxury of theoretical distance to compensate for their physical immersion in polyglot Brooklyn. The ghetto did not remain within a neatly bounded space, to be savored or reviled in safety. Contact with the people of the ghetto activated denigrative opinions of the minorities and hardened preexisting ones. A few Canarsians lumped all blacks together as if they were an alien species, dissolving their individual qualities in the primordium of race. An Italian worker stressed, "All the social classes don't mix. Take the blacks for example. Their culture is different from ours." He recalled the words of a former official: "We got to find a formula to mix two vegetables without making us nauseous," but he rejected that advice. "*I* say, don't put animals in the street without training. I seen what happens, and you don't put the animals with the civilized people. Does a cat and a dog mix? I can't see it. You can't drink milk and scotch. Certain mixes don't mix."

An ominous biological imagery stained the animal metaphors. One conventional way to explain white complaints about black sexuality, family life, and criminality is to look at the needs of the blamers themselves. Is deeming an entire race deficient in some primal substance a way to enhance a faltering sense of self? Canarsians seemed to agree with those Andalusians who believed that "it is always the people of the next-door town who are the cause of the trouble, who come stealing the crops, whose wives are unfaithful, who swear more foully, are more often drunk, more addicted to vice and who do one down in business."[2]

The strangers act as scapegoats and warnings; projecting forbidden wishes onto others works like an exorcism. "The tensions of the internal structure are projected outside the group where they serve, as an exterior threat, to strengthen the group's solidarity."[3] The projective metaphor illuminates some dark corners of the mind, but it is plagued by a variety of problems, only one of which need concern us here: the downplaying of real differences between groups. Great disparities of class, color, and culture divide Canarsians from the people of the ghetto. Like the Andalusians, they presume that the villagers next door steal more, suffer greater family breakdown, and are more addicted to vice—but the presumption is undoubtedly true.

The subtleties of vernacular epithets disclose the dangers of deciphering racial judgments without reference to the settings in which they are uttered. Lifting a phrase out of context obscures shades of meaning buried in the tacit understandings of conversation. A noteworthy feature of "natural talk" about race in Canarsie was the line frequently drawn between blacks and "niggers." A Jewish antibusing activist elaborated upon that distinction. "Back then in 1948," he began, "there was none of this 'I'm black and you're white' stuff. New Yorkers were New Yorkers." He fondly remembered his army days in Texas, where he and his pals had run up against the taboos of southern racial etiquette. "One day, I was with ten of my army buddies, and we sat down in the back of the bus." The driver told them, "We're not starting the bus until you move out of the back, that's for the coloreds." The man and his New York colleagues told the driver, "See, we're not going to move nowhere. We come from New York and we don't know from blacks in the back of the bus." A black woman got on the bus. "She was clapping her hands and yelling, 'Praise the Lord, white peoples is in the back of the bus.' Who cared if they were black? I still don't care."

His sufferance did not extend to the poor blacks of the ghetto. Middle-income blacks he saw as "just like me ... But if they are going to send shit from Brownsville down here, it's a different ballgame. You're not talking the language I knew growing up." Vernacular usage, then, did not always coincide with the approved usage of the broader society. The distinction between niggers and blacks was the foundation of a ranking of the profligate lifestyles of lower-income blacks and the respectable lifestyles of middle-income blacks. Beneath the surface of apparently racial judgments was the ineluctable reality of class cultures in conflict.[4]

To be sure, breeding shaped the way Canarsians talked about that reality. Plebeian Italians more often resorted to pungent language, with few restraints on coarse word like "nigger." Canarsie also had its fair share of Jews who were not unlike the unpolished *prosteh* of the eastern European shtetl. "To 'talk like a *proster*' means not only to talk inelegantly and ungrammatically but also that one is not above using 'ugly words.' "[5] The distinctions made by an educated Jewish housewife did not differ in kind from those of her *prost* neighbors, except that the contrast of refined and unrefined replaced a more vulgar idiom. "It's really a class problem. I don't care about the color of a person if they're nice people. The black parents in the school programs I work with are beautiful and refined people. They're like us."

The images of the ghetto held by both crude and cultivated whites were formed and reinforced in encounters with blacks. Many Canarsians viewed black street slang as a sign of blacks' reluctance to observe the most basic proprieties. An Italian working-class couple complained that the blacks failed to maintain the accepted division of social life into a vulgar male sphere of work and a respectable female sphere of home. "These maniacs, the way they walk the streets and the language they use, forget it! UGGGH! They curse the way we say 'Hello, how are you?' " Working-class culture provided a masculine realm of raunchiness untamed by female gentility, but cursing in public violated the norms of demeanor. The husband, who was free with profanity in the presence of other men, described the rules. "I never walked around the house cursing. It's unreal the way they talk, 'motherfucker this,' 'cocksucker that.' The way they talk to you in the streets is the way they talk in their houses! All right, if you're out on a job with your friends, it's okay. But you don't bring it home. I wasn't brought up going 'motherfucker,' 'motherfucker,' 'motherfucker.' "

Sometimes blacks hurled the language against whites like a weapon, untempered by the rules that cushion repartee in the black rhyming ritual of insult, the Dozens. An Italian salesman hated driving across Brooklyn. "These colored bums, they bang on your hood when you're waiting at red lights. My wife and I were called 'white motherfuckers' just driving across the ghetto."

Changes in the visual landscape accompanied the barbs of language. The display of black folk art on the side of a Brownsville tenement injected an anomalous presence into Canarsians' visual space, just as the large transistors favored by ghetto youths invaded their auditory space. An Italian worker considered a mural depicting scenes from slavery as the triumph of an alien people. It was as if the blacks' need to reclaim a portion of their suppressed history could be gratified only at the expense of the dignity of his white tradition. "I seen one painting of a girl with a slit in her dress and hustling and two dudes. But that's not the drawings of a middle class area. A lot of this stuff is displayed as art, they say that people are expressing themselves or saying something. But I can't read it. It's not what I want to see. They even have black schools where kids paint pictures of kids picking cotton! But this is 1976, not 1876."

The profusion of graffiti on the city's subways and buildings, which Canarsians attributed mainly to ghetto vandals, added to the visual estrangement. Some cosmopolitans read graffiti therapeutically as a symptom of urban alienation or aesthetically as minority art nouveau, a primitivism broken free of stuffy formalism. Canarsians, however, viewed graffiti moralistically. "You want to lock them up!" cried a Jewish man. "It's disgusting, I'm appalled by it," said another.

The spread of the arabesques onto the face of the city marked sinister forces crossing the line between public rules and private whim. Even the picturesque examples struck many as the acts of predators who violated the rules of place that reassure pedestrians in anonymous urban spaces. "Graffiti don't belong there. If they want to be artists, there are plenty of schools for it. Put it back on the canvas where it belongs." The defacement seemed to show a willingness to defy the unstated rituals that underlie the impression that "everything is okay here." Canarsians translated ugly scrawls and obscenities as a form of sensory mayhem carried out against the public. "It's a senseless defacement of property," claimed one man. "Nobody has the right to destroy things of others. We never had this graffiti stuff when we were growing up, and we didn't have muggings back then either. It's destructive, these are sick people who have no respect." The ultimate message of graffiti was that the public sphere was full of unseen dangers and no longer belonged to the law-abiding.

Canarsians reached their judgment about the people of the ghetto by reading such palpable signs. The slums of Brownsville give it an unruly appearance. Canarsie is neat and trim, a grid of repetition, the landscape of order. When whites looked north across Linden Boulevard, the chaos transfixed them. Memories of the old immigrant neighborhoods forced them to compare the ghetto and Canarsie, but also the Brownsville they knew from their youth and what confronted them now. Like archeologists of moral life, they peeled back the layers of time and read signs of vice and virtue in the crumbling buildings. One Jewish craftsman mused, "I can't help thinking of the immigrants. I mean, they tried to make a living, they sacrificed so the next generation could live a better life. They gave their family values. Don't shit where you eat. My grandfather lived in Brownville, and look what they did there! He had a little garden in back, but now it all looks like a science fiction movie. The niggers have ruined it. They have no pride. Just because you're poor doesn't mean you have to live in filth."

The judgments of shame entered the folklore as received truth. An Italian youth, surrounded by his buddies, mostly the sons of plumbers, electricians, and carpenters, said blacks were "pigs who just throw their shit around." His parents, who grew up in East New York, told him "how in East New York and Brownsville, you know, the niggers moved in slow and sure, and the white people didn't want to live there no more." His father wondered aloud at dinner, "How could people live like those animals?" The kids took in the contemptuous tone along with the content and vented that indignation second hand. "The way they leave the streets, there ain't no excuse for that shit. Look at the way they make those houses! What about the white people who used to live in those houses? Those houses were clean! But now you think somebody's mother or father would want to live there or walk around there?"

Canarsie's image of ghetto culture crystallized out of all the visual gleanings, fleeting encounters, and racist presumptions. Lower-class blacks lacked industry, lived for momentary erotic pleasure, and, in their mystique of soul, glorified the fashions of a high-stepping street life.[6] The hundreds of thousands of female-headed minority households in New York City, and the spiraling rate of illegitimate births, reinforced the impression that ghetto women were immoral. A Jewish shopkeeper in Brownsville was sure that black women were given to sexual excess. "I know this black, see, and he told me, 'My sisters are not blacks but niggers. All they like is boozing and getting laid.' "

The verdict of immorality also applied to ghetto men, who were said to be aficionados of the "going-out life" of bars, hustling, and pimping. A young Italian man compared the "normal married guy— his concerns are making sure the bills are paid and coming home to the family"—to his minority-group workmates. "It's a drag to say it, but most of your blacks and Puerto Ricans are a little different. Getting out on that Friday night is very important to them, and having that bottle of whiskey. It's very hard to put it across the board, because I know blacks and Puerto Ricans who are very strong family people, but there's quite a few of them, their main thing is for girlfriends on the side when they're married."

People apprehend their own identity most keenly through encounters with the forbidden. As Kai Erikson has crisply defined the seeming paradox of that interplay, "Deviant forms of behavior, by marking the outer edges of group life, give the inner structure its special character."[7] Canarsians felt most like family people when they railed against "the element"; all the separate accusations—blacks loved to party, used profane language in public, did not take care of their dwellings—formed an indictment of the weak ghetto family. A Jewish salesman claimed, "I had the same problems they did, but few of them niggers want to make much of their life. Flashy cars, booze, and broads is all they care about. They don't even want to get ahead for their families!"

Racism, which primed whites to select fragments of reality that confirmed their prejudgments, accounts for a good measure of such distorted and mean-spirited claims. But that interpretation suffers from at least three drawbacks. First, it neglects the social forces that shape racial judgments. Canarsians' obsession with the worst in ghetto life reflected ghetto realities: a high proportion of lower-class blacks and soaring rates of drug addiction, family breakdown, and criminality. The high life is only one of the lifestyles in the ghetto repertoire, which also includes righteous and respectable, but the signs of pathology were florid enough to distract even the casual observer. The evidence of the streets was jarringly accessible, while the interior scenes of family life remained dim and opaque.

The seamy aspects of ghetto life were so vivid that they overwhelmed the ability of whites to note all the other aspects that did not conform to the stereotypes. A Jewish businessman urged minorities to perfect the politics of impression management and to punish wayward members who tainted the collectivity. As he saw it, only cohesive ethnic organization could filter out the negative messages:

> It only takes five bad black kids in a project of 140 to spoil the group image . . . I always thought Eddie Cantor and Liebowitz were great. You need someone to look up to, you have to show your heroes. The problem is you only see the *schvartzes'* bad side, you only see people getting handouts. Now we Jews, we never showed the outside world our worst face. We showed the doctors, the lawyers, the scientists. But the blacks send their worst element, the fighting kids, out into the world. They ought to get their Reverends, and if they catch a kid messing around, then beat the living shit out of him, because he's harming the group image.[8]

Each Canarsian's round of work and play led to contacts with minorities that qualified or embellished the shared imagery. Middle-class Jews and Italians met black teachers, office workers, and civil servants, but a Jewish bill collector's job took him deep into the inner sanctums of the underclass. "I'd immediately see the difference between a nigger and a negro when I was collecting. In the nigger's case, you walk in and the kids are on the floor, the bedroom door is wide open, and the mother is banging away with a guy right in front of the kids. Of course, the kid is going to grow up haywire like that, but I don't want my kid around that element."

A second problem with the emphasis on racism is that it neglects the cultural rule that breaches of moral norms must be punished. When provincial Jews and Italians recoiled from the riven families of the ghetto, they were prisoners of ancient notions of right as well as vituperative passion. "The blacks have ten kids to a family," the Italian wife of a city worker observed. "Their overpopulation is a problem. The wrong people are having children. You see, it's the quality that's important, not the quantity. Bring up a few, give them love and education." She compared the apparent licentiousness of ghetto dwellers with the moral density of immigrant life, which shrouded the self in a blanket of family obligations. "Our parents came from Europe with the feeling of working hard and paying their own way, and it was all for the family. You see, we did what we *had* to. We worked hard and lived right. It's not right that they think they can do what they *want* to. I mean, who doesn't want six or seven children, but we couldn't be conscientious about that many."

The contrast of quantity and quality, like doing what you want and living right, repeated the primal contrasts of appetite and obligation. In traditional Italian culture, "give them education" meant the lessons of family honor. The woman who failed to perform her role as the center of *la famiglia,* like the mother of illegitimate children, risked censure as a *disgraziata.*[9]

The final drawback of the emphasis on racism is that it downplays the desire, which was contained in all the racial classifying, to decipher enigmas. It is hard to exaggerate the bewilderment Canarsians felt when they considered the family patterns of the ghetto. To be without a family in southern Italy "was to be truly a non-being, *un saccu vacante* (an empty sack) as Sicilians say, *un nuddu miscatu cu nenti* (a nobody mixed with nothing)."[10] As Canarsie Jews and Italians saw it, many ghetto dwellers *were* nobodies mixed with nothing. "They are different from us Jews and Italians," an Italian plumber reflected. "You see, we were poor, but we helped one another. But the colored don't have that family life like we used to. I don't know what it is with them. I can't understand them people."

The common patterns of desertion, transiency, and illegitimacy reinforced Canarsians' impression of the volatility of ghetto family life. The loosely joined families seemed to lack the distinct positions that Jews and Italians relied on to define the very existence of a family. "Their families are strange," said one man. "I don't like the shenanigans going on with all these families living together. Where are the morals? Where is the father? Does he go out with another woman and just leave the family?"

Canarsians often attributed the pathologies of the ghetto to the nature of the family rather than to sin, genes, poverty, environment, or exploitation. "I'll tell you why I don't believe in this environment stuff," began a member of the Knights of Columbus. "I used to run a drugstore on Cambria Street, that's in Bedford Stuyvesant, and I knew plenty of black people who brought their kids up right even though they were poor, they were as good as my kids, and I bring mine up right, good kids who are decent and want to earn a living and be good citizens, kids from families with seven or eight kids. So I don't think it's so much environment. It's more the family and the habits you learn." The contention that blacks lacked a normal family life reflected the need to hold poverty constant to distinguish the effects of ethnicity. If poor Jewish and Italian immigrant families had not suffered catastrophic levels of breakdown, was it unreasonable for Canarsians to conclude that the black family was different from the families of other immigrant groups?[11]

Not all residents reckoned causality in the same way. Some emphasized the moral failings of ghetto dwellers, others had more sociological discourse at their disposal. One day three PTA leaders—two Italian and one Jewish—sat around a dinette table discussing white immigrants and black ghetto dwellers. The Jewish woman said of blacks, "The problem with them is that their culture is a matriarchy." Her two sidekicks razzed her with affectionate sarcasm, "Hey, I like that fancy word," thereby marking the border between two symbolic communities, each with its own code of speaking. The more educated white-collar Jews were the fancy speech community; the less learned blue-collar Italians were the down-home speech group.

The culture of the blamer as well as that of the blamed thus helped shape the process of appraisal. A Jewish elected official in the

Jefferson Democratic Club said, "I'm not smart enough to figure out how you solve the problem, but it's really one of socialization. You have sociological problems that are vast. Take the blacks and Hispanics and counterculture them. Create a kibbutz to break up their matriarchal society. You can't start integration with blacks when they don't have the family structure. In order for whites to live with blacks, you have to change their sociology."

What separates reflections about "matriarchy" from philippics about "shenanigans"? The substance is identical: poor blacks suffer from brittle family ties. The difference lies in the strength of taboos on vulgarity, the degree of self-consciousness about generalizing, the sophistication of the lingo. "Matriarchy" did not change the reality covered by claims that blacks "ain't got no family"; it merely translated it into a more respectable idiom. Regardless of any differences in their levels of racism or precariousness of status, the educated had resources of theory and discourse available to them which the provincial could not claim.

There is a unity tying together many of the complaints leveled by Canarsians against ghetto dwellers. "The element" had unbridled appetites. Their culture, considered an anticulture, devalued the respect and duties that convert natural beings into civilized people. Rather than abstaining from the joys of the flesh, ghetto dwellers were seen as abstaining from the restraints that socialize instinct and create a body politic.[12]

The white Canarsians' self-righteousness, whatever its sources, punished the black poor and diminished whites by submerging their generous impulses. It clouded the complex reality of the ghetto, the diversity of its lifestyles, and the valiant struggles of black people to survive. And it hurt the larger social order, dividing citizens who were dependent on each other without forging a conception of the public good. Living so close to the ghetto, Canarsians might have developed compassion for the ghetto dwellers and sensitivity to the forces that strangled their life chances. They too had descended from poor minorities, had toiled hard and suffered long. Unfortunately, physical closeness to blacks widened the moral and social chasm between them. The legendary sacrifices of Jewish and Italian immigrants nourished contempt for poor blacks, who seemingly failed to bust their chops as had the forebears of the whites. Some whites became excited by primal fantasies of sex and violence. In a sorry repetition of history, blacks, already victims of words like shit and pigs, became the casualties of white moralism and spite. Violence was no less real for being symbolic.

Crime in the Streets

"It's a physical reality. You have to protect your
body and your children."

An official in the Jefferson Democratic Club once described the people of Canarsie as "gun shy" refugees who had suffered "financial beatings" when they fled the old neighborhoods. They also risked actual beatings and real armed robberies, even after moving into their new community. Street crime united all residents in fear. On a cool autumn night in the mid-1970s some citizens met to discuss a rash of muggings in Canarsie. A survivor of the Nazi death camps declared, "It's like Hitler's time. I am still not free. I have not been liberated yet." The analogy had a special Jewish flavor, yet it conveyed the intensity of all Canarsians' concerns about lawlessness.

Demagogues inflamed popular fears about crime, turning "law and order" into a talisman. The adept orator could speak the unspeakable with a wink, leaving little doubt that he was talking about "niggers." When would-be avengers recited the phrase, some residents heard a promise to satisfy their fantasies of reprisals against blacks. Racism does not exhaust all the meanings encompassed by "law and order." In a world of changing morals, traditionalists used the formulation to affirm a world of discipline and decency. Garry Wills has described the yearning for timeless verities contained in the phrase. "The desire for 'law and order' is nothing so simple as a code word for racism; it is a cry, as things begin to break up, for stability, for stopping history in mid-dissolution. Hammer the structure back together; anchor it down; bring nails and bolts and clamps to keep it from collapsing. There is a slide of things—queasy seasickness . . ."[13]

One did not have to reach far to discover the basic appeal of law and order: simply put, there was less of it than there used to be.[14] Like virtually all of his neighbors, an Orthodox Jewish man saw the contraction of safe and usable space as a mockery of a liberal society. What good were constitutional rights if danger made it impossible to enjoy them? He was methodical in work and worship, and transgression of the law offended his vision of a well-ordered universe. "People's homes are their prisons," he said late one night, as we sat on the deck of his home, looking down into the street. "If I can't sleep and I want to go out on the street for a walk at four in the morning, I am not permitted to do that. It's the fear. We live in a degenerate society. Why are there so many criminals? They kill people like they would kill a fly."

Canarsie suffered a rise in burglaries and muggings in the late 1970s, but most local police considered the neighborhood relatively safe. However, the residents could not sequester themselves away from the rest of the metropolis. They lived next door to some of the highest crime areas in the entire city. To work, to visit, and to shop, they had to travel back and forth through the city, and their mobility made them vulnerable to attack. I met few residents who were strangers to street crime. If they had not been victimized, usually only one link in the chain of intimacy separated them from the victims—kin, neighbors, and friends. Canarsians spoke about crime with more unanimity than they achieved on any other subject, and they spoke often and forcefully. Most had a favorite story of horror. A trucker remembered defecating in his pants a few years earlier when five black youths cornered him in an elevator and placed a knifeblade against his throat. "They got two hundred dollars and a gold watch. They told me, 'Listen you white motherfucker, you ain't calling the law.' I ran and got in my car and set off the alarm. A group of blacks got around the car. If anybody made a move, I'd have run them over. The police came and we caught one of them. The judge gave them a fucking two-year probation." The experience left an indelible imprint. He still relived the humiliation of soiling himself.

Neighbors occasionally tried to best each other in duels of grotesque incidents. "Forget about that," a utility worker broke into his wife's account of her mugging. "Did you see what they did to the guy who gives you the tokens up near Van Sinderen Avenue? They took the money off the guy, but then they didn't leave him alone. They poured gasoline on him and threw a match inside the cage, and they barbecued him."

The vicariously lived suffering of kin was almost as injurious as one's own. In spite of entreaties by his daughter, a mulish old Jew living in an ancient building in Brownsville refused to budge from his home. In areas like that, the few remaining elderly Jews were sometimes mugged on the way to Friday night services, an especially senseless crime since the Orthodox do not carry money on the Sabbath. In a number of cases splashed across the pages of the tabloids, the enraged hoodlums had killed these pious people. But the old man refused to relocate; in fact, he berated his daughter for racism when she warned that "the schvartzes" were going to kill him. "My own daughter, how dare you speak like that! I am ashamed for you. You should feel compassion for your fellow man."

People's rounds of work extended the radius of liability beyond the neighborhood and expanded the reach of rumors about crime. Police work especially breeds an intimacy with urban danger that forces cops to refine suspiciousness into a fine art. By concealing their intentions, predators stage faked presentations of the impression that 'nothing is happening here.' Hiding the clues that recommend caution or avoidance, they exploit the dramatic possibilities of social life. To compensate for such scams, police too can adopt the theatrical ploys of miscreants. The veiling of official appearances in undercover work or a stint on the "granny squad" was a chance to play a confidence game in reverse.

One police officer explained that he earned his living by getting mugged. On his roving beat he had been mugged hundreds of times in five years. "I only been mugged by a white guy one time. All right, one instance, I went to the Brooklyn Navy Yard. They got a huge mugging rate there. I was dressed like an old man, a scar on my face, a little blood dripping like I was just in an accident, a cast on my arm, wearing old clothes." He had been out on the street for barely five or ten minutes when a band of black youths approached him. "The first words I heard were, 'Get the old white man.' Somebody got around me, I got kicked, I got punched, one guy says, 'Grab him, let's take his wallet,' I got stabbed in the hand. It was a savage thing. I also found that it was because I was white. 'Look at the old white guy,' 'Let's get the old white guy,' 'Get the fucking white scumbag.' What the hell does 'white' mean?"

The cop told his story in the Knights of Columbus lodge. The nods and shouts of his audience were part of a process that recurred in other jobs. Those who worked in and around the ghetto were involved in or heard about incidents, and these trickled back to Canarsie. Bringing home their stories of risk to kin, neighbors, and friends, workers formed an information network linking external sources of danger to the locale. At both the work and neighborhood ends of the chain, talk collectivized the experience of danger.

The police, as emissaries of the state, were trained in the craft of violence, reinforced by the majesty of law, and compensated for risk. Yet many residents worked in ghetto areas as bill collectors, merchants, landlords, teachers, delivery men, cabbies, salespeople, firemen, utility workers, social workers, or repairmen. Their livelihoods did not permit easy flight or evasion. One worker displayed the fearsome knife that was his badge of a dangerous occupation. "If I come home and tell the little woman stories," he said, dropping his voice to a hushed whisper as his wife hovered in the kitchen, "her hair would stand on end. You know, I carry this knife with me the whole time I been working in the ghetto." In an eerie rhythm he chanted, "I figure I got a chance, I got a chance, I got a chance. At least I'm going to take somebody with me if I gotta go, believe me."

When there were riots in the ghetto, whites tended to fuse the political violence of black protest with the ordinary criminality of the underclass. A Jewish schoolteacher who had worked for a national civil rights organization lamented the change in the movement. "It's a pity that pressure was required for blacks to get anywhere. In the beginning it was bloodless, they followed the Gandhian philosophy. But later it became more bloody, and I felt conflicted emotionally and intellectually. I think there's a belligerence about blacks today. They are always yelling, 'Why you pickin' on us blacks?' "

By the middle of the 1960s the image of violence had tarnished the positive reputation earned by black protesters earlier. When asked in 1966, "Would you say that the actions Negroes have taken to get things they want have been generally violent or generally peaceful" during the past year, 68 percent of a Brooklyn sample, more than half Jewish, said "generally violent." Of the New York "backlash" Italians queried by Louis Harris and Bert Swanson in the spring of 1969, 49 percent felt blacks wanted to tear down white society; only 22 percent disputed that verdict.[15]

Fear of black vengeance prompted some whites to take a dim view of *Roots,* the television dramatization of Alex Haley's search for his African origins. One woman had wanted to suppress its airing as an inflammatory program. "Did you watch *Roots*? Well I watched every one of them, and if they keep shoving that stuff down our throats, there's never going to be peace. What upset me was they rehashed history, but *history is dead!*" Her objection came from a fear that slavery remained a vibrant memory for many blacks, who might hold whites responsible for it. "And I expect this summer the blacks will be out there on the streets with axes to cut off white feet. It's going to be pushed and pushed and pushed how they were mistreated, and there will be a holocaust. This was over two hundred years ago that this slavery bit was! Yet *Roots* showed all the violence, and how the white people were mean to them. The blacks were treated worse than animals, they were taken up from their own happy soil." But, she added, "They don't need to be reminded of that."

Such dark thoughts were not confined to conservative or hysterical Canarsians. A liberal Jewish teacher praised *Roots* as a needed education for blacks and whites but admitted, almost sheepishly, to a nagging thought. "I was concerned, frankly, on the first day of school about any kind of reaction from unstable hoodlum groups." Another Jewish teacher who felt that "George Wallace filled the bill of a racist dictator, he was everything I despised" also expected racial turmoil, "and it happened in some Brooklyn schools since *Roots* was shown. Black kids, twelve and thirteen years old, are using the name Kinte Kunte, and they have called white students 'white murderers.' They had to call in the police at one school."

Writers have pointed out the presumptions that frame people's view of social life and have written of the power of demagogues and the media to frame perceptions, but Canarsians' understanding of crime and protest was shaped by actual contingencies in the environment. Proximity to the ghetto gave black power an immediacy from which those at a remove from the underclass were shielded. Vulnerability forced on the residents of New York City's boroughs interpretive strategies that differed from those of secure suburbanites, as well as of scholars exposed to academic black nationalism.

Many Canarsians, concluding that vast stretches of Brooklyn had become dangerous places, nervously shifted their patterns of movement through the city or retreated into protective asylums. Evasion established a reluctant trade: forgoing the enjoyment of public places like subways, parks, and streets, refusing the risks of lonely dispersion in anonymous urban spaces, and getting in return the safety of a less random, yet less stimulating, environment.

Whites ceded many areas of the city, but crime followed them into Canarsie. Social policy and administrative decisions, such as housing for the poor in middle-income neighborhoods, school zoning and busing schemes, and the inadequate screening practices of public housing projects, increased the permeability of the community. By forcing mutually suspicious groups to mingle together, such mandates disrupted local rituals that served to prevent disputes, thereby increasing the chances of racial abrasion.[16]

Tensions between black and white students in a Canarsie junior high school in the mid-1970s exemplified the sometimes unhappy consequences of mixing black and white children under structurally inauspicious circumstances. Wilson Junior High drew its one-third black enrollment from the low-income Breukelen Houses project and students bused in from Brownsville and East New York. During an outbreak of racial fighting, a melancholy Jewish girl peered out the front door of the school. As police cars circled the block, she said poignantly, "I'm afraid to go outside, because it's white against black. The whites are prejudiced because of what's happened. The black kids have their protection rackets and their shakedowns. I still have my black girlfriends, but if it comes to a fight, I'll have to go with my own. I'll have to stay with the whites."

A key source of opposition to busing lay in the apprehensions of white parents about exposing their children to tough lower-class kids. While racism and hysteria inflated those fears, the nervousness was based on a realistic grasp of the greater proficiency of lower-class children in violence. The painful lessons her children learned from racial contact depressed a progressive Jewish woman. "Most Canarsians are against busing. They're afraid their property values will decline, but they're also afraid their kids will be killed in the hallways." She ruefully described the chasm of the generations. "Our kids' experience in mixed schools hasn't been positive. My daughters are extremely bigoted, they tell me, 'I hate the niggers.' You see, they've had frightening experiences. It's funny, but the racial feeling is generational. I was more liberal than they are, but I didn't have to deal with the dangers they face."

Danger forced many parents to revise their views of child-rearing. Comparing the perceived violence of ghetto kids with white defenselessness, they wondered if they had prepared their children for city life. Genteel residents reluctantly embraced reprisal. Realism came more easily to street-smart Jews and Italians who knew by heart the lessons of the piers, the sweatshops, the poolroom. One merchant advised a course of study at odds with Talmudic edification. "It's a problem of education. Our kids just aren't educated to fight. I was tough. My parents were from Kiev, and I grew up on the Lower East Side, so I can take care of myself. But my kids?" He remembered back to the antibusing protests of 1972. "I used to carry a gun, and the blacks saw I had a gun. But my kids ain't tough like that."

Both Jews and Italians began to see liberalism as being out of key with the requirements of urban living and to equate it with a self-destructive idealism. In this revised interpretation liberalism did not embody a vision of transcendent justice; rather, it ignored the demands of bodily survival. "The Concerned Citizens of Canarsie are too extreme," a Jewish teacher argued; she referred to the militant organization that had arisen during the busing crisis of 1972–73 as a "fascist" group with "racist" leanings. "But the problem is that we Jews are too liberal and moderate and soft. We don't want out kids to fight. The Wilson Junior High [black] kids who come from Brownsville and East New York sweep our kids into the gutter. It's a physical reality. You have to protect your body and your children."

The structure of this woman's analysis, split in half with that intrusive, hedging "but," exemplified the growing dissociation between the principled force of a liberal tradition on one side and the demands of everyday life on the other. Sympathy for the minorities was an emotional requirement of political closeness between blacks and whites. Black threat, however, diminished the ratio of positive to negative contacts with blacks that nurtured that sympathy.[17] Abrasive encounters with specific blacks began to dwarf abstract notions of support for blacks in general, and the image of blacks as victims yielded to an image of them as victimizers. Physical realities did not entirely vanquish liberalism; they did force many residents to engage in agile maneuvers to reconcile physical realities with moral principles, or they drove liberalism underground for a time.

In Canarsie High School, violence between the races had broken the peace recurrently since the school was completed in the 1960s. By 1977 the student population was 27 percent black. The school was not a wildly dangerous place, nor did antagonism prevent friendships from forming across the barrier of race, and students were not all equally likely to become embroiled in disputes. Yet the mixing of adolescent boys from different economic and racial backgrounds created a tinderbox in which a simple dispute could turn into full-fledged racial war. In the absence of agreement on territorial rights, hostile factions vied for primacy in hallways, classrooms, stairwells, bathrooms, the lunchroom, playgrounds, and exits. Italian boys often inveighed against the incursion of blacks, and their gait and mien. Depending on the context, the references to "niggers" might mean "all black people" or they might mean the particular blacks uppermost in the boys' mind at the time. "We only bother with the ones that are like friends with us. But then there's always them fucking arrogant ones that, the only way, if you don't kill them, they'll kill you."

Nodding off in a drug-induced haze, one youth slurred:

> The blacks are trying to take over Canarsie High School. The teachers are afraid of them. That's why the whites get blamed for every little thing. I seen *Roots,* man, you know, I say it's not really our fault in a way, 'cause it was really the English who tortured them. The niggers hint it to you, like you're responsible. In history class we talked about it. They just look at you and start talking about *Roots,* "these honkies this" and "these honkies that." They shouldn't have put the blacks in slavery then. They should do it now! Keep 'em in hand!

A common opinion among the tough Italian boys was that blacks violated the ethical character of disputing defined by "a fair one." One protagonist in a racial battle claimed, "That's another thing with them niggers, like, they are such pussies, that if I was to go up against a guy who's six foot tall, I mean he would pull a knife out on me or some kind of weapon. Being that he's six feet tall, he should be able to kick my ass. Like, he'll pull out a knife, because they're like yellow dogs. I never carry a weapon on me. In their own neighborhoods they got to carry guns. That's how *baaad* they are! We don't carry no pieces on us when we hang out." Another youth chimed in, using the colloquial phrase "having words" for disputing, "The only thing we share is words and punches." A third boy crossed over into a parody of black slang. "The niggers all got that attitude— *baaaaaaad!*"

Greil Marcus wrote of the black ideal of "badness," personified by the mythic story of Stagger Lee, "That bad man, Oh, cruel Stagolee." "Locked in the images of a thousand versions of the tale is an archetype that speaks to fantasies of casual violence and violent sex, lust and hatred, ease and mastery, a fantasy of style and steppin' high. At a deeper level, it is a fantasy of no-limits for a people who live within a labyrinth of limits every day of their lives, and who can transgress them only among themselves."[18] But the bad style of some ghetto teens quickly crossed the threshold of provocation formed by the Italian boys' tetchy sensitivity to slight.

The accumulation of incidents and stories of crime inside and outside of Canarsie weakened the credibility of appearances. An Italian politician described the average constituent's reasoning about crime.

"He doesn't philosophize *why* it was a Negro mugger. His experience is being mugged by blacks, so all blacks are muggers or potential muggers. The syllogism is there." An act of violence sabotaged the victim's sense of reality and left a diffuse sense of mistrust. As Erving Goffman observed, "It seems that the surround is constructed out of elements easily seen as members of classes, and the tendency is to generalize from one member of a class to the other members. If one chair breaks under the individual, he begins to suspect the others."[19] One fearful Canarsie woman lamented, "It would be different if I could walk down the streets without worrying, if I didn't have to stop to say to myself, 'Hey, that Negro man coming down here, is he going to knife me 'cause he's looking for revenge [on whites], or is he my friend?' It would be okay if I could feel they were my friends, just as much as I am their friend."

Canarsie's chief attraction was the immunity it promised from the dangerous classes. After a flurry of muggings by black youths around the subway station near the low-income project, the residents were especially unnerved. All the classifications of safe and dangerous places they relied on for an illusion of order were thrown into turmoil. One evening dozens of people crowded into a synagogue basement to discuss the muggings. The rabbi sermonized, "We need another night to be in synagogue just to deal with those hoodlums on the streets. Five blacks broke the ribs and shoulder bone of the last person who was attacked. The entire perimeter of the project has become hazardous."

A congregant said with sanguine equanimity, "I'm sure that the [precinct] captain will enlighten us." The captain, parrying the request for illumination with a hopeless language of bottom lines, deployment formulas, and fiscal crisis, failed to assuage the crowd's demand for consolation. In a thick Yiddish accent, a man cried, "We are handicapped. So broken ribs and shoulders are not enough? We need a murder too?" A man in a skullcap declaimed, "The answer is vigilantes. We had vigilantes in Crown Heights, and we stopped the niggers there. The community has to do it ourselves." An elected official said, "Look, off the record, I carry a baseball bat under my car seat." The rabbi added, "I was driven from the Bronx. I know. How much is your home worth if you can't tell your friends to get off at the 105th Street subway station?" Someone else interjected with crisp finality, "Club them to death! You have that right!" An elderly somber-faced woman sitting near me drew a historial parallel that electrified the gathering. "I am locked up like in the ghettos of Europe. I am afraid of people knocking down my door. I still am not free."

All across urban Middle America, citizens performed such acts of communion. From a distance the gatherings seem like the folly of the horde, but emotional contagion does not do full justice to their meaning. They also formed fleeting moments of culture-building, in which residents helped one another work out new definitions of permissible and forbidden behavior.

Fear of a menacing environment had produced heated political discussions by the middle of the 1960s. A referendum in 1966 asked New York City voters to weigh the merits of establishing a civilian grievance board to hear charges of police brutality. The question quickly supplanted its stated purpose—to assuage the concerns of minorities about sadistic police practices—and became a verdict on the civil rights movement.

The precincts most opposed to civilian review all lay within Italian Old Canarsie, but the referendum failed to gain a majority in any Canarsie precinct. As much as 90 percent of the Italians voted against the board, approximating the boroughwide figures for Irish and Italian Catholics. The four most antireview precincts had given William Buckley, the Conservative party's 1965 mayoral candidate, about 20 percent of the vote in a three-way race, and Barry Goldwater had received more than 40 percent of the presidential vote in his 1964 crusade against liberalism. Such developments marked the potential appeal of a New Right populism among Catholic lower middle-class voters who liked muscular responses to racial and global danger.

Civilian review did best in Jewish areas of Canarsie where Buckley received only 5 percent of the vote in the 1965 mayoral race, and Goldwater had taken barely 10 percent in 1964. Yet even in the precincts most sympathetic to the CRB, support crested only at 40 percent; in most Jewish precincts, one-third or less voted for the board. This level of endorsement was consistent with the pattern detected by a team of scholars who took soundings of the Brooklyn electorate in 1966. While 30 percent of Jews with high school or grade school education voted for the board, 54 percent of those with a college education supported civilian review.[20]

Brooklyn residents who were most nervous about crime, the same survey revealed, tended to oppose the civil rights movement. But what about liberals who admired Martin Luther King and approved of the Miranda ruling yet feared crime? Fervent ideology pulled

them in one direction, physical realities in another. Among strong
Jewish supporters of the civil rights movement, 55 percent of those
who said they felt safe supported the review board. Only 38 percent
of those who felt in jeopardy did the same. "The attitudes of liberals
on social and economic equality, civil liberties, and procedural rights
had such a low correlation with their attitudes towards the CRB
that it suggests just how disassociated these values were in the
minds of rank-and-file voters."[21]

The vote against the review board dealt a stunning blow to the liberal forces that had dominated New York politics for a generation.
Andrew Hacker wrote, "It brought to the surface some issues which
had hitherto been considered off limits in election campaigns . . . But
once civilian review of the police reached the ballot, it made visible a
division that would affect almost all later elections."[22] The vote disclosed the first breach in Jewish unity, divided conservative lower-
middle-class Jews in the other boroughs from the liberal Jewish gen-
try in Manhattan, and moved the Jewish and Catholic petty
bourgeoisie closer together.

Throughout the decade after 1966 lower-middle-class Jews parted
company with their affluent brethren on a range of racial issues.
Some writers have attributed this class division to internal dispositions of the enlightened and the know-nothing. Upper-middle-class
professionals are said to have a flair for abstractions, an ability to
rise above self-interest to empathize with others, and faith in using
trained intelligence to solve social problems. The argument has
some truth, but Milton Himmelfarb has captured the potential
abuses of such a claim. "In 1966, was it chiefly education that
prompted Jews to vote for the civilian review board, and lack of
education to vote against it? Perhaps it was prosperity and lack of
prosperity. The prosperous could afford their votes. The unpros-
perous (and elderly), living in apartment houses without doormen
and riding subways rather than taxis, may have voted as they did,
not because of ignorance but because of concerns explicable by the
reality of their lives—a reality against which prosperity shields the
prosperous."[23]

The political fallout of crime was evident in a less precisely mea-
surable decline in support for an oppressed group. An older Catholic
woman stated:

I didn't have such hatred before. I started disliking the blacks
about ten years ago, in 1967. I was on a subway and got mugged.

I still don't know why they slashed my face with a razor. It was a black girl and a Puerto Rican that done it. That finished me feeling sorry for them. And once I was on the "J" train [of the subway], and a black boy came up and kicked me, so I says, "What was that for?" and he tells me, "Your feet are in my way," so I kicked him back. That's the pay-off you get. They won't even let you sit in your seat in peace. I don't mistreat them, so why do they mistreat me? It's sad. Did you know that I used to help the blacks back during the Depression? I used to try to get their rents lowered. They were being exploited by the landlords, this was on President and Nivens streets in South Brooklyn, so I went to the OPA office to protest because I felt so bad about how they were treated.

Through the reflections of many Jewish liberals on the civil rights movement ran a strain of betrayal, a growing suspicion that they had been suckered and played for fools. A person who had been mugged by a black found it hard to feel sanguine about race relations or proud of past acts of support. A beating in exchange for sympathy seemed an uncharitable restitution. Crime turned liberalism into a synonym for masochism: the indulgence of one's victimizers.

An Italian construction worker in 1977, observing his Jewish neighbors with wry detachment, noted their liberalism, but also a new anger. "The Jews have been crucified a lot now by the blacks, they've been having a lot of trouble with them the last ten years. My neighbor next door was mugged. She's a schoolteacher, she used to be real pro-black before, but she hates them now. The blacks were about to kill her the other night. You can see how she's changed. She used to be, let's put it, broad-minded, right, very liberal, and now she has no use for the blacks."

An adviser to a Canarsie politician, sitting in the back of the synagogue on the frenetic night described earlier, analyzed the impact of environment on ideology. "What we are witnessing," he said portentously, "is the deliberalization of people with pronounced liberal tendencies." The insight was a good summary of the result of crime in the streets in Canarsie. Physical reality explained the urgency of the demand for law and order. Racists simply added their own hateful emotions to a concern that gripped everyone. Residents liked to regale a stranger with the popular aphorism, "A conservative is a liberal who's been mugged." Occasionally a sardonic raconteur would twist the standard form to dramatize the utter certainty that blacks would deliver harm: "A liberal is a conservative who hasn't been mugged—yet!"

Neighborhood Integration

"Maybe they used to be liberals, but not after they were scared out of East Flatbush."

Real and imaginary threats to property values and racial balance quickened the struggle over territory. Resistance to integration went beyond cupidity, but the economics of land, housing capital, and debt payments best explain the residents' fear of racial change. A school official, who once had cheered George Wallace at a Madison Square Garden rally, described to me one source of Canarsians' demonic perceptions in the mid-1970s. "With the economy so bad, people are getting crazy. If busing goes in, they figure, 'Hey, I can't make a living, I'm falling behind and now they're going to ram this busing down my throat and take my house away.'"

The apparent racial stability of Canarsie did not console its nervous residents. For two decades they had been watching white Brooklyn shrink down to a thin sliver along its south shore, extending from Bay Ridge in the west to Bensonhurst, Sheepshead Bay, and lower Flatbush in the center, to Canarsie in the east. "We're finished here in Brooklyn, I tell you," one man avowed. "It's like we're the Israelis. They are surrounded by fifty million Arabs, they have to fight, but there's no place to retreat. Their back is against the water. Well the white middle class in Canarsie is up against the same wall."

Signs of incipient change in the late 1970s lent some credence to the fear of engulfment. The central core of Canarsie remained lily white. In all but seven of its thirty-three census tracts between 1970 and 1980, the number of blacks remained constant at zero or increased from two or three to less than a dozen. Yet change was coming to the peripheral tracts that abutted adjacent neighborhoods and to anomalous zones like the two projects.

Bayview Homes, a middle-income high-rise public project, went from 15 to 22 percent black in the 1970s, and the increase in Puerto Rican tenants brought the minority population to one-third. At the northwestern threshold of Canarsie, in a tract that looked across Ralph Avenue toward East Flatbush, the black population of 47 quadrupled, rising by 1980 to 161 blacks, or 4 percent of the total. In Canarsie's northeastern quadrant north of Flatlands Avenue, a striking exodus of whites left the low-income Breukelen Houses a minority enclave of youth gangs, female-headed households, and welfare recipients. The halo effect of the project touched the surrounding blocks. Directly to the west was a buffer zone between the project and all-white Italian Old Canarsie across Rockaway Parkway; that tract jumped from a dozen to four hundred blacks in a decade. Most ominously to Canarsians, the commercial strip along the south side of Flatlands Avenue across from the project had an increasingly seedy and abandoned appearance. And dozens of middle-income black and Hispanic families were moving into the eleven front-line blocks south of Flatlands Avenue opposite the project. They had penetrated only one block deep into the heartland of eastern Canarsie, but the direction of movement, south toward Seaview Village and Jamaica Bay, was obvious.

People's forebodings varied with the steepness of their investment, their reserves, and their options for disengagement. One Jewish woman had lived most of her life in walkup apartments and middle-income projects in Brownsville before buying a home in Canarsie in the early 1960s. "Canarsie people don't have a lot of money. We got a little house and it's a big achievement. We don't want to lose what it took our entire life to build."

Caution underwrote stiff resistance to integration. In 1976, at the first meeting of a block association in the central section of New Canarsie, a speaker told the audience, "Jimmy Carter used the phrase 'ethnic purity' and had to apologize for it. But I use the term and I won't apologize for it. I am not a racist. I just want to keep my community pure. I sunk every dime I have into my house and I don't want to be chased. I won't be chased."

Canarsians had an earthy, materialistic view of the link between attitudes and property. A carpenter dismissed his sister's self-righteousness as the luxury of transience. "She don't even care who lives next door to her. She wouldn't care if an Eskimo moved into the neighborhood. But what do you expect? She lives in an apartment in Manhattan." To some extent, attitudes toward laws against discrimination in selling homes reflect property interests. The motives that created an informal version of apartheid in Canarsie, however, cannot be reduced to the racist greed of a privileged segment of the housing market trying to hang onto its advantages. White views of blacks moving in resulted from forces of ideology and environment as well as of investment, and all three forces influenced the others.[24]

Nationally, urban Catholics score respectably high on measures of integrationist sympathy when compared to nonsouthern Protestants. They come close to the stereotype of know-nothing ethnics only when compared to Jews, whose support for civil rights laws is striking.[25] A Jewish teacher insisted that race was an invidious, even un-American, criterion for selecting a home buyer—adding the proviso that the buyer should have attained the same level of social rank and respectability as she had. "It's the American way. Minorities should live where they want. It's part of our philosophy: life, liberty, and freedom for all." In contrast to this universalist statement is the virtually phobic fear expressed by an Italian machinest. "I bag all the niggers together. They do nothing for themselves. They are a useless people. They have different traits from us. I don't want to mingle with them."

Comparing a Jewish teacher with a master's degree, whose father was a Socialist tailor, to an Italian machinest with eight years of education, whose father liked Joseph McCarthy, hardly offers a fair test of ethnicity, a tag that partially hides influences of education, class, and occupation. Surveys permit the analyst to weigh factors that may remain hidden from the ethnographer; their drawback, however, is that the respondents are treated as lonely atoms with no ties to local communities that impart to their members distinct moral learning.

The commandments and taboos that pervaded the speech of Jewish political and school leaders signaled the vibrancy of a public culture of democracy. A PTA leader stated, "Of course it's the blacks' right to move in. Everybody has the right to civil rights." Her tolerance was not a mysterious gift, something she had merely by virtue of being Jewish. Cultural teachers, by harping on a set of precious "shoulds," had imbued her with a self-conscious striving toward universalism. "I try not to see color. I wouldn't care if a black bought a house next to me. You should take each person on their own merits."

Italian leaders in the Republican party, the North Canarsie Civic Association, and the Conservative party had different notions of "should." Unabashedly defending the exclusion of blacks from Canarsie, they affirmed the personal wishes of kith and kin rather than the canons of formal law.[26] The acceptance of prejudice as inevitable upheld a strict division between the rights of citizenship, which prevailed in the larger society, and the rights of settlement, which applied to the smaller world of community. "Some prejudice is legal," insisted one Italian man who was active in Old Canarsie civic affairs. "You have to do it to keep out undesirables. It's a cooperative effort of neighbors. They have the right to pick their neighbors. The social and the business world are two entirely different things." Citing human nature rather than human rights, a Republican leader rejected the perfectionist ideal of law as an instrument of social change or guarantor of liberty. "The government is trying to equalize the races by moving people around, but law can't accomplish this sort of thing. Brothers like to be close to brothers. People moved into communities because they wanted to be close to people who are like them. It's not up to the government to throw things over."

His claim evokes the naturalistic sensibility that weakens the persuasiveness of law in provincial neighborhoods, as well as the realistic ethos that lies at the core of white ethnic culture. A far cry from individualism, ethnic provincialism views life as a field of social entanglements. Its conservatism rests on deference to communal prejudices, on the belief in the natural quality of personal ties, and on its suspicion of the formal remedies of strangers, including those of the state.

Provincial people tend to shy away from airy generalities in favor of judgments conditioned by local context and immediate experience. "That's completely different out there on [Long] Island with those blacks," exclaimed an Italian blue-collar worker, who moments before had insisted, "We don't want them blacks in Canarsie, I tell you, I wouldn't want to live next door to them." The material differences between the worlds of here and there made the comparison academic. "The [black] ones who live out on the Island, you never hear of an incident out there. Not really." Incidents, his euphemism for crime, was the relevant issue, not race. "The only incidents you ever hear of is right here—in Bedford Stuyvesant, the ghetto, East New York, and Brownsville. All the incidents are mostly out this way."

A policeman's mistrust of abstract moralism made him angry over sanctimonious condemnations of white racism:

> We aren't racist pigs. We are only people looking out for the survival of our community and children. Did you ever notice anyone who talks of an area being prejudiced? I love this, I look at this: We had a Nyquist on the Board of Regents. Where does he live? Where does his kid go to school? They ain't never lived in Brooklyn, they ain't never lived in East New York. A Kennedy

who says this, "Oh, we got to live together, we'll have busing," or a Nyquist, why do you live out in Long Island, why is there an eight-foot fence around your property with armed guards, how come your kids don't go to public schools?

The world close at hand affected the theoretically adept as well as those with a penchant for concrete thinking. An odd collusion emerged among lofty democrats who affirmed the rights of mankind, race-baiters who berated blacks with all their might, and the shrewd ones, indifferent to the abridgment of rights, who loved their property more than they disliked blacks. They all distinguished between ideal states and the exigencies of the environment. The common denominator was aversion to risk. Fearful that morality or legality might prove too costly, given the chancy guarantees, even supporters of equal rights trimmed their commitments. A home-owning humanist who had grown up in Brownsville cited the Declaration of Independence. "It's the minority's right to move where they want. I wouldn't mind if a colored family moved next door if they were upstanding and fine like me. Educated and intelligent blacks, why not? They are people. Color shouldn't have any place there." A few moments later, she backtracked to physical realities. "But I don't want trash who will frighten me. My problem is walking in the streets and seeing people in the street who I don't know whether they are going to bother me. There is no reason to walk in fear."

Restrictionism was accompanied for some by guilt or regret, for others by glee, and for still others by indifference. A Jewish civic leader resorted to the most convoluted apologetics to justify exclusion: "The black is infringing on the right of those who don't want him. I understand his reason for leaving the ghetto, but he has to understand my reasons for not wanting him. I wouldn't want to move into a neighborhood where I wasn't wanted. If I wanted to live in East New York, I couldn't. My rights are abridged in that way too." A realtor found in that logic the handy grounds for defining "good blacks" and "bad blacks." "I showed one black around who wanted to move into the East 80s, near Flatlands Avenue. He got the idea real quick. The good blacks don't want to move in. Only troublemakers demand a house in Canarsie. But they usually get the message."

History reinforced the residents' vigilance. A woman trenchantly defined the difference between novices and veterans of displacement. "I'm for anyone buying a home as long as they're neat and clean and they don't ruin the block. Their race really doesn't matter to me. But many Canarsians are bigots because of what happened to them in East Flatbush and Brownsville. Lower-class blacks pushed them out. They talked about *schvartzes.* They never knew the middle-class blacks. But the two of us are different. We weren't pushed out. We don't have that hate."

The experience of Jews from different milieus explains the gulf between a national Jewish commitment to equal housing and Brooklyn Jewish fears of integration. A comparison of answers to questions about concrete situations rather than abstract values sharply modifies the stereotype of pure Jewish enlightenment. In Manhattan 39 percent of the Jews said they would be nervous if more blacks moved into their neighborhood; 63 percent of Jews in Brooklyn felt alarm at the prospect. Of the Manhattan Jews, 70 percent hoped for an integrated society, but only 43 percent of those in Brooklyn shared that hope.[27]

The new buyers in Canarsie who fled East Flatbush in the early 1970s plunged into heavy debt. One realtor in 1973 estimated that buyers made down payments of $15,000 to $20,000 on a $45,000 home, which locked them into twenty-five years of mortgage payments at $400 a month. Property taxes took another bite, of between $700 and $1,500 annually. Families with incomes between $10,000 and $20,000 a year felt the pressure. "Maybe they used to be liberals," said the realtor, "but not after they were scared out of East Flatbush and put every cent they had into a house and went up to their necks in debt . . . When a guy makes those kinds of sacrifices, you can't push him around."[28]

Like survivors of a disaster, veterans of displacement kept reliving the experience, as if they could glimpse no future beyond a compulsive repetition of the past.[29] In a fleeting moment of relaxation they might say, "It's a rough problem, the blacks would like to live in a nice community," but then they would fret, "What if the merchants in Canarsie run as fast as they ran from Pitkin Avenue?" Or they would whisper to themselves, "I better get out before something happens I can't control." A Canarsie man who had vivid memories of the binge of blockbusting that had swept through his East Flatbush neighborhood replayed this scenario in his mind. "We're not just talking about a few blacks. At first, it would be ten, then it would be twenty, and then who knows what might happen? We've run from neighborhoods that changed overnight. How do we know Canarsie will be viable five years from now? We're scared to death."

In reckoning the risks of integration, whites performed a kind of exorcism. Tipping is a self-fulfilling prophecy, the outcome of white susceptibility to superstition more than an inherent dynamic of integration. But whites displaced onto blacks responsibility for the stampede touched off by white fear. Yet the imagery of irrationality should not be extended too far. Individual residents who did not mind the idea of blacks as neighbors had to mull over the likely responses of their panicky neighbors as well as the objective qualities of a black buyer.[30] Once a certain number of stampedes had taken place, realism obliged the cool-headed to read the legacy of flight as a portent of things to come. Experience showed that after the "good element" arrived, the "bad element" followed. That sequence happened mainly because whites panicked, but as investors primarily concerned with limiting their risk, Canarsians did not bother about the whys. One housing activist asked bitterly, "People have the right to move in if they can afford it, but you tell me, what happens after the black doctors come in and the others panic and we lose everything? You tell me *that!*"

This local reading of selling panic suggested a need for a preemptive strike; middle-class blacks were excluded not as the goal of white supremacy but as a means of keeping the lower class from entering the neighborhood. Once again the residents of Canarsie proved to be highly selective in their devotion to free markets. The exclusion of worthy blacks was the price paid to immunize whites against the risk created by their own fright and racism.

Perceptual obstacles added to apprehensions of instability. According to many whites, blacks ignored the familiar norms that informed their own language, gesture, and action. The apparent diffusion of black styles of dress, laughter, handshakes, dancing, and gait across class lines created opportunities for misreading. As a Jewish carpenter defined it, "The problem is that we see blacks as a mass. It is unfortunate. We can't tell the difference between a black pimp and a black mailman. When I look at a white man, I can tell what social class he is, but if he is colored, I can't tell."

An array of social and political factors diminished the faith of whites that they were able to size up the character and status of black buyers. The active members of home-owner groups were well versed in the arcana of FHA provisions, which allowed certain categories of buyers to purchase homes with virtually no down payment. In a few instances three or four marginally middle-income black families had pooled their funds to try to buy a two-family home in

Canarsie. Even those who had the money to buy a home were not necessarily trusted by some residents. Many middle-income blacks were not "really middle class," said an Italian police detective, "because they are often in civil service, and they get there by special methods [affirmative action], so they are not necessarily any more industrious than ghetto blacks."

A buyer's chains of association complicated the guessing game. Homeowners are exposed to danger by their neighbors, but also by the neighbors' kin, clients, associates, enemies, and poor cousins, as well as impostors. The sprawl of a person's networks diminishes the control neighbors can exert, the caliber of the people who visit the community, and its general tone. One realtor captured the residents' apprehension. "You see, they know the new blacks have pride in ownership. They tell you that. But they're afraid the Brownsville blacks will hang around and blend in, and they don't know the good ones from the bad ones. You can't tell. The bad ones bring down the good ones. Before, when there weren't as many middle-income blacks, you could tell who belonged in the neighborhood. You saw people and knew they didn't belong. But now you can't tell." Social change made the familiar hunches obsolescent. The ambiguous position of the new blacks deprived white residents of adequate strategies for promoting their own well-being, deciphering the environment, and appraising risk.

More than a tiresome slight, the notion that one could not tell blacks apart bespeaks the intricate way urban dwellers scan their environment, sift visual and other clues for forecasts of danger, and make guesses about the intentions of strangers. People generalize from experience to reduce uncertainty and manage alarm. Employers, pedestrians, and home owners do not operate on the presumption of innocence that lies at the core of legal reasoning. They associate individuals with classes of events and merge past incidents with hunches about repetition. Erving Goffman has summarized the essence of this "design of vulnerability." "We need not concern ourselves with anxieties about the not possibly real. Recent bedevilments of the environment have introduced enough real issues, and each real possibility breeds its own set of unjustly suspected appearances."[31]

In their concern for false appearances, in the attempt to seek out fakeries, in the vigilance to signs, Canarsians resembled the subjects of fancy philosophic theories who must sort out a wink from a rehearsal of a wink from a parody of a rehearsal of a wink. But all the mental gymnastics were more than exegesis for its own sake. The attempts to define righteous neighbors had a practical aim.[32]

Residents tried to keep an eye on hysterical whites as well as hypothetical black buyers. After all, a "bad sale" involved an incompetent, panicky, or "disloyal" seller as much as an unknown or unwanted buyer. Betrayers included well-intentioned liberals who were glad to sell to blacks, speculative realtors wanting to exploit a selling wave, and neighbors wishing to liquidate their holdings on the most favorable terms.

The transiency of a neighbor's tenure in Canarsie weakened the reciprocal bonds among home owners who ostensibly shared common interests. A neighbor's decision to move meant a precipitous break in status, transforming a reliable neighbor into a restive seller seeking to maximize gain or cut losses. An Italian vigilante who had squelched a number of sales of houses to blacks captured the risks created by the conflicting interests of movers and stayers. "Sometimes you have to use forceful methods with them, you have to be firm with the sellers. You explain to them, 'Hey look, you raised your kids, you're on your way to Florida, but many of us still have children here. You got your price, but I need mine.' You make threats over the telephone, you threaten their children. That's okay, 'cause they are threatening other people's children. It's self-protection for the staying."

A seller's relationships with others on the block could enhance or diminish the jeopardy movers imposed on stayers. A loner, for example, was presumed to be immune to local wishes; that wary distance from others might permit either the seller's avarice or integrationist sympathies to sway his selling behavior. A man who was involved in organized efforts to prevent integration complained of the sale of a house to a black family in Old Canarsie, although the transaction was reversed by a delegation of local men who prevailed upon the realtor with unmistakable warnings. "Now I blame this on the civic organization in that area, they should have been in on it and talked to the seller to bring in our own kind. You got to deter a sale like that. It's the shut-ins, they're the ones most likely to sell black, the ones who don't have a lot of friends in Canarsie or have much to do with people on the block."

Involvement in the neighborhood provided a crude measure of reliability. Respect for the wishes of neighbors or knowledge of possible reprisals often led residents who loathed racism to selectively practice discrimination. In this sense the anxiety or racism of a small but active and organized minority controlled the behavior of more democratic segments of the community. "I have a black friend who's a vice president of a New York bank," explained a Canarsie attorney who was married to a progressive schoolteacher, "and I told him, 'Look, I wouldn't sell you my house. I don't care, but my neighbors would kill me.' "

Civic leaders also bowed to the imagined wishes of the neighborhood. The first black family on one Canarsie block did not attend the block association meeting, and the head of the group felt chagrin at what he thought had prompted their stand-offish attitude. "The black family wasn't invited to the block party last summer, which was a bad mistake on my part. Some of the people said, 'Don't do it, don't invite him.' You gotta go by what the majority of the people want. So I think maybe the blacks said, 'They didn't invite us to the block party, and now he's inviting us to the meeting,' maybe there's a little animosity for what I did to them." The black family had been a credit to the block. "They keep their house better than a couple of white people round here. They're polite people. I went to their house, I was amazed, they kept everything clean." The block leader resolved never again to yield to public objection. "I'm ashamed of the other people around here. But now this block party we have for the summer coming up, I'm going to invite them, because they live on the block, and they showed me they want to live here and keep it clean and they're good people."

When nervous residents began to detect the early signs of racial change, even local block pressures could not restrain an owner's temptation to "sell black" while the asking price was high, either as a hedge against loss or a chance to score a handsome profit. Then the charade of a unified neighborhood quickly fell apart. In one such situation in the late 1970s, as middle-class blacks began to buy homes on the blocks south of Flatlands Avenue across from the Breukelen project, a panicky woman warned, "They're getting scared in the Flatlands Avenue area. We have an obligation to tell them to hold tight." A community watchdog informed a gathering of conservative activists, "The neighborhood is starting to move out and they're selling to blacks now. The [black] people whose house was bombed are still moving in." A neighbor reported, "A Puerto Rican rented on 105th Street. And an absentee landlord threatened to sell to 'what you consider objectionable elements.' " A housewife retrieved the image of jittery residents, eager to jump ship. "The average person on 103rd Street is waiting for it to turn black, so they won't feel bad when they sell. People want to sell, but they are asking incredible prices. I hear them saying out loud now, if they can't get white, they'll take black. Those people who won't sell at reasonable prices are reserving the right to screw their neighbors."

A right to screw their neighbors speaks a plain truth: most talk of a united Canarsie was hype or hyperbole. Economic cunning, not good neighborly feeling, was the prime factor in selling. Put a shade differently, neighborliness depended on shared financial destiny. After one block near the projects registered six black buys in a row, a local resident described the shakiness of the norm of neighborliness. "It's all over now. Originally, I gave the block seven years, but it will be all black in two. The stigma of selling black is gone." The high interest rates of the late 1970s would slow the pace of her prediction. Nonetheless, between 1970 and 1980 the number of blacks in the three census tracts south of Flatlands Avenue and east of Rockaway Parkway increased dramatically: from 12 blacks (0.6 percent) to 286 (17 percent), from 28 (1 percent) to 349 (14 percent), and from 21 (0.8 percent) to 317 (12 percent).

In countless ways Canarsians denied blacks the equal opportunity they were always trumpeting as the virtuous route to success. That transparent guile did not escape one Canarsie black man. Typical of many in the black middle class, he blended pride in his blackness with a yearning for respectability. His definition of betrayal came from transcendent ideals, not the venal turf of homeowners. Treachery for him meant subverting the Constitution, not selling a neighbor short. He remembered his dream of becoming a home owner:

In 1962, I found a basically racist community in Canarsie. I tried to buy a house in Seaview Village and I was denied that. This racism is even more widespread in 1976 in the Northeast among liberals than it was in the South. I can't understand Jews who persecute black citizens. They say that the Jews understand about persecution. In 1962 my wife and I were earning $25,000 when we wanted to buy in Canarsie. Isn't that middle class? There was no justification for what they did. I understand that they don't want a low wage earner. I don't want what I don't deserve. I only want what I am entitled to. I say, don't exclude anyone from the things you want. I want the same things they want. But I won't become a racist to achieve my ends. I understand the fears of white people in Canarsie, but their appeal is one-sided. How can they justify it? I'm not wrecking homes and hurting anyone. I'm an architect! I construct!

Memories of White Brooklyn

"In 1956 . . . it was one big happy Flatbush family.
But now? Ninety-five percent of them have been
mugged and moved away."

The vulnerabilities of place pushed Jews and Italians, regardless of their personal or ideological bent, toward wariness. However, people have more dimensions than simple adaptation or risk aversion. They dramatize their experience in bursts of gratuitous symbolic action. They invest the material world with sentiment. The residents had staked emotion in their old homes as well as money in the new ones. Fond images of an older Brooklyn produced home-grown versions of the urban elegy. There is a poetics of place as well as a politics of place.

The present physical desolation of their old Brooklyn neighborhoods had special meaning for the Jews and Italians who had lived there. For elderly first-generation Jews and Italians, looking back at the tenements was not just a blasé judgment about a strange people who seemed not to respect themselves enough to take care of the buildings. The destruction they saw was an insult to their memories of childhood and ancestors. As a result, the shock of racial transition could not so easily be put away as an emotion of the past. Proximity kept the old wounds active and made them an uncanny part of the present.

Some residents would swerve from the most direct route to their destinations in order to drive by the old homestead. Their children would often listen to parental reveries with impatience or tired bemusement. "I remember my old place in Crown Heights fondly; I ride by it and the kids get annoyed when I say, 'That's my candy store!' " Pilgrims to childhood homes were incredulous. "I couldn't believe it. The houses were all marked up, the streets were filthy, and there was garbage and graffiti everywhere. There was no respect for property. It was very sad. I started to cry." Tears welled up as she told of her journey, suggesting the truth of a relationship Marc Fried has glimpsed among mourning, neighborhood change, and residential dispersion. "For the majority it seems quite precise to speak of their reactions as expressions of *grief*."[33] Crying was a constant in the experience of the returnees. "When I moved from Brownsville, I left my whole life behind me. That was where I grew up. My parents passed away there, but it wasn't the same place any more. By 1960 you could see the changes on Pitkin Avenue. It makes me nostalgic to think of it. I'd say to myself, 'What happened to that store that used to be here?' The delis were bodegas, there were no Jewish people, it was completely changed. I felt sad. It left me with a depressed feeling."

Her melancholy signals the complexity of people's relationships to neighborhood. Morris Janowitz has shown how some people treat their surround as a community of limited liability from which it is easy to sever their ties and disengage. Others treat their neighborhood as a place of expansive involvement and insoluble commitments; they invest emotion as well as money in their communities.[34] They trust and love the kith and kin who reside there. A stage of life, a style of living, or a scrap of culture is associated with the physical stage on which it is enacted. Evoking that close symbolic tie among home, loss, and attachment, Gaston Bachelard wrote, "The houses that were lost forever continue to live on in us ... they insist in us in order to live again."[35]

It was hard for the elderly who had grown up in the immigrant villages of East New York and Brownsville to separate a beloved physical world, no longer accessible, from a cherished cultural world. "They were magic days in Brownsville. That's where my mother settled when she came to America from Pavel. It was such a beautiful place back in the 1930s, you could hear the sound of Yiddish everywhere. We would walk to get fresh goat's milk." This woman had made what felt like a great odyssey across Brooklyn to live in public housing near the East River. "You won't believe this, but it was the first time I had lived in a non-Jewish neighborhood. I had lived in a ghetto my whole life. I went home to East New York and said, 'There are the hills of my home.'"

Speakers often fell into a hushed, wistful mood as they gave themselves over to memories of childhood places. In *The Poetics of Space* Bachelard described the primitivism of such states. "We should therefore have to say how we inhabit our vital space ... How we take root, day after day, in a 'corner of the world.' For our house

is our corner of the world. As has often been said, it is our first universe, a real cosmos in every sense of the word . . . All real inhabited
space bears the essence of the notion of home . . . An entire past
comes to dwell in a new house . . . Through dreams, the various
dwelling-places in our lives co-penetrate and retain the treasures of
former days."[36]

The loss of those first corners of the world often incited a wish to
punish the villains who had ruined them. A devout liberal shook
with anger at the blacks she blamed for destroying Eastern Parkway.
Her mourning for the death of her father merged with sadness at the
passing of the old neighborhood. The squalor of her former neighborhood deprived her of the chance to say with pride, "That's where
I grew up." With passion breaking through her words, she said, "The
colored people made it like that! They chopped the steps off. They
didn't get that way on their own. That was malicious behavior, they
made a slum out of it, they infested it with vermin. We had such a
lovely childhood there, there was no reason it had to go like that."

Yiddishkeit provided some check on the virulence of the woman's
diatribe. At the least the culprits—"colored people"—never crossed
that loathsome threshold and became "niggers." But one trucker
jabbed, "I look back on the neighborhood [of Bushwick] and I
mourn for it. I seen the house my father built with his own hands, I
seen the niggers come into that house and destroy it. The niggers
done this, the niggers ruined it. I seen the porch he built ripped
down, not in a normal aspect, but this was malicious acts that destroyed it. They ruined it! The doorways, the fixtures, the windows—the works."

Occasionally the disjointed complaints about vulnerable places
formed into a clear understanding that there had been an Edenic
time once, before ghetto crime, racial tipping, and white flight. The
encroachment of blacks and Hispanics became the epic event in the
history of recent time and space. An extremely resentful Italian
worker launched into a withering discourse on the civil rights movement, which had crashed down upon his world of safety:

Back in 1960 I was for civil rights and the love of all. But they
threw out the literacy test and gave the animals a vote and they
voted for the guy who gives them the most welfare. I mingled
with the niggers in school when I was growing up. They were
nicer back then, more relaxed and if you bumped into one of
them by mistake, it would be okay. But now? A hustler stabbed

a Greek friend of mine in Times Square, but the hustler got away in a gypsy cab. Those god-damn gypsy cabs! I'm not a racist 'cause I don't want to live with them who cause the rapings and stabbings. These people enjoy the blood pouring out of a white man. It's unfortunate. The only way to solve it is all-out war, and I won't run from it. What's it all come to? You tell me. It's all black on Flatbush Avenue now. I used to walk Flatbush Avenue when I was dating my wife. It was all white then. I remember joyous occasions. In 1956 the Dodgers beat the Yankees in the World Series. I was at Flatbush and Church avenues, thousands of people were in the street enjoying themselves all night long. It was one big happy Flatbush family. But now? Ninety-five percent of them have been mugged and moved away. Is it my fault?

His nostalgia for the cosy Flatbush family shows how race may serve as a metaphor for vague indignities. The romance of the past betrayed the man's loyalty to a rhythm of daily life that had vanished along with the Dodgers and white invincibility. The more he mulled over the state of the nation, the more his resentment over changes in patriotic devotion and family life became fixated on the darkening complexion of Flatbush Avenue, which made him bitter and poisoned his feelings toward blacks. Anxiety about race was only the most palpable form of the threat that weighed on him. Race was a kind of shorthand for an array of social, cultural, and economic deprivals. In the midst of that elision, blacks were transformed from adversaries, or from beings with unique personalities, or from scapegoats who drained away hostility, into signs: an easy way to represent change. To borrow from Claude Lévi-Strauss, blacks were good to think with as well as to hate with.

Even if this Italian worker unwittingly used the vulnerabilities of place to dramatize other areas of vulnerability, the overdetermined quality of his elegies does not mean that his complaints about the decline of Brooklyn were masquerades or symptoms or pretexts for something else. The feeling of homelessness came from accurate memories of the old neighborhoods and from a true exile from a safe, comfortable, and enjoyable space. With characteristic absolutism, the man voiced a popular longing for a Brooklyn that used to be.

Mourning did not enable whites to imagine how it felt to be on the receiving end of exclusion. One Canarsie black man, though, retained the power of double vision. He knew the sting of discrimination, yet he could imaginatively enter the world of the people who wounded him. "Ten years ago, maybe twenty, East New York and Brownsville were Jewish ghettos. Blacks moved in and the whites fled." He granted the truth of white nostalgia. "The people of Canarsie are right to be nostalgic. The neighborhoods *were* terrific. They were fabulous neighborhoods. The people would sit out on their porches and visit their neighbors." He advised a realistic approach. "It's like growing up with a doll which you no longer have. You shed a tear. Now it's not the same as they knew it in the 1950s, so they mourn for it. It's a shame. But there's only one problem with that, I mean, the Canarsie people forget one thing: *I* didn't destroy *their* Brownsville."

4. The Lost People

Class Consciousness

*"It's okay to talk about the welfare classes, but the
real problem is the middle-class squeeze. You get
it from top and bottom."*

Canarsians' feelings of vulnerability violated their expectations that
their lives of striving would be rewarded. They felt they had a right
to avoid entanglement in the affairs of the larger society. Garry Wills
has described Richard Nixon's ingenious appeal to that belief in the
frantic election year of 1968. "Nixon's success was not offered in
Miami as a theme for mere self-congratulation. It was a pledge to
others, a pledge that he would not rob them of the fruits of their success: 'You can see why I believe so deeply in the American dream.
For most of us the American Revolution has been won; the American dream has come true.' "[1]

The promise echoed William Jennings Bryan's celebration of a
similar notion of privatism. Bryan came to New York City to reassure the 1896 Democratic convention that his intentions were not
subversive. Like 1968, 1896 was a time of social upheaval, when the
old faiths no longer seemed apt and partisan loyalties had gone
slack. "Our campaign has not for its object the reconstruction of society," the Great Redeemer told the convention. "We cannot insure
to the vicious the fruits of a virtuous life; we would not invade the
home of the provident in order to supply the wants of the spendthrift; we do not propose to transfer the rewards of industry to the
laps of indolence."[2]

The speech would have been well received in Canarsie three-quarters of a century later. The residents thought racial quotas trans-

ferred the rewards of industry to the laps of indolence, welfare raided the home of the provident to supply the wants of the spendthrift, and rioting was insurance for the vicious. Policies designed to help minorities challenged the social place of middle-income people. The policies were enforced, not by actual muscle but by the symbolic muscle of government. One aide to a Canarsie elected official, a conservative Democrat who detested "limousine liberals," drew the parallel between threats to physical and to social place in a comment on the impact of the civil rights movement: "The whole middle class is suffering from a proverbial mugging."

The civil rights movement was a heroic phase of American history. In their effort to achieve basic constitutional rights, blacks claimed the title of the injured party. But the more blacks fought for a place in society, the more whites resisted, seizing for themselves the identity of the injured. The reasons for the change in the terms of that racial debate are complex, but in part they stemmed from a shift in the strategy of the civil rights movement. A national consensus in the early 1960s sustained black demands for legal rights and equal opportunity. But as blacks pressed for social and economic equality, complex questions of status, justice, and domination were raised.[3]

Just as Canarsians were closer geographically to the underclasses than were affluent suburbanites, so they were closer socially to the black lower- and middle-income classes.[4] The basic fact of life for the residents of Canarsie was the precariousness of their hold on middle-class status, the recency of their arrival in that exalted position, and the intense fear that it might be taken from them. The cramped quality of lower middle-class life was evident in their abstentions and forfeitures. It galled Canarsians that poor blacks and Hispanics used food stamps to buy "luxury items" while they had to scrimp to get by. "I go to the supermarket and I see the welfare lady splurging and I'm abstaining," complained an insurance salesman. "It makes you mad because you been working so hard, and you have to give up things, and they don't work and get things you can't afford."

"I'd like to take a real vacation," said another man at the pressed margin of the middle class. "What we call a vacation is going to an aunt or uncle or something like that, where there's no hotel expenses. My wife and I, we'd like to go where nobody knows us, go to a show or a nightclub or something, do this or that, that's a vacation, really relaxing." But his take-home pay of $150 a week always seemed to lag behind the spiraling expenses of rent bills, utility bills, feeding the family.

When his wife thought about growing old and getting sick, the future looked grim. The plight of an old Jewish woman whom she and her husband had visited in a city hospital offered a sad portent. The patient lay in her own waste because the nurses wouldn't change the bed linen. "A bowl of soup for a woman who's put her whole life into this country! I know she's not outstanding, but do you have to be an outstanding, well-known person to be taken care of? I'm sure Rockefeller, if anything happened to him, boy, he's not going to want. They'll rush him to the best hospital. Not that I'm saying we need the best hospitals. But they should take care of us properly. We bleed just like Rockefeller bleeds."

Fiscal pressures fortified the feeling of deprivation. An Italian worker offered his own sardonic version of class consciousness. "There is no more middle class any more. I'll give you my interpretation. I don't believe in low, middle and high class. There's high income and there's low income." He argued that thanks to transfer payments, tax policy, and mortgage payments, "The average guy who makes $20,000 a year is basically coming out with the same amount as the guy on welfare. So what does that make him? That makes him low. Middle income is a federal term to make people feel good before they pick their pockets."[5]

Rivalry for jobs dissolved magnanimous impulses. If the employed felt nervous about the security of their jobs, unemployment sometimes produced feelings of white panic and bitterness. An unemployed Jewish salesman saw blacks as his personal tormentors. "The blacks want my job, they want to take my little box of a house, they won't leave me alone!" A Jewish politician explained in 1977, "All over Canarsie, people feel others are eroding what they have gained. Today, with the economy so bad, there's a greater feeling, people are saying, 'Blacks are coming in and taking our jobs.' Of course they had security when only whites were in the job market."

Canarsians saw the workplace as only one of many arenas of threat created by liberal reform, the civil rights movement, and black assertiveness.[6] All facets of black and white relations seemed to impose strains on the lower middle classes: on their ability to remain financially solvent, on their ability to believe that life was just, on their ability to withstand privation. A Jewish educator in Canar-

sie described the pressures placed on his neighbors by the overthrow
of white dominance:

> These efforts to help blacks reached a plateau. It's like a rub-
> ber band. I don't know the moral or legal limits on stretching
> the middle class, how far and how much they will pay the price.
> I don't know, to tell you the truth, if we've stretched the limits
> far enough. But I do know that since 1964, the vast majority of
> Canarsie feels that they've been stretched to the limits of their
> endurance.

The image of being stretched had many variants connoting
pressure, discomfort, and pain; blacks were not the only source of
hurt. Residents said they were choking from and groaning under and
gagging on the costs of efforts to help the poor. Others said they were
being "raped," "fucked up the ass," or "screwed" by utility rates, the
tax system, or busing. Men sometimes described a vague, malevolent
force that was breaking their balls. A sophisticated analyst of lower-
middle-class rage captured the dangers that pressed his neighbors.
"Canarsie is up against the wall. That's what the lower middle and
middle classes feel pressing on them. They feel the pressure, like
everything is fading away. It's all in danger: the house you always
wanted is in danger, the kids are in danger, the neighborhood is in
danger. It's all slipping away."

The real keyword of middle-class lamentation was *squeeze*. A
merchant depicted his plight as follows. "Someone is coming in and
squeezing us and taking it all away. That is what is unifying our community. The squeezing is wrong, it's so wrong. You are looking at
a man who hurts. First, they squeeze my pocketbook, so I can't
do anything. Then they come in with busing and squeeze my
kids." Squeeze indicated the position of the middle classes betwixt
and between the impoverished and the affluent. A self-professed
conservative Democrat pinpointed the vulnerability of the middle
class:

> It's okay to talk about the welfare classes, but the real problem
> is the middle-class squeeze. You get it from top and bottom. It's
> not only welfare, but the multinational corporations who are
> ripping us off, taking our jobs away and sending employment to
> the South and the West. The middle classes are the lost people.

We don't have the wherewithal to fight back, because we aren't rich enough, and we're not poor enough to get the advantages that go to the poor. We suffer.

That the elected officials in the Jefferson Democratic Club evinced a hearty progressive streak is not surprising, given their strong New Deal loyalties. Yet Italian leaders in the Republican and Conservative parties voiced similar notions of status radicalism. Whatever else their conservatism entailed, it did not include affection for corporate business. "Oil, steel, insurance, and the banks run this country," exclaimed a Nixon loyalist in the Italian-American Civil Rights League. "I'd go for public ownership of the oil companies if I didn't think the national politicians were a bunch of thieves."

Canarsians' resentment was directed as well at privileged portions of the middle classes. The special perquisites, or "lulus," given to state legislators, the escalator clauses in AFL-CIO union contracts, and the sweetheart deals negotiated by city workers provoked their anger. A dockworker whose union guaranteed him employment did not consider municipal unions instruments of popular justice. "These cops are paid overtime on fringe benefits in their last year before they retire, and that's what they get as a pension. I'm a working guy and I can't imagine getting that. It's not fair. I'm paying money on my house and mortgage, and I just can't make it."

The lines of antagonism, then, were not fixed or simple. Rivalry between blacks and whites, between public and private workers, between business and labor—each was only one of many shifting points of conflict and concord. Canarsians mistrusted privileged blocs of all sorts, including the organized sectors of their own class.

How much squeezing would the citizens absorb before lashing back? Can one detect in the identity of the little man an ominous harbinger of fascism? When a volatile, two-fisted worker used the word, *squeeze* could be the language of the body, unmediated by thought. The word conjures up the image of intense pressure building to a vindictive climax. Historically, the middle classes have felt deeply betrayed when their wants have outpaced expectations or their aspirations have been thwarted by austerity. Betrayal easily turns into soured cynicism or, worse, nationalist mania and race-baiting. Michael Rogin has aptly described the baneful downside of American hopefulness as "the punitive consequences of frustrated optimism." In Seymour Martin Lipset's classic formulation, a crushed middle class succumbs to populist forms of right-wing extremism.[7]

An Italian construction worker warned of the dangerous propensities of riled "average people." "We're working men, and we don't bow our heads in humility. We fight and say to the blacks, 'Keep out of our neighborhood.' We never bullshit. We call a spade a spade." He was equally capable of denouncing large corporations, and the privileged in general, who crushed "little nobodies like us, just average people trying to survive. How the hell can you keep surviving with Con Ed and Brooklyn Gas Company preying on you?" And there were the blacks on welfare, the demands for quotas, and the black felons who paraded across his television on the nightly news. Sometimes it was just too much to endure, and he felt an urge to take out all his different frustrations on one scapegoat. "You know how the Jews were put in concentration camps? Well, people will get angry and reactionary and put the blacks in concentration camps. If we whites are constantly frustrated, there will be a racial conflagration."

One should be wary of a mechanistic equation of strain and right-wing mania. The development of reactionary protest was not a foregone conclusion. Various personal, moral, and political restraints inhibit the direct translation of frustration into authoritarian rage. While racist and nationalist binges remain a latent tendency in American society, that tendency has diminished. Whether middle-class frustration surges to the right or to the left depends significantly on the political leaders and institutions that channel anger. The retributive consequences of frustrated optimism remain a propensity more than a destiny.[8]

Canarsians for decades had felt beleaguered by the forces of corporate avarice and special interests. They had always seen themselves as little people. The forgotten men of the Depression are not that different from the average working people heralded by George Wallace. To the old rhetoric the passions of race added new threats and more vivid culprits. Now Canarsians had to contend with organized minorities and powerful liberalism as well as organized labor and big business. The residents used the categories they inherited from immigrant life and the New Deal, but they stretched them to make room for black and Hispanic rivals and their patrons in academia, the suburbs, the media, the judiciary, the bureaucracy, and the Democratic party.

Welfare

"Who's feeling sorry for me? The colored have
gotten enough. Let them do for themselves
like we do."

The middle classes hurled blame down on those who enjoyed the in-dulgence of dependency and up against those who enjoyed the im-munities of affluence, yet their focus remained on the minority poor. Before detailing the conceptions of justice and character that shaped their response to the welfare classes, we must examine two major recent changes in the fiscal and political environment that contrib-uted to that fixation. One involves the change in the welfare func-tions of government and the proportion of those on welfare in Brooklyn and in New York City. As William J. Wilson has argued, competition between blacks and whites has moved from the sphere of jobs to the enjoyment of public goods, like schools and entitle-ments. The growth in the expense and diversity of claims on munici-pal and national treasuries, including Aid to Families with Dependent Children and antipoverty programs, enhanced middle-class upset about black dependency. Between 1965 and 1971 the per-centage of the population on welfare in minority neighborhoods near Canarsie soared: from 23 percent to 38 percent in Brownsville, from less than 8 percent to a startling 31 percent in East New York.[9]

Changes in publicity accompanied the growth of entitlements; the government's initiatives became more visible, the cries of the claim-ants louder. The clamor reached a peak in New York City during the 1960s, when the Welfare Rights Organization launched a controver-sial campaign to enroll eligible clients. "The campaign of disruption was in full swing. There was a three-day sit-in at the commissioner's office, and unruly demonstrators closed [welfare] centers throughout the city. One sit-in reportedly netted $135,000 in new grants." These changes in publicity and dependency gave new meaning to the con-cept of transfer payments. "Instead of merely granting the poor a continued share of a growing economy, the massive expansion of the rolls began to approach actual redistribution of income from the middle class to the poor."[10]

Canarsians often showed their hostility to people on welfare by contrasting parasites and producers. The head of a conservative civic group wrote in its newspaper, "For years, we have witnessed the appeasement of nonproductive and counter-productive 'leeches' at the expense of New York's middle class work force." He reported on his field trip to the ghetto on "check day." "The first thing that caught my eye . . . was the 8:00 A.M. opening of all the Liquor Stores, who spend their entire morning . . . bracing for the brisk day's business. It's a crude fact that the liquor stores cater to continuous LINES of people, from morning to night on days that welfare checks are received."[11]

A receptive reader could take double pleasure from the editorial. It pledged to exact retribution from the profligate in a disinterested act of upholding morality. And it reminded the readers of their superiority, as plucky bootstrappers, to the hapless leeches, a word that bypassed the equivocations of thought and went right for the guts. A city worker, practically beside himself, exploded, "These welfare people get as much as I do and I work my ass off and come home dead tired. They get up late and they can shack up all day long and watch the tube. With their welfare and food stamps, they come out better than me . . . So why should I work? I go shopping with my wife and I see them with their forty dollars of food stamps in the supermarket, living and eating better than me . . . And they got this escalator clause too, so they keep getting more. Let them tighten their belts like we have to."

Was "leeches" an expression of racist contempt? Can an envy of splurging be detected in the animus toward those who lie around and "shack up all day?" Did the call for belt-tightening express a secret wish to squeeze the welfare people as tightly as the speaker felt squeezed by all the privations in his life? Self-denial often produces an attitude of stingy misanthropy. As one man inveighed, "Who's feeling sorry for me? The colored have gotten enough. Let them do for themselves like we do!" His question hinted at the close link between fatiguing sacrifice and greedy self-absorption. The economy of scarcity is emotional as well as political.

The complexity of hostility to welfare becomes lost if we focus on racist passion or on the stinginess induced by financial vulnerability. The first position, which views resentment of the dole as a displacement of inner tensions, succumbs to a false psychologism. The second position, which views the tension between the productive and the dependent classes as a fight for personal advantage, succumbs to a false materialism.[12] Both fail to represent the full range of Canarsians' emotional repertoire. As all the middle-class chants of "It's not fair, it's not right" suggest, one of the key emotions in fiscal backlash is indignation, an emotion born of the perception of injustice. Along with the political and psychic economies of welfare, there is a moral economy of welfare.

The voracity of the word "leech" contrasts sharply with benevolent nurture. It conjures up a creature that sucks the sustenance of others. Unlike those who embrace the ethos of reciprocity, the leech receives without returning, takes but does not give, devours but refuses to contribute. More than a disguise for self-interest, a symptom of envy, or a euphemism for racism, the leech is a symbol of violated justice.

Regardless of where they fell along the spectrum of ideology, most Canarsians reproached what they saw as the deformation of welfare rather than the giving as such. They bemoaned the devolution of a rightful guarantee of subsistence into a pride-corroding, dependency-enhancing system of giveaways. They specifically condemned the way welfare was administered. A liberal Jewish woman argued, "I don't think the problem is we give too much welfare, but how it's handled. We do it poorly. Medicaid and the school lunch program are full of waste and fraud. I worked for the welfare department, and I know that much of it is not proper." The residents said that the aged, the worthy poor, both white and black, and the crippled did not receive adequate recompense. Some of the most conservative enemies of giveaways argued for an expansion of government initiatives in creating jobs, insuring health care, and protecting the environment.[13]

In searching for a model of just giving, the residents cited the system they imagined they knew best. A local civic leader offered this version of the prevailing wisdom. "For scores of years, welfare has served as a dignified alternative to starvation . . . for the individual who has been truly unable to produce, but who obviously would produce if able." The wizardry of the old welfare system was its ability to satisfy a variety of desiderata, both practical and moral. Above all, the man believed, it worked in harmony with, not in opposition to, prized cultural values. "It has served to help our ancestors 'get on their feet' financially after arriving here penniless, so that they could assert their pride and determination, and go on with the business of raising a family and earning a legitimate living."

State aid had sustained many residents of Canarsie, or their friends, relatives, and neighbors. Beneficence, however, did not mean munificence. According to the romance of history, relief extended a modest provision hedged by the client's shame, by the moral sanctions of the local community in which the recipient lived, and by widespread acceptance of the system's authority to place restrictions on giving. An Italian Republican leader said, "Welfare is a necessity, but there are the extravagances, the items allowable. And there's the continuous cycle of generation after generation on welfare."

He migrated back in time. "Years ago my father died and left my mother with eight children. We went on welfare and we were visited by a welfare worker at our home periodically, to see if my mother was buying foolishly." Current talk about forming a union of welfare recipients struck him as arrogant, in contrast to his family's humble deference to the intrusions of a paternalistic state. "We weren't allowed to buy a telephone or linoleum. We had to ask. You need these controls on public funds. When my older sister got a job after she graduated from Midwood High School, they reduced the welfare. And when my second sister went to work, we went off welfare. Welfare helped us, and it was right and just they did. Then we could shift for ourselves."

The ideal of governmental sternness went beyond the chilly withholding of care; it defined the best interests of clients, parallelling folk notions of the best interests of children. The residents saw liberal permissiveness as an abdication of concern, which left children and welfare clients incapable of self-direction and worse off for it. An Italian Reaganite Republican voiced a common opinion: "Blacks have been made the political football of the Democratic party. The Democrats offer the blacks so much welfare that it impairs them. They never give them an opportunity to lift themselves up. Welfare destroys them. They must learn to fend for themselves. You can't always run to papa." In good universalist fashion, the man applied the same lesson to his children. Would not softness spoil them, he asked, and unfit them for life in a world that required steely character? "A child should begin to stand on his own two feet. Don't hand them everything on a silver platter."

Provincial Italians were convinced that leniency encouraged welfare recipients to make extravagant claims, just as they thought permissive child-rearing encouraged kids to make wild libidinal claims on the world. In both cases, they reasoned, if given one inch, human beings would *naturally* go for the whole foot. "I blame this welfare mess on the government," a policeman said after describing a system that seemed self-perpetuating when it should have been self-cancelling. "Now this is only telling me one thing. If you're getting welfare for the first generation, the second generation is just gonna say,

'What the hell do I have to work for? I'll just carry on the same thing,' and it moves down the line. If you're gonna give somebody something for nothing, let's say you tell 'em, 'We'll pay for your house, we'll pay for your rent, we'll pay for your food,' why should you want to work?"

Liberal Democrats in Canarsie were no more enthusiastic about the welfare system than were conservative Republicans. The remnant of Debsean socialists no less than acquisitive vulgarians worshiped self-reliance. Pulling one's own weight was a natural complement to a cooperative society in which all shouldered their burdens. "Bums," "parasites," and "takers" offended that notion of reciprocity, which obliged citizens not to slough off their duties onto others. A leftist saw dependency as a violation of her humanist belief in individual development:

> Some of the problems of poor blacks is their cultural background. It's the way they have lived in America. I don't know about Africa, but dependency has become ingrained in their culture. The attitude is, "Let others take care of me." There's a lack of self-reliance. But there has been much black progress despite the bad methods. I see it where I work. People are put into jobs they are not qualified for, but they learn from being in the situation. Learning to contribute makes you less satisfied about being given things.

The division of the world into producers and parasites objectified basic principles of right living. All the adages of lower-middle-class life celebrated the values of get up and go, busting chops, doing for yourself.[14] "Face it," said one Jewish merchant, "the Haitians and the Jamaicans and the other islanders down in Flatbush don't consider themselves black. These island people are producing people, they're up early sweeping their stoops and taking care of their homes. They're producing people like we are! But the black lower element don't contribute to society, they just take. In my view, you should get what you put into. You have to contribute."

Welfare violated notions of distributive as well as contributive justice by circulating burdens and rewards inequitably. When he measured the rewards that accrued to indolence against those produced by effort, an Italian worker felt like a consummate chump. Only his analytic streak and sense of humor saved him from wild resentment. "The average person on welfare, let's say they make

$10,000 a year, with all the school benefits and food stamps. I make $20,000 a year. But I am taxed and taxed and taxed, close to $6,000 worth. So I'm down to $14,000 already. You take that fourteen and someone's getting ten, he's making only four thousand less than I am, and he's not working. Interesting idea? I'm just trying to put you in my category."

Garry Wills has argued that "the American fanatic has always suffered moral disorientation at the mere thought of anyone 'getting something for nothing.' " Americans, however, are not the only fanatics. Marcel Mauss wrote, "The essence of potlatch is the obligation of worthy return." Virginia Yans-McGlouglan has written, "The Mezzogiorno peasants were not accustomed to getting 'something for nothing.' "[15] At least the old system of welfare, according to the conventional wisdom, accomplished an implicit trade of something for something. "In essence, the very person that received welfare soon would be paying taxes, so that the city would constantly replace its outlay of funds. He had become a productive citizen."[16] In contrast, the present system seemed to encourage multigenerational welfare families, undermining the public's trust in eventual symbolic or material repayment.

Resentment of the injustice of the tax system reinforced the image of one-sided exchange. Canarsians believed that tax penalties were heaped on working people while the affluent got off scot-free. "The very poor have nothing economically," claimed a housewife, "but they reap the benefits of our hard work. My husband works hard, and the taxes keep going up. The taxes go to the poor, not to us. And the rich have their tax accountants. The middle-income people are carrying the cost of liberal social programs on their backs. The rich can afford to be liberal. They won't be touched by liberalized programs."

The reckoning of fiscal right and wrong originated not only in mean-spirited individualism but also in a practical ethics that tallied the ability to pay, the effectiveness of the welfare system, the worthiness of the clients, the distribution of burdens, and the discretionary margin of savings. Canarsians resembled earthy peasants the world over who must decide which claims on their labor are permissible. As James Scott has argued, kin ties, the state, and patron-client relations may help peasants in times of need but also burden them with demands on their meager resources. The key to the legitimacy of such claims lies in "the timing, size and scope of their contributions and claims to peasant resources."[17]

Unrestrained giving seemed to be the signature of the paternalistic liberalism that emerged in the 1960s. It was presented as generosity, but Canarsians thought it a prescription for irresponsibility. On the one hand, it confiscated the paltry surplus of lower-middle-class bootstrappers; on the other, it showed lack of mettle by caving in to clients' demands. Once, giving had symbolized responsible caring; now it meant decadent promiscuity. A self-professed conservative, who had participated in CIO sit-down strikes in the 1930s, pronounced, "A liberal is a giveaway: too much, too fast, too easy. A conservative is the reverse: too little, too seldom, too hard." A few residents even saw the liberal as kindred spirit of the notorious "easy" girl from the old neighborhood. She was cheap, gave it away without exacting a return. Perhaps she was good for a tumble, but a tumble did not earn the respect of those who exploited her favors. An Italian craftsman expressed a similar thought in slightly different terms. "It's like the old maid and the prostitute. Well, liberals are like the prostitute."

Affirmative Action

*"Two hundred years after the inception of our
'Great American Dream' the middle class now
finds itself in the midst of a 'Great American
Nightmare.' "*

Welfare was unpopular in Canarsie, but it was familiar, and it did not interfere in the competitive results of the marketplace. But the government's remedies for past economic injuries of the black poor did not achieve legitimacy through custom. Affirmative action, busing, quotas, model cities programs, bilingual education, and community control of schools were novel instruments in the effort to redress economic inequality and legal and political discrimination.

Gradually the perception had spread among the people of Canarsie that they were being asked to atone for some unconfirmed wrong. The enlightened called it redress; many Canarsians considered it little more than extortion. It seemed that the middle classes, the government, and the minorities had struck a bargain, yet benefits flowed in only one direction, from the middle to the lower classes, and the middle classes had precious little say in setting up that exchange.

"Taking" connoted the cost of benevolence for the poor, the injustice that government generosity imposed on the middle-income classes, and the illegitimacy of the methods of redress. A Jewish teacher who could not send his son to a private college because scholarship awards were restricted to the most needy complained: "I work hard for my money, but they are taking from me to give to someone else. This taking is killing the creativity of the middle class. We are terribly abused."

"Taking" referred to all forms of illicitly captured rewards—hustling, blackmail, rioting, quotas, busing, and muggings. During a mugging a scrappy daughter of "union people" fought back to hang onto her handbag. On reflection, the experience seemed to her a graphic form of the deranged exchanges that characterized the economic strategy of the underclass. "I was hurt, but I fought back and resisted. I was angry, I thought, 'It's mine and I don't want to let it go. I work hard for it and I don't want you to take it.' "

The civil disorders of the 1960s represented such a mugging in a dramatic collective form. Canarsians tended to view rioting not as an outcry against grievous wrong but as a manifestation of the ghetto dwellers' tendency to scream for benefits, to wallow in self-pity about exploitation long past, and to use lofty ideals to mask thuggery. Instead of taking responsibility for themselves, rioters took the hard-earned surplus of others.[18]

A Jewish baker defined a liberal as "someone whose goal is the most good for the most people. Today's conservatives masquerade as liberals. They tell people what's good for themselves is good for all people." A voracious reader of political news, the man had watched the drama of southern desegregation with excitement. Despite his deep emotional investment in black emancipation, black militance struck him as coercive. "It was a form of the iron fist: 'You give me this, or else.' "

Worse still for many residents, liberals seemed entranced by theories that justified plunder. An activist in Mario Procaccino's 1969 campaign to unseat Mayor John V. Lindsay blamed Lindsay, and liberals generally, for an intellectual permissiveness that endangered middle-class homeowners and tacitly sanctioned blackmail. "He took the nightstick away from the police. He said, 'If the blacks riot, don't hurt them, they have reasons for it.' " The man spoke the word "reasons" with strain, as though he had switched to a foreign tongue which carried an alien set of values. To accept reasons for rioting was to take cockamamie excuses and *ferkocta* double-talk at face value. Such a reading of lawlessness indicated that liberals were suckers easily gulled by the underclasses and unworthy of respect.

The currency of terms like "environment" to explain social problems marked a new conception of equality, a change Garry Wills dubbed "refiguring the calculus." Lyndon Johnson, in a speech at Howard University in 1965, expressed the new thinking: "You do not take a person who, for years, has been hobbled by chains and liberate him, bring him to the starting line of a race and then say, 'You are free to compete with all the others,' and still justly believe that you have been completely fair." As Wills commented, "People must not only be admitted to the race; they must also be equipped for the race."[19] In one fell swoop Johnson defined the flaw in Canarsie's mobility myth without addressing its status as revealed truth. The residents viewed concepts like compensation and affirmative action as fancy versions of robbery that maliciously harmed the middle class, both in an absolute sense and also relative to their innocence, their ability to pay, and the exemptions of the wealthy. Anger was sharpest in the vulnerable, provincial reaches of the lower middle class. An unemployed construction worker who had tried to become a fireman fumed, "It's humiliating for a white guy to go on welfare. He's harassed while the boons get it for free. I was turned down for a fire department job, I was number two thousand on the civil service list, and I got a notice that says for every two acceptances, there's got to be one minority."

The residents anticipated future harm and vicariously experienced the harm meted out to their circle of intimates. A self-described former liberal insisted, "I liked John Kennedy, and I liked the early civil rights movement. I was a liberal. I used to fight for the *schvartzes'* rights. I thought, all people have a right to public accommodations, to jobs according to ability. But, if my kid has a ninety-nine average, why should he be deprived? He has one life to lead. What's fair is fair. The *schvartzes* want to get ahead. They *should* get ahead. But not on my kid's back. Blacks are taking advantage."

Affirmative action depleted people's trust in social appearances. A Jewish school administrator vowed, "I'd never vote to return to throwing money down the drain, although I supported LBJ's programs at the time. Now I feel we must teach responsibility. But don't just give money and jobs to blacks. They take black administrators in the school system who aren't qualified. They have tainted credentials." These suspicions were often magical explanations for white setbacks earned honestly in the marketplace. "Say my son was qualified doing one thing, and he went for that job, and the quotas was for another black man, and the black man didn't have the quality. They would have to take the black man. Otherwise, the blacks would claim discrimination."

Out of the precipitate of lower-middle-class anger there began to crystallize a fierce Jewish backlash against reverse discrimination. Resentment flared in the insecure regions of the petty bourgeoisie, among those shielded from contact with progressive milieus, in the Orthodox circles where communal self-absorption encouraged members to compute a distinctively Jewish interest. One Jewish woman, a paraprofessional married to a salesman, felt financially strapped. "I have to work now, it takes two incomes to make what it used to with one. So you want to know how I became a bigot? I'll tell you. The blacks have options we don't. The Jews never had a civil rights movement. We fought for everything ourselves. When my parents came over here, they didn't have signs in Yiddish and Italian, they were only in English. And those giveaway programs. I'm not getting any! This is how I became a bigot. I'm tired of it. I want equal opportunity, not this sixty-forty business."

The rise of Jewish backlash created a generational chasm between this woman and her father. She could not express her resentment without guilt. Although the New Deal was but a faint memory to her generation and hardly germane to her present concerns, it endured as the antiquated lore of her parents. "I voted for Stevenson in 1956," she recalled, "but that was because I was indoctrinated with my father's Democratic loyalty. He always told us, 'It's the Democrats, do or die. They are for the working class and the Republicans are for big business.'" She and her father would quarrel and sometimes she would provoke him, saying that Roosevelt had started the Holocaust or that she was thinking of voting for Nixon in 1972. "But my father gets mad when he hears that. He says I'm not thinking, he says, 'I'm a worker and a union man and I'm for the Democrats.'" Her liberal sister also hectored her and looked down on Canarsie resentment as "low-class" behavior unbecoming to Jews.

Despite the commonalities in middle-income complaints, subtle differences characterized the narratives. Jewish resentment was less absolute than the Italian variety and was hedged by taboo and tradition. The ambivalence was not just a psychological affliction but the result of contact with forces of restraint and disagreement. Hesitation was imposed from outside as well as self-inflicted. The Jews' resentment contained more conditionals, elaborate apologetics, and wordy defensiveness, in part because the liberal views of relatives, friends, and acquaintances forced them to justify what Italian workers more often could take for granted.

Information about reverse discrimination was an amalgam of fantasy, truth, and rumor that reached Canarsians through many circuitous pathways. The rise of backlash organizations altered the process of transmission. Whatever motives residents had for joining, participation had its own consequences. Members of such groups may have been more alarmed than others about reverse discrimination, not only because they were more anxious about their social standing but because the groups served as clearing houses of grievance, nodes where rumors collected, and relay points for disseminating information to the community.[20] The meetings offered a revival-meeting atmosphere in which the aggrieved could raise their consciousness. Visits from leaders and members of similar groups in other neighborhoods broadened the parochial perspective.

One night a group of right-wing activists from Queens traveled to Canarsie to speak before a band of their Brooklyn counterparts. One of the visitors exhorted the Canarsie people, "We need a power bloc and organization to fight for white civil rights. There are no civil rights laws to protect *us*." The man instructed the audience in the arts of public relations. "The Jewish Defense League is good at dramatizing their hatred of quotas. The New York State education system was eighty percent Jewish, and now they must be twenty percent black, but they didn't say they had to have ten percent Italians!" He told of a JDL stunt. "They dressed a four-eyed, bookish, square, Jewish-looking kid and put him in front of Shea Stadium with a sign demanding a quota for Jewish baseball players. Merit is crucial. We have to end the muddleheadedness of the quota system. Blacks without credentials are getting into Brooklyn College and hurting the chances of whites."

The charge of reverse discrimination expressed an ethical critique of remedies like compensation. Indignation was the dominant emotion in the rejection of sixty-forty exchanges, in the complaints that blacks were climbing ahead on the backs of whites, in the never-ceasing choruses of "what's fair is fair." Black demands for equality of results rather than of opportunity began to alienate even fervent supporters of the black struggle for justice. Their new status as opponents of civil rights measures pained countless progressive Jews, who felt torn not simply between cupidity and ethics but between commitment to justice for blacks and disapproval of specific means of redress. One Jewish educator specified the visceral universalism that he felt should guide the good society:

> As a Jew, I believed anything that helped someone getting the short end of the stick would help the Jews. I couldn't go to medical school because of the quotas . . . I was pro-civil rights. I supported the Selma march, and the civil rights movement in its early phase. But, when someones tries to take something from me to benefit others, I'll fight it. I'm against compensation. I changed with the notion of not offering equal rights and opportunities, but compensation. That's reverse discrimination. It's a gut reaction with me.

Primal emotions fed the belief in the sanctity of voluntarism. One antibusing leader, drawing to the end of a speech with great flourish, referred to a local civil rights official he had debated on the radio. "Ramsey of the NAACP told us we had to pay the price for those years of slavery. But I ask you, who will pay the Jews for two thousand years of slavery? Who will compensate the Italians for all the ditches they dug?" The audience was stirred by the conception of justice on which, it believed, their immigrant forebears had built their modest successes. Quotas, open enrollments, rioting, busing, and reparations violated a standard of justice rooted in those mythical precedents of earning. Seen from the long view of immigrant history, singling out blacks for special help violated the canons of equity. Affirmative action compensated only a few deprived groups, and its champions were charged with having double standards. Why should one group be blessed with exemptions that were denied earlier groups? "These bilingual signs drive me crazy. The old Jews and Italians didn't have their language on signs. If this is a melting pot, let them melt. If there are materials in Spanish, there is no incentive to melt into a harmonious family. Bilingualism wasn't done for any other ethnic background. There's no precedent for it."

Affirmative action seemed to bump blacks ahead of white ethnic groups who believed they had been standing in a hypothetical queue of immigrants waiting to join middle-class society. But determining one's place in line obliged a controversial ranking of the order in which rival claims should be satisfied. Were blacks ahead of Jews and Italians by virtue of slavery? Should the clock be set running for blacks at the emergence from Jim Crow society after World War II? Those questions demanded judgments about the origins, duration, and end of the period of time-serving. Canarsians had little hesitation in defining blacks as being at the beginning of the ritual ordeal from which immigrant whites had just been liberated. "A lot of things went wrong for us, you know, for the Jewish people. What happened to the blacks happened to us too. We had to push hard in the beginning too."[21]

Sentimentality deformed ancestor worship and slighted the power of labor markets and impersonal forces in shaping destiny. The analogy of climbing up the ethnic ladder, invoked to condemn black shiftlessness—"We made it, why can't they?"—was flawed by a false universality. As Roland Barthes has written, "Myth has the task of giving an historical intention a natural justification, and making contingency appear eternal." But the contingencies faced by blacks in America have been immeasurably more punitive than those faced by the white immigrants.[22] Nonetheless, the myth conformed to the evidence of personal memory, neighborhood legend, and life history. That view of the possible defined the limits of the permissible: If I was poor and did not go out and mug, if I managed to pull myself up by my socks without signs in Yiddish or quotas, then the environment cannot possibly explain persisting impoverishment and criminal behavior.

Italian Americans were highly skeptical of claims that blacks had suffered special burdens or that they needed government aid to pull themselves up. In the mid-1960s, before racial tensions reached their apogee in the borough, 45 percent of Brooklyn residents said blacks had not been denied equal opportunities for advancement; among Irish and Italian Catholics, the measure of disbelief was 60 percent. The limited contacts of provincial Catholics created barriers to sympathetic identification with strangers, shielded them from the social circles that disseminate sociological conceptions of reality, and discouraged them from acquiring detailed knowledge about black history.[23]

Local Italian leaders in Republican and Conservative circles, in the Italian-American Civil Rights League, and in the North Canarsie civic groups did nothing to change the beliefs of the rank and file. They were akin to the literate scribes of urban antiquity who straddled the line between community and society. Rather than subject folk intuitions to the relativizing scrutiny of cosmopolitanism, they gave the folk learning a more searching formulation. A leader in the Italian League scoffed at the claims of "so-called exploitation." "The problems of the blacks are their own fault. It's their ignorance. Jobs are created for everyone, but their own laziness keeps them from going after it. The common black, his problem is laziness and his upbringing. The Civil War was over one hundred years ago. They were given the fruits of the land and they haven't done much with them since."

Once again, the sharp division between less educated Italian opponents of black demands and more educated Jewish proponents neglects the equivocation that gripped Brooklyn Jews who supported the civil rights movement. In 1965, 63 percent of Brooklyn Jews, a full 23 percent more than Brooklyn Catholics, maintained that blacks had not received equal treatment, but only 23 percent felt that blacks "have used their opportunities for advancement as well as other groups."[24]

A Jewish teacher's analysis suggests the ambiguities of voluntarism. The woman greatly believed in the egalitarian tenets of kibbutz socialism, which she thought meant "it's inequitable for some to have so much. There should be no cutthroat competition. And we should all work together. There's too much concern with private interests, too much greed. We've lost idealism. Now, for most people, it's 'my family only.' " The Jewish identification with slaves had a paradoxical effect. "A lot of Jewish people I know in Canarsie commented about the television show *Roots.* They had great empathy for blacks, because blacks were slaves also." She granted that blacks faced special hurdles, but she felt that deprived people were obliged to jump those hurdles. Yet blacks were mired in a lower-class culture of dependency that denied them the internal resources and group supports to overcome limitation. "We Jews were able to rise above it, and the blacks should too. I agree with that up to a certain point. But there's a tremendous difference. One was so many years ago. We have had to wait a thousand years to see results for the Jews. And our background is different. Our families were more intact than theirs. Our cultural background is different."

Italians were the vanguard, Jews the laggards, in the movement toward backlash. The force of Jewish tradition slowed it but could not arrest it. Eventually, a few Jewish leaders tried to provide more explicit rationales for casting off the fetters of the political past. Alan Erlichman, a leader of the antibusing insurgency of 1972–73, wrote the "Chairman's Column" in *The Citizens News,* the newsletter of the Concerned Citizens of Canarsie, in which he developed a theory of the betrayals of liberalism. The essays—"Fatal Affliction: (A Medical Diagnosis of New York's Middle Class)," "Unjust Justice,"

"Liberal Crunch," and "Great American Nightmare"—extolled the virtues of Middle America.[25]

Erlichman voiced the faith and the fear of Canarsie's most resentful elements. First and foremost a polemicist, he rarely strayed far from his audience's primal resentments. He played to the issues that made them flinch and churn, not because he was a demagogue, as his detractors charged, but because he, too, flinched and churned. He spent his youth playing ball and digging the sounds of 1950s rhythm and blues with his buddies in Bensonhurst. Over the years he had managed a diner, been a hair stylist, worked with his father-in-law in a fabric store, and sold real estate.

In "Fatal Affliction," Erlichman depicted the white middle class as sickly. "The disease that has embodied itself within the structure of 'Middle New York' is no less severe than the cancer that had dwelled within the bodies of many of our lost, loved ones." The mandates handed down by imperious bureaucrats to integrate Canarsie's schools were a symptom of a grave illness. "We have been stricken by the cells of 'blind power,' given to a chosen few, that are tearing down our institutions of learning, and are now beginning to destroy our communities."

The chosen few were the mandarin elect composed of affluent liberals driven by a misplaced affection for the poor, who "see fit to 'save' the underprivileged, at the expense of the dwindling middle class." Erlichman took note of the "injustice [that] holds us responsible for the inequities within the minority classes." Without flinching, he hurled the blame back onto the sanctimonious liberals, social planners, and suburbanites who had "embarked upon a search and destroy mission of [middle-class] schools, cultures, and finally its residences." Returning to the medical imagery, Erlichman admonished his audiences that "to delay our medical treatment, would be to commit 'class suicide.' " More than any other catch phrase, "class suicide" proclaimed the middle class's fears of its fading powers, the terminal prognosis for the illness created by liberal reform, and the masochism in complying with one's own annihilation.

"Unjust Justice" seized on the judiciary as tyrannical agents of middle-class destruction hiding behind the veil of benevolence. Erlichman's immediate targets were two judges, Bruce "Let-them-loose" Wright and Federal District Court Judge Jack B. Weinstein, who had ordered busing of black children into Bensonhurst and Coney Island. They were attacked for mollifying the black community while sacrificing middle-income whites. Erlichman generalized about class formation: like his colleagues across the nation, he had been forced by "inequities" to "selfishly fight for the causes that protect [the middle class], for this is the life, the blood and the substance of our Nation. In essence, that is what the Concerned Citizens of Canarsie stand for, middle America."

In "Liberal Crunch," written in 1975, when the busing rebellion had begun to fade from Canarsie's memory, the enemy had become a "liberal wrecking ball" swinging through middle-class enclaves in Queens and Brooklyn. "The liberal politician, be his party Liberal, Democratic, or Republican, must allow the blame for our crisis to fall at his feet and begin to adjust his thinking. His blind support for the welfare leech and the misguided educational priorities will only serve to turn New York into a town that is totally void of financial resources and a viable middle class. When this comes to pass, he will then reign over a society of parasites that is completely incapable of sustaining any sort of economy or social establishment."

In "Great American Nightmare," Erlichman told how, in a perverse trade, whites had exchanged places with blacks, who enjoyed supreme status in a society tilted in their favor. In the name of fair play and reparations, social engineers had "sold out the middle class and relegated us to the role of whimpering, frightened, second class citizens." The leeches played a sinister role in a universe in which the American dream was inverted to become the American nightmare. Echoing William Jennings Bryan, Erlichman wrote that "the hard worker is overtaxed so that the idle can be 'rewarded' for their non-productive existence." Meanwhile, the good burghers of Canarsie, who "broke their backs building fine communities are penalized by the introduction of high-rise scatter-site housing," another reward for the leeches. The perversity of the social order reached a peak of allocational madness. White workers fell behind, and leeches got all the advantages. If resplendent portions of welfare did not sate their maniacal appetites, they could take the life of virtuous citizens and gain the rewards of prisons offering "the finest of recreational and nutritional advantages."

From lenient judges to racial quotas, the American dream had gone sour. The tension between the moods of promise and disenchantment framed Middle American bitterness. Erlichman's faith still lingered that America was the exceptional land, "the greatest nation on earth and still the only place where an underdog can make his way back to the top." Canarsie might still make it back too, but the image of underdog highlighted the subversion that necessitated the comeback. "Why the 'pitch' for basic American Rights? Simple! We've lost them. Two hundred years after the inception of our 'Great American Dream' the middle class now finds itself in the midst of a 'Great American Nightmare.' "

The "Chairman's Column" revealed the essence of middle-class conservatism. It defined no vision of the good society beyond the spontaneity of the marketplace, the pluck of bootstrapping, and the sacredness of middle-class advantage. The editorials held out no cure for social misfortune, which boiled down to the leeches' lack of intestinal fortitude. They provided no insight into the suffering of the black poor or the forces rendering voluntarism an inadequate solution.

The psychology of middle-class pain thus inhered in its ideology. Both were part of an embracing self-concern. What distinguished Middle American resentment was neither its racism nor the radicalism of its solutions, which varied a good deal with the person and the segment of the middle classes. The extremity consisted of the uncompromising nature of its self-preoccupation.

The Citizens News purveyed only one version of middle-class protectionism. An Italian policeman epitomized another brand of preservatism. Though hardly enamored of quotas, "give-away" programs, or busing, he was sympathetic to the poor and committed to New Deal principles. His world centered on the Catholic church, Holy Name societies in the police department, and the Knights of Columbus. No stranger to poverty, he had climbed out of dependency on welfare and a broken home. The experience had marked him deeply, leaving a tremendous faith in his powers of self-regeneration but also a compassion for the weak and the injured. He took the ideal of brotherhood as an imperative of daily life, not as a homily confined to the extramundane. "People's selfishness is the big problem. Their resentment falls on the lower classes. 'The check collectors' is how they perceive them. They lose the Christian precepts of 'helping thy neighbor.' They feel, 'I made my way up, now you make yours.' I don't have that feeling, but I undestand how they feel."

At a Sunday brunch a congressional candidate waved the red flag of race, exalting "the white middle class." The cop was angry. "The phrase 'white middle class' is a racist statement to me. Of course it's okay for blacks to move next door. The question is one of intrusion and the problems that come with the intruders, not because they are black, but because they are not middle class. That goes for everything between black and white. This is primarily a class struggle, and the people of Canarsie are trying to save what they have. They are trying to remain middle class."

The wish to remain middle class did not always mean vindictive scapegoating, and racial disputing was not necessarily tantamount to racism. Throughout the 1960s and 1970s racial tolerance and norms of equality grew, alongside white resentment of specific aspects of liberal reform and of the civil rights movement.[26]

A melancholy cabby, distressed about crime, quotas, and busing, still managed to retrieve from the immigrant experience a common base of identification. "It was hard for the Italians forty-five years ago, and all they could get was sweeping jobs 'cause nobody else wanted it. There were areas we couldn't move to 'cause people thought they were better than us and wouldn't let us. So I sympathize with the decent, law-abiding blacks, regardless of what their color is." An unemployed Jewish hardhat, who sometimes vented a nasty racism, in more sanguine moments foresaw a social order in which black and white workers advanced together rather than in opposition. "Those quotas and Philadelphia plans made us angry. They should create plans to help both sides. Create jobs, but don't take from one to give the other and create bitterness." Such expressions of empathy and fairness belie the image of ineluctable ruthlessness at the point of racial struggle.

A strain of biracial populism, a local version of the national black and white coalition assembled by Jimmy Carter in 1976, remained a submerged yet latent and probably growing current in Canarsie life. It rested on the grievances shared by middle-income whites and blacks over crime, utility bills, and welfare cheats. One backlash activist argued, "I think the rich get too much in this society, and the poor blacks get too much, but the black pharmacist is being swallowed up the same as I am. I can't define the difference between black and white middle income. We're both swallowed up by this illegitimate taking." Across America, large numbers of blacks rejected busing as a remedy for de facto segregation, endorsed strict controls over the disbursement of welfare funds, and disliked affirmative action in the form of explicit racial quotas.[27] An alliance of middle-income blacks and whites might not remedy the plight of the black underclasses; it risked replacing the meanness of race with the meanness of class. But at least the common interests between the races could provide a foundation on which to reconstruct a politics of generosity.

Racial friction and racial harmony depended on specific policies championed by politicians as much as on the irreconcilable exclusiveness of black and white interests. Unfortunately, liberal reform set up an apparent world of scarcity, which naturally led each group to seek its own rewards. "I see this country pitting group against group," argued an Italian lawyer in the Jefferson Democratic Club. "We never join the have-a-littles with the have-nots to fight the haves. We make sure the have-a-littles fight the have-nots. That's the shame of it. The have-a-littles, the Canarsie people, they don't see the have-a-lots. They can only see the have-nots. So the have-a-little Canarsieite says, 'Don't deny me, don't take my future away from me.' "

Liberalism's special enthusiasm for the poor fortified the belief that it worked against middle-class survival. Deriding lower-middle-class nervousness as racism, many reformers saw Middle America as a defiant stumbling block to an enlightened society. That verdict was only a partial truth. When they performed that moral excision, left-liberals abandoned much of the traditional mass base of the Democratic party.

Black Pride, White Pride

"When I become an 'other,' I get furious."

Backlash cannot be reduced to class struggle. Civil rights legislation celebrated the sanctity of the person through its argument that segregation placed fetters on the ability of individuals to compete in meritocratic races. And quotas put forth not class or the individual but race as a proper basis for making claims on the state or on the conscience of private institutions. The specific arguments about remedy merged with a tangled debate of immense philosophic and practical moment. What should be the place of race and ethnicity in American life?

A consensus prevailed in Canarsie on the rightful place of ethnicity in a democratic society. The local theory of pluralism forbade the dominance of a single group in public life, defined the individual as the proper unit in affairs of state, and reserved a space in private life for regional culture, ethnocentric prejudice, and communal lifestyle.[28] But as they nervously watched the twists and turns of the civil rights movement, Canarsians became persuaded that a different, and quite dangerous, notion of race had triumphed in public discourse, in the policies of court, in the requirements of government. The use of explicit terms of race to allocate goods, assign blame, and apportion respect threatened to rend the fabric of society with communal passion. Concepts like compensation and restitution imposed more than financial burdens. By implying that all whites shared equal liability for past wrongs, racial remedies bestowed judgments of guilt and innocence, shame and virtue.

Canarsians were too close to their own humble origins to think of themselves as exploiters. An Italian cabby believed that the collective dishonor black leaders meted out to whites did not distinguish between the holders of slaves and the descendants of near-serfs. "I couldn't see the blacks rising up because of what happened when they were slaves. So what happened four hundred years ago, all those whites who whipped them and beat them, are we responsible for it? I didn't even have anything to do with slavery. What's past is past. Nobody can give them what they owe them."

Accusations of white racism produced a curious inversion: whites believed that *they* were the victims of black racism and slander. That turnabout undermined the corrective maneuvers individuals use to fend off threats to the equilibrium of face-to-face encounters. As Erving Goffman observed, "The person shows respect and politeness, making sure to extend to others any ceremonial treatment that might be their due." Or "he may provide explanations as to why the others ought not to be affronted by" an act that will offend. If the explanations fail, "he can still attempt to maintain the fiction that no threat to face has occurred."[29] Black nationalism, however, struck many Canarsians as a refusal to honor those polite fictions.

An Orthodox Jew who was a fierce Zionist drew a line between ethnic self-love and malignant tribalism. "The greatest achievement the Black Panthers gave the black people was the sense that black is beautiful, pride in being black." He maintained that "Jewish is gorgeous," and his vision of cultural pluralism was a mixture of platitudes, ethnic loyalty, and fair play. The true virtue of America, he thought, was a universality that came from a tolerance of particularism. "The American way of life is the ability of different ideas to be discussed, arranged, and worked together, with a mutual respect for each other's differences, and giving to the other guy the same rights and privileges and freedoms that you want for yourself." Black power, he argued, violated that respectful vision. "If blacks are hollering black power, then unfortunately the racial tone of black power is such that the corollary to that is white power, and it becomes a racial thing out in the open. The Black Panthers took that black pride movement, which was positive, and turned it into a hate whitey movement, which was negative."

Ethnic nationalism raised vexing problems of cultural equity. Demands for the recognition of black culture or Hispanic language retrieved from the smorgasbord of American traditions a few for special validation while presuming that all white ethnics drew on a common fund. But the residents of Canarsie viewed themselves not as abstract whites but as members of specific ethnic groups. As a result, they felt blacks were demanding unfair helpings of cultural dignity. A housewife sketched an elemental ideal of justice. "If you close schools on Martin Luther King Day, or Black Solidarity Day, then you must close the schools for Jewish Solidarity Day and Italian Solidarity Day. It's all a matter of fairness. I believe in black pride, but don't step on my white Italian pride. We've all been discriminated against."

The demand for equal cultural time showed a lack of understanding of the violence inflicted by American history on black culture and psyche, yet when lofty arguments about *négritude* trickled down to the grassroots, they were stripped of their theoretical nuances and context. An Italian lawyer astutely described that translation:

They see black news and they feel, "Why can't there be a white news?" They don't see it in the macro. Here's a race that's been held down for two hundred years, and fucked over for those two hundred years in every imaginable way, who feel they must fight for what they need. Who can argue with the legitimacy of blacks feeling that? But the Canarsie people see it all in the micro. They say, "Don't call me a bigot if you have a problem. I don't want my kid hassled. You're throwing my ass away."

The first cries of black power touched off cries for Jewish rights, white purity, Italian pride. The exhortations of one backlash leader, who liberally borrowed from black doctrines of race pride, showed an extreme form of white vulnerability. "When the blacks say 'Black power,' 'Black this,' 'Black that,' it has a religious connotation. Now take the word white. We are white, and we have to fight for what they are taking from us. White is also a religious term. Let's take back what is ours." A dynamic of mimetic revenge was often at work, as if some citizens were saying, "Okay, so you want to yell black is beautiful, I'll show you, I'll yell back that white is beautiful."

At one gathering of a backlash group, the values of ethnic supremacy and the values of Italian voluntarism and Jewish meritocracy collided. The organization had set up a scholarship to recognize high school students who contributed to the community, and a debate broke out about whether the funds could go to black students or only to whites. A Catholic woman argued, "Look, you all know how I feel about the niggers, but I'm not against the blacks. As long as they are a conscientious black trying to better themselves, as long as they are qualified, they should get the scholarship." A Jewish woman disagreed. "There are hundreds of Negro scholarships for the blacks!"

When the group met with other conservative civic and homeowner groups, it spoke of building a coalition to preserve "white middle-class ethnic rights." The phrase indicated the theoretical muddiness of the group's endeavor. There was much brave talk about forming a National Association for the Advancement of White People. "We will use the NAACP bylaws word for word, except for the black to white change. If we have to go to court, we will make sure they can't hurt us or they will have to invalidate the NAACP." The speaker swerved to a new idiom of ethnicity. "But we will insist that they abide by the concept that a Jew, Italian, Irish, Polish are minorities, and come under the same claims and benefits as ethnic American minorities." He shifted back to the idiom of race and class. "We will tell it like it is, we will fight for the white middle class . . . We'll protect 'our' people." He changed tack again. "He's an Italian, so he's a minority. And we want these benefits, not as whites but as a Jew or as an Italian, as *ethnics*." At that point, one hopelessly confused man proclaimed, "It's a black-white issue." A leader interceded. "No," he said pointedly, "We're *minorities*."

That forceful correction suggests that developing ethnic consciousness is much like becoming class conscious, which Frank Parkin has likened to "learning a foreign language: that is, it presents men with a new vocabulary and a new set of concepts which permit a different translation of the meaning of inequality from that encouraged by the conventional vocabulary of society."[30]

Never the dominant impulse in Canarsie politics and culture, ethnic nationalism was one small expression of a pervasive feeling of racial dispossession. That sense of ethnic jeopardy took on special meaning for Brooklyn Jews. At some indeterminate point in the

1960s, they began to see themselves as specifically *Jewish* victims of black nationalists, and blacks in general. The perception was diffuse, time had to pass before it acquired the clarity of words, but it did acquire them.

In the early 1970s almost half of a sample of Brooklyn Jews believed that anti-Semitism was a serious threat, and most perceived blacks as the chief culprits. Among Jews with no religious affiliation, 33 percent agreed that "unless black militants are put in their place, there will be a lot more anti-Semitism," and 58 percent of Reform Jews, 68 percent of Conservative Jews, and 77 percent of Orthodox Jews agreed. Altogether, almost 20 percent more Brooklyn Jews (65 percent) had those worries than did Manhattan Jews. The East River defined the regional limits of Jewish liberalism; Jews in Manhattan and Brooklyn lived in different ecological, symbolic, and social worlds.[31]

The Ocean Hill–Brownsville school crisis of 1968 had inflated those Jewish fears. The minority-controlled school board of that part of Brooklyn insisted, in a brief demanding autonomy for the black community, "We will have to write our own rules for our own schools. Enforcement of these rules will have to be carried out by the people of the community."[32] That experiment in self-determination reflected a larger black disenchantment in the late 1960s with the integrationist ideals of the early civil rights movement. More practically, many blacks viewed the white educational establishment as an obstacle to innovation and justice in teaching. But breaking its hold, even if it might release the creative energy of black ghetto children, boldly challenged school officials and teachers, as well as their vested interest in controlling certification, work routines, and employment. It also entailed taking on the sacred principles that justified those privileges—professional expertise, the independence of the civil service, municipal unionism.

Events came to a head when the governing board of Ocean Hill–Brownsville fired nineteen teachers and supervisors—most of whom were Jewish—including two chapter chairmen of the United Federation of Teachers. Rhody McCoy, the unit administrator of the school district, declared, "Not one of these teachers will be allowed to teach anywhere in this city. The black community will see to that."[33] Viewing the ouster of the teachers as a provocative attack on their due-process rights and ultimately on the foundation of the teachers' union, the UFT began a citywide strike that pitted a heavily Jewish union against the minority community.

Unmistakable episodes of anti-Semitism, as well as false rumors, accompanied the crisis. "It was an anti-Semitic thing," said an Orthodox Jewish salesman. "It wasn't get whitey teacher out, it was get Jew whitey out." A decade later an Italian policeman recalled, "It's like Ocean Hill–Brownsville. They had a big protest there, the blacks said, 'Remove those teachers, they're white trash, they're Jewish, we don't want them Jew teachers in our schools.' So what happened two years later? The blacks said, 'We want to go to Canarsie schools.' And those teachers in the Canarsie schools were the same ones who had been thrown out of the Brownsville schools!"

The Ocean Hill–Brownsville uproar prompted a rethinking of conventional truths. A Canarsie rabbi defined the introspective hesitancy that was one of its legacies. "I can tell you that the masses of people in Canarsie saw the Ocean Hill–Brownsville struggle as a black-Jewish struggle. Here we were, Jews marching for civil rights, really gung ho, marching along in Selma, Alabama, but it came to the public schools and it became, 'Get out of my community, I want your job.' It started a lot of people thinking."

The Jewish Defense League understood that aspect of the crisis of liberalism. As spokesman for "Jewish Jews," they were accustomed to thinking in terms of "what's good for the Jews." One JDL member said, of his conversion in the 1960s, "I used to be quite a way-out liberal, until twelve or fifteen years ago. But more and more I became aware of Jewish nonrights. I came to the full realization that the problems of the Jewish people were the results of Jewish liberalism." The man identified the source of the problem in the Jewish inability to fight back against enemies:

We Jews have been subjected to thousands of years of persecution, and we have adopted a second-class attitude. We try to help those who would harm us. The Jew has always been the liberal in any community, historically speaking. If there were liberals, then the Jews were ultra-liberals. If there were conservatives, then we were the liberals. We were always one step ahead of everyone else in doing for everyone else, and generally at the expense of our community. So, we led the way for black civil rights, we led the way for Puerto Rican civil rights, we led the way for Chicano civil rights. And those very same Jews and Jewish leaders who sacrificed down South for Martin Luther King, we have never seen them in any rally for Soviet Jewry. And that is the downfall and deception of the Jewish people, because we Jews do not consider that we also have problems, and so we worry about everyone else, and everyone else worries about everyone else, so nobody worries about us, so when the shouts for and demands for rights and benefits are there, there is no Jewish demand for rights and benefits, so everybody else gets at the expense of the Jew.

The frustration of Canarsie's working men and women sometimes spilled over into a form of racial banter that had a decidedly less Talmudic flavor than the complaints of the JDL member. An ultra-conservative Italian insurance salesman waxed indignant as he spoke to a small group of racially aggrieved residents. "Did you see what they did in Harlem? They changed the name of the La Guardia School and named it after some Puerto Rican revolutionary." The change of name formalized white displacement, and the man retaliated with a macabre form of reciprocity: "We should put James Earl Ray's name on the sign at Wilson Junior High!" The laughter that ratified his suggestion made palpable the impotent rage of his listeners, who included some of Canarsie's most ferocious backlash activists. The image of a united minority community, in which black and Hispanic tormentors blurred together in a single cabal, expressed the belief that minorities were poised to take over the city.

Even among the most aggrieved, backlash had a less hysterical side. The very division of the militant faction into ranters and rationalists has a neat simplicity rarely found in reality. The outbursts of the resentful are one instant filtered out from many others. Finally, the repulsive language distracts from the content of the statements. Transfixed by diatribes that offend good taste, the observer skips over the substance of complaint to concentrate on the style in which it is voiced. Once racist invective is removed from its conversational context, its status as culturally sanctioned speech becomes blurred.

The acceptability of racist talk in some Canarsie circles shows the difficulty of separating emotion from learning. At a home-owners' meeting, two men discussed the *New York Times* coverage of Professor James Coleman's alleged recanting of his position on the merits of busing. "Coleman wants intermarriage now," a salesman said. "He says that busing doesn't work." His comrade laughed. "Well, let him start with his daughter. She's probably going out with a nigger now. He's just trying to justify his own shortcomings." A member of the Conservative party mentioned that a civil rights leader had called for an army of American blacks to liberate Angola.

"That's a great idea," his friend told him. "Let him take all the niggers he wants with him." Another activist warned a friend who was about to make a public appearance: "Hey, make sure you don't slip and say nigger in public."

The ability to shift codes of speaking marked an awareness of the various etiquettes that regulated talk about racial matters. Unlike middle-class ideals of respectability, important strains in plebeian culture mock the standard that hostility must be expressed in a sublimated idiom, give moral permission to rowdy nose-thumbing at established society, and allow the use of emotion-laden, pungent words that are forbidden in polite society. The enjoyment of racially offensive joking provided one sign of inclusion in that vulgar moral community. Frank hostility, like racism, was more than uncontrollable passion. It was ethically validated behavior.[34]

The feeling of second-class citizenship grew among whites of all kinds. For warm-hearted democrats, the sense of stigma came reluctantly. For the vindictive, it came early, even eagerly, and some of the unhinged really thought that the paramount intention of the civil rights movement was the humiliation of the white race. Few things better symbolized their discontent than their response to the ethnic census.

In the middle 1970s the U.S. Department of Health, Education, and Welfare directed the Brooklyn schools to determine the racial makeup of their staffs and student bodies. The form, it was widely rumored, included separate categories for blacks and Hispanics but lumped whites indiscriminately under the rubric of "others." A Jewish educator refused to comply with the census. "It smacks of Nazi Germany. I think of Idi Amin, identifying people by race! The solution is not juggling people like numbers, but changing human beings."

In the more vindictive reaches of the Jewish and Italian lower middle classes, the anger was uncut by cosmopolitan detachment. At a gathering of backlash activists, a Jewish woman cried out, "We built this city and now we've become the 'other'!" Her companion declared, "That's why we're here, because of all the inequities in this country. Like the politicians, the United Federation of Teachers is afraid of blacks, because the blacks can get pretty rough. Do you know what we're up against? We're up against HEW. Can't *we* yell racism and discrimination? You have to do something. If you don't take a stand, the blacks will take over *everything*."

In a quieter moment later that evening, one of the women reflected, "We weren't aware of color when we were kids. And our kids weren't aware of color. Then in the fifth grade a black girl told them, 'My mother says we are blacks now, and we're different, and we can't play with you.' You see, they used to have black friends, but after that they became wary. And now they're shoving this ethnic census down our throats. I'll tell you one thing, when I become an 'other,' I get furious."

She was not referring, of course, to Jean-Paul Sartre's definition of the "other" as "projected evil,"[35] yet that definition was not far from what she meant. The HEW form seemed to relegate all whites to a residual category of otherness and to reserve the dignity of a name for groups officially designated as deprived. The state left itself open to the impression that it championed a particular rather than a general interest.

The diversity of complaints about dispossession suggests that white feelings of insignificance were more than the panic of people susceptible to paranoid thinking, dizzied by change, or full of misplaced dread about their status. Realistically perceived breaks with precedent—in ethnic ideology, in social policy, in political discourse—aroused the ire of the white middle-income classes.

Ethnicity, then, was a language to be chosen as well as an identity to be discovered. Ethnic identity did not come only from the givens of biological nature or the passions of racism. It was equally the product of a tense opposition, a reaction to the attempts of rivals to name themselves and to identify their enemies. The identities of Jew, white, and Italian required the inspiration of external threat— the orders of a judge, the remedies of the state, slots on administrative forms, a playmate's rejection, polemical accusation—to give them inner form. Ethnicity was a way Canarsians learned to talk, to direct their attention, to do battle. It had to be constantly formed and reformed in real and imaginary dialogues with enemies and neighbors.[36]

White ethnicity revealed one facet of a creole identity that combined aspects of race, class, person, and ethnicity. Canarsians were like code-switchers; they could address irate tax-payers as middle-income people, laud the powers of the individual in sermons on striving, wave the banner of race before ethnocentric audiences, and invoke Italian or Jewish pride in applying to the city for program funding. Sometimes speakers used a jumble of metaphors of race, class, and ethnicity in the same breathless sentence. The constant was the feeling of precariousness. A school administrator who lived in Canarsie diagnosed the blended qualities of the patois. "Canarsie's priority is to maintain the socioeconomic, the cultural, and the political status quo. Basically, Canarsie would like to erect a great wall around it and keep all that Canarsie produces and gains for itself. They use the Jewish imagery of Diaspora from East New York, but it's not basically or only Jewish. The Jews and the Italians have allied themselves in an effort to hold on to what they have."

The readiness of both Jews and Italians to chastise the liberal betrayers of middle-class interests was expressed in their hostile view of Mayor John Lindsay's bid for a second term in 1969. His opponents included the backlash Democrat Mario Procaccino and the candidate of the Conservative and Republican parties, John Marchi. An Italian attorney considered Marchi a conservative Italian variant of Adlai Stevenson. "It's a shame. Marchi belongs in a university. He's a metaphysical existentialist." Procaccino suffered no such disabilities. The raw scourge of limousine liberalism, he once told a black audience whose suspicions he was trying to allay, "My heart is as black as yours." Lindsay won reelection but did not achieve a majority. While his Italian rivals split the conservative vote, he squeaked by with a plurality of 42 percent to Procaccino's 35 percent and Marchi's 23 percent.

In Canarsie, Procaccino took between 50 and 60 percent of the vote in both Italian and Jewish precincts. The move toward a backlash Democrat was the shared tendency in the vote; the subcurrents, a liberal Jewish stream on the left for Lindsay and a conservative Italian stream on the right for Marchi, pointed to the enduring differences.

Only four years earlier, in a three-way race with regular Democrat Abe Beame and Conservative William Buckley, Lindsay had won a plurality of better than 40 percent in many Old Canarsie Italian precincts, not far from the normal Republican vote minus the defections to Buckley. But in 1969 Lindsay plummeted nearly 30 percentage points, bottoming out at the pro–Civilian Review Board nadir of 10 to 15 percent. Retrospective appraisals caught the characterological failure that ethnic conservatives saw as the essence of liberalism. "I didn't like his pacifist ways," said one resident. "He was the ruination of the blacks, he paid them not to riot," said another. The wife of a city worker offered this eloquent piece of symmetry. "Lindsay was soft on the criminals and hard on the police."

Milton Himmelfarb has written of the plight of New York Jews who disliked the left liberalism of the "new classes" yet were repelled by the crudity of racially overwrought conservatives like Procaccino. "For the Jewish-Jewish middle-class Lindsay voters, Lindsay had worked hard to appease their resentment. He had eaten crow. Like the Emperor Henry IV, he had gone to Canossa—a friend of mine has said that Lindsay went to Canarsie."[37] On his journey to the boroughs Lindsay made a plea for absolution, The pro-Lindsay Jewish vote in Canarsie, double to triple that in the Italian precincts, still reached only between 30 and 36 percent in the most liberal areas. Despite their misgivings about Lindsay, many advisers, candidates, and officials in the Jefferson Democratic Club could not bring themselves to vote for a Democratic racial punisher. "Not that they liked Mordecai, says the Talmud, but that they disliked Haman: not that Lindsay won those Jews, but that Procaccino lost them."[38]

More striking was that so many lower-middle-class Jews reversed the priorities of their liberal brethren. One bitter man who had fled East Flatbush claimed, "I was a loser because of the liberal philosophy. I lived in a nice part of East Flatbush during the time Lindsay was dealing with the liberals and the black militants and the minorities. He didn't do a damn thing for the middle class." In the Orthodox community the conviction that Lindsay was anti-Jewish prompted many to vote for Procaccino. "It was under John Lindsay that the Jewish community in New York City suffered its greatest decline." And a resentful Jewish home owner saw in the muscular Catholic tradition an adaptive solution to risk. "I voted for Procaccino because I thought an Italian would knock the blacks out after Pretty Boy Lindsay had let them in."

In the pedagogy of exchange, Jewish acolytes learned from Italian mentors. Francesco Guicciardini, the Italian philosopher, would have struck a responsive chord in Brooklyn Jewish audiences. "Those men conduct their affairs well who keep in front of their eyes their own private interest." Luigi Barzini has observed that Italians do not need to read the philosopher's work. "They learned long ago to beware privately of their own show and to be sober and clear-eyed realists in all circumstances ... They are incredulous: they do not want to be fooled by seductive appearances and honeyed words. They cannot afford to be carried away by emotions."[39]

The Italians knew early on where their interest lay in the upheavals of race. The Jews computed their interest in a more oblique fashion, which permitted a measure of idealism based on an abstract rendering of their particular interest as the interest of all of mankind's forgotten, abused children. Countless Jews had been drawn to the millenial cadences of Martin Luther King in the early 1960s. In his "Letter from Birmingham Jail," King had declared, "I am in Birmingham because injustice is here. Just as the prophets of the eighth century B.C. left their villages and carried their 'Thus saith the Lord' far beyond the boundaries of their home towns . . . so am I compelled to carry the gospel of freedom beyond my own home town."[40]

Wary of strangers, southern Italians might have told King, "Stay in your own village, tend your own garden." And many Orthodox Jews preferred to remain sequestered in their ritual communities. But scores of Canarsie Jews had approved of King's defense of the outside spiritual agitator, reinforced by the image of the wandering prophetic Jew. One of those supporters, a PTA leader, reflected in 1976, "Recently, we saw reruns on TV of the civil rights marches and the pictures of state troopers hurting old black people. It was sad. I felt like crying. I had a favorable impression of King, he wanted equality, who can argue with that? It's a pity what happened to him. He could have done so much more." She concluded sadly, "We Jews are our worst enemies. We have always been liberal, but it backfired when we took the side of the black movement."

Jews of every stripe had inched closer to the Orthodox Jews in Canarsie, whom their rabbi described in the language of distributive justice:

> You can find in the Prophets written over and over, the Jewish mission to bring light unto the world, to be an example, to show people there is care. But most Orthodox Jews in Canarsie—and most Jews in Canarsie, period—are feeling, 'Nobody cares about me, why should I care about them? When everyone cares about me, I will worry about others. When everybody worries about Israel, then I will worry about Biafra. The Jews would love to be the champions of the weak, they would love to help the deprived, but that does not seem to help them. We Jews are more pragmatic than we used to be. We were always happy to help, we were always happy to do for others, but we hoped for something in return. We did not expect to get shot in the back or that someone would take our jobs. Should it be, "I nurse you and you shoot me?" Even liberals in Canarsie feel that liberalism has turned against them. You'd like to help, but . . .

Resentful Jews turned against limousine liberalism. The more secure, and those tied to progressive and cosmopolitan circles, voiced a more chastened critique of reform. They did not think it was they who had changed, but liberalism.

Whatever the difference between the Orthodox and the secular, between *prost* and *edel* Jews, the differences between Jews and Italians remained vivid. Italians warned against threat with unembarrassed candor. They did not so often apologize for seeming mean or unenlightened. Puzzled by the tenacity of Jewish liberalism, the Italians railed against it from across a vast divide, as if liberalism were a strange poltergeist. For Jews it could not be so simple. They were wrestling with a buried part of their past that seemed to have turned against them, or with the live pressures of parents and rich relatives on the West Side of Manhattan, on the campuses, in the Great Neck suburbs. A simple coding of responses misses the caveats, the little hesitations, the tortuous reasoning in the Jewish search for an appropriate political idiom. The fine shadings, the timbre of voice, the intricacy of the apologetic—all these things point to a world of critical differences in the meaning of liberal betrayal.

5. The Reverence Is Gone

The Permissive Society

*"Today it's all your rights ... You got a right to
this, and you got a right to that. In other words,
you do as you damned well please."*

"There's been a crisis of authority over the last fifteen years, from
the top all the way down to the bottom of society," one Canarsie
moralist complained in 1976. "It's a wave of disrespect, everybody
wants to be free, no one wants to be told." Traditionalists in Canarsie felt besieged by a tide of permissiveness in family life, jurisprudence, school curricula, patriotic observance, sexual relations, and
religious matters. Braless women, antiwar veterans, communal living, wife-swapping, flagrant homosexuality, the unruly, androgynous
hair of the hippies, the American flag customized with peace decals—
all these things were bizarre signs, as if a mocking deity had tampered with the primal order of things.

The new morality undermined Canarsians' world views more than
it threatened their financial security or territorial safety, and for
most residents, these symbolic dangers felt less unsettling than material threats. For one thing, the state's role in promoting unwanted
lifestyles was less obvious than its responsibility for changes in race
relations. Moreover, while both provincial and cosmopolitan Canarsians worried about crime and quotas, the community was a good
deal more divided in its opinions on issues like the sexual revolution.
In order to capture the distress created by cultural change, then, I
will focus in this chapter on Canarsie's most traditionalist residents.

Politicians vied to capitalize on the moral anxiety of Middle Americans. They tapped volatile feelings about ultimate values, equating a
vote against the Equal Rights Amendment, for example, with an af-

firmation of tradition in general. As James Sundquist noted, "In the public's perception, all these things merged. Ghetto riots, campus riots, street crime, anti-Vietnam marches, poor people's marches, drugs, pornography, welfarism, rising taxes, all had a common thread: the breakdown of family and social discipline, of order, of concepts of duty, of respect for law, of public and private morality." This politics of culture, uniting white ethnic Catholics, evangelical Protestants, and Orthodox Jews in an alliance against change, exemplified Clifford Geertz's observation, "Culture, here, is not cults and customs, but the structure of meaning through which men give shape to their experience; and politics is not coups and constitutions, but one of the principal arenas in which such structures publicly unfold."[1]

The struggle between cultures of release and of restraint inspired a Brooklyn version of the "quondam complex," which Seymour Martin Lipset and Earl Raab described as "a preponderance of symbolic investment in the past, related to some past group identity which has declined in symbolic significance." Convinced that their values and lifestyles have been mocked and defiled, watching with anguish as new social groups are celebrated at their expense, "the dispossessed" succumb to nostalgia for past glories, intimations of conspiracy, and vengeful attacks against satanic forces. The clinging to fundamental truths, whether the literal truth of Biblical revelation or the unchanging truth of traditional moral and family forms, serves as consolation for cultural loss.[2]

Cultural threat sometimes induced a state of mania in Canarsie's most hidebound residents. As children, they had been taught to obey fixed rules; as adults, they watched as the grammar of social life was transformed into the voluntary practices of personal argot. "Do your own thing" was a paradoxical imperative. What did it prohibit, what did it require? Traditionalists compared the chaos of liberation to the clear canons of the past and concluded that alien values had triumphed. As they talked, the complaints sometimes blurred together in a breathless sense of confusion, summed up in the pithy comment, "Respect, it's been lost." An Italian worker lamented:

We were strict and we respected our parents, but now? . . . This sexual permissiveness is disgraceful, it's like dogs in the street. And homosexuals? Homosexuals are sick. If they want to be like that, then it's their prerogative, but don't announce it . . . It's wrong for a woman to step over a man's boundary. The husband should be understanding, but he's the authority, the man is the stronger arm ... Back then we communicated with relatives, there was terrific home life, but today they have the idiot box. We are losing respect for the family ... The way of living today, there are no values. People drift further and further apart. We are becoming cannibalized ... I remember standing on Albany Street by the candy store. We didn't sass the policeman when he told us to move. Now in school they call teachers "mother-fucker."

The concept of a quondam complex has considerable merits, but it needs to be applied with a light touch. The agitation of cultural traditionalists is not always the last spasm of an atavistic remnant. It may also be a sensible response to the loss of a cherished status. The celebration of new heroes and lifestyles often does detract from the respect accorded older moralities. Unless one clings to an unyieldingly materialist view of human needs, fighting back in defense of those values seems a reasonable thing to do. The true flaw of overly psychological analyses of restorationist cultural movements is that they reduce popular philosophic debate to masquerades for other phenomena—like the fear of change. But such movements are explicable not only as psychological flight but also as a positive expression of vernacular moral codes.[3]

A Brooklyn priest provided a clue to the quickening struggle between the codes of ethnic traditionalists and the cosmopolitan classes. A loyalist of the old order, the father wanted to discipline the self by imposing clear distinctions between the forbidden and the permitted, by stressing the primacy of external rules over inner feeling. "These days the church is influenced by the Piaget-Kohlberg theories of pedagogy, but I'm against Piaget-Kohlberg. I think things have become too permissive. Kids need guidance, they want to grow to discipline. You have to guide kids, but the trends of the church since Vatican Two, they don't guide at all. We need rules. You have to regiment kids. Authoritarianism is okay if it teaches."

In the father's view, events after 1960 had destroyed spiritual authority in a carnival of rights and self-seeking. He contrasted the old fasting rules with a "new stunt" at a Brooklyn church where the priests permitted the nuns to administer the sacraments. "You must maintain respect for the sacraments. Familiarity breeds contempt. When I was a kid, I never touched the vessel. Now the altar boys touch the sacred vessels. The awe is gone, the reverence is gone."

"At no point in Catholic doctrine," Guy Swanson observed in *Religion and Regime,* "is an immanental belief more dramatically evident than in the tenet concerning Christ's presence in the Eucharistic bread and wine." Embodying sacred values in material tokens, "an immanent order leaves open less ground for purely secular concerns."[4] As the supreme values that are immanent in tangible symbols suffuse the physical world, the space left over for self-expression contracts. Thus the change in the Eucharist from a channel of grace imbued with mystery to a merely commemorative sign was no small matter. It was one phase of an ongoing development: the toppling of high gods, God's retreat from the mundane world, the growth of critical rationality.

Countless Italian Catholics favored the clarities of hierarchy over the cloudy revisions of tradition. But the allure of secular pleasure had preempted the esteem of self-denial. "Years ago religion required dedication. You had to get up on Sunday and to follow all those ritual things. It takes time. Today people lose religious interest because it interferes with their lifestyle. Now people say, 'I'll worship God in my heart, not according to the church.' But there's no God if you bring it down to your level. It's not God as it's supposed to be."

The growing slack in formerly strict codes symbolized the way personal needs had supplanted duty. The expanded role of the worshiper in bestowing legitimacy on religious commands marked the leveling of spiritual authority. One Italian traditionalist cited the image of "chocolate-covered matzos" as a debased amalgam of sacred and secular. "Religion has lost its meaning. Take Passover. They've changed the observances. And the priest says it's okay to eat meat on Friday. They've changed the prayers to meet peoples' needs."

Italian Catholic leaders of the local Republican and Conservative parties molded the diffuse nostalgias of ordinary people into critiques of secularism. One Republican leader condemned the church for its modern-day concessions: "I don't like the liberalization of the church. It's a question of psychology. Today it's not faith that's important but mentality. Mysticism held them close, but now with all the modern changes like the English mass, the words no longer hold the mystery of the language of God. I don't like this understanding of everything. You need ties to the origins. Human nature needs a link to the past."

The capitulation of the church to temporal fashion denied their longing for unchanging verities. As social, religious, and familial rules were transformed into mere conventions, subject to veto, play, and choice, they lost the power to channel human energies in a compelling and coercive way. "The church changed their attitudes on the basics," the man continued. "You used to look to them for guidance, they were a solid stone to rely on, but now they sway. There's no longer unanimity on what is permissible and not permissible."

Another Italian civic leader contrasted the pernicious effects of decadence with the human need for rules that guide, punish, steer. "I think of the Machiavellian philosophy," he mused. "Religion is the moral aspect of a person, it controls the animal part of man. So much concentration on pleasure and materialism, it becomes the whole purpose of life for people today. I sense an analogy to the destruction of the Roman Empire."

Italian Americans were in the forefront of the cultural counterrevolution, and not just on religious matters. The vibrancy of Italian diatribes against the permissive society reflected the enduring hold of provincialism as well as the tension between familism and self-fulfillment. A perceptive Jewish official caught the difference between the Jews of New Canarsie and the Italians of Old Canarsie, as well as the differences between old and new Italians. "The Old Canarsie Italians are still living in the generation of my parents. They have the same relationship with their parents and world that we Jews had with ours back in Brownsville one generation ago."

In the swirl of changing morals, liberalism acquired the pejorative label of a doctrine that made the satisfaction of appetites easy, legitimate, and cheap. For an Italian cop, liberalism defined all kinds of "looseness," from graffiti artists to gypsy cab drivers to "flagrant-like" homosexuals. After a few hours of wandering about the topic of morality, he fell upon the metaphor of the traffic grid to express his vision of society and propriety.[5] "Take this analogy. You got a society like New York City, okay? And you got the complexity of a heavily trafficked area, well-disciplined with stop signs. It's regimented. If you place that heavily trafficked area in Lebanon, there will be complete chaos, with destruction of life. It's the same with young people today, they've relaxed discipline. And it's the same with blacks. They lack discipline. It's all shiftlessness with them. They have no values or respect."

Fear of the untrammeled self stemmed from a conviction that individuals depend on the moral community to keep them on the straight and narrow path. The censure of "looseness" was thus more than umbrage over individual sin or immorality; it described a structural condition of weak norms and absent sanctions. When they carried on about shiftless blacks, dissolute hippies, or their own wayward children, Canarsians were equally blaming the lenient codes that produced their distasteful behavior. It was not the case, then, that the upper middle classes had a monopoly on "environmental" ways of thinking. Rather, the ethnic lower middle classes had an earthier vision of impulse life, and the environment they invoked referred to the sanctions delivered in small social circles.

If the traffic grid evoked the virtues of form, graffiti pointed to a world of chaos in which feisty impulses spilled over the containers of norm and politesse. The brutal splashes of color curling across the face of the city traced out the community's inability to tame antisocial desires. An Italian worker insisted, "It's beyond me how a person can do it and be allowed to get away with it without being punished. It's unbelievable! You see, the more you can get away with something, the more you do something. I don't subscribe to the philosophy that they're expressing themselves." Celebration of misconduct as self-expression led to an unashamed—and virtually unshameable—openness about impropriety, thereby destroying the buffers that kept private vice from public view.

The unsettlement of many traditionalists came less from the transgression than from its flamboyance. Privacy functions as an automatic mechanism of conflict resolution, by keeping moral antagonists in the dark about each other's heresies. The new publicity of television, the streets, the movies made it difficult for opposed cultural factions to evade the abrasive contact point between them. In the confessional morality of the 1960s everyone was supposed to drop the pretenses and etiquette that kept inner secrets and fantasies from escaping into the open. That visibility intensified Middle American feelings of loss of control over the public culture. An Italian unionist's anguish about depravity was no revivalistic desire to root out sin, and it coexisted with an attitude of tolerance:

If they want to live together and not be married, that's fine. If they want to read pornographic books and see pornographic movies, that's okay. I believe you should not infringe on people's rights. But if it's on television, and I don't like how they're doing it, I would turn my television off, and if I found the product that's sponsoring it, I wouldn't even buy it. I would use my power of boycott. And if I have to, I will write a letter and let these people know that I disagree. Because I really believe that this business of people living together is fine as long as they don't *broadcast* it to the point of making it an outright thing on television or in the newspapers. They talk about these things as if they were nothing!

Flaunting proclaimed the right to indulge oneself by breaking moral rules. The diffusion of such cultural innovations provided a growing audience for critiques of narcissism, of secular humanism, and of sociological jurisprudence, which formerly had been the staple of right-wing traditionalists. But as unsettling lifestyles penetrated the consciousness of Middle America, average citizens began to apply the vocabulary of the state to matters of morality. "Today it's all your rights, your rights, everything is your rights," complained a cabby. "You got a right to this, and you got a right to that. In other words, you do as you damned well please."

To one Republican leader, no corner of life seemed impervious to the entrancements of liberty, and he applied the phrase "law and order" to events taking place in sexual relations, in politics, and in family life. "There was more pulling together in families in the 1940s and 1950s," he asserted, "but in the 1960s, it became the civil rights of every individual, and authority started to collapse. See? It was a *complete* civil rights movement, not just for blacks, but for *everyone!*" The plaint of a man out of key with his changing environment was no irrational lashing out at a society that remained opaque to him. He had a realistic understanding of the emerging struggle between living right and individual rights, and his own position of relative decline. Disagreement with that emerging cultural regimen, not confusion over its meaning, was the noteworthy characteristic of his lament.[6]

Some Canarsians criticized particular elements in modern culture, while others seemed to repudiate the very process of change. Traditionalism flourished in the heart of the Italian working class, in part because the values of Italian familism instilled a suspicion of modernism, in part because forces of occupation, association, and education restricted exposure to the relativizing influences of diverse cultural teachings. The Jews of Canarsie were less shrouded in provincialism than Italians, reflecting the tenets of Jewish culture, the cosmopolitan influence of Jewish occupations and education, and the greater diversity of the Jews living there.[7]

A schoolteacher epitomized the more cosmopolitan reaches of Jewish Canarsie. She deemed the sexual revolution on balance a great step forward for mankind, despite the quirky excesses that accompanied it. "There are always the swings of the pendulum," she said philosophically, "but I'm for greater liberal thinking and freedom. The new morality has made for more freedom and choice, it has liberated us from the set, arbitrary restrictions of Calvinism. It's meant the freedom to enjoy, the freedom to think, the freedom to be."

Unlike the Italian Republican and Conservative officials who affirmed the "pro-family" virtues of Old Canarsie, the Jewish officials in the Jefferson Democratic Club represented a more secular view. "A lot of this talk of tradition," argued one elected official, "is nostalgic looking back. We shouldn't hold traditional values sacrosanct. Change is positive and exciting." But enthusiasm for change was hardly universal among Jews. The majority of those in Canarsie had been raised in morally restrictive households, and they recited the same litany of virtues as other lower-middle-class Americans: work, family, law, duty, patriotism, marriage, achievement, success, respect. A Jewish woman complained of the breakdown of sexual discretion. "Only bad people live together before marriage. What is this age coming to! Pornography is getting respectable! These new morals are terrible."

Even Jews with pretensions to enlightenment had been brought up in provincial milieus. A Jewish woman who hesitated to endorse premarital sex for young women straddled the line between an intellectual belief that one should give up old taboos and a visceral inability to do so, concluding almost apologetically, "That goes back to East New York." She sketched a moral community forged on the stoops, where close-knit relations relayed the communal conscience through the neighborhood: "In East New York, the Jewish values were passed on from generation to generation. We never dreamed of doing other than those values, and we were aghast when people didn't do as they should. We still talk about these things. A girl having an illegitimate child, or a girl getting a divorce, it was unheard of, you just didn't have it. You knew all on the block, the street was like a small town: you knew who was doing this and who was doing that."

The Orthodox rabbinate and laity viewed much of the cultural innovation of recent decades as a thin cover for narcissism. A devout

Jewish man rejected the word *taboo* and the implications it carried. "It depends on what you want to call a taboo. Either you have basic beliefs which come from somewhere or you make up your own set of rules and mores which don't have any basis for anything other than you do what you damned well feel like doing." Canarsie had never had large numbers of Orthodox and Hasidic Jews, but the smaller numbers of the observant were just as mistrustful of the encroachment of secular modernism. "In Judaism," the man explained, "we have a basic set of rules. We believe God gave us free will, we can choose to do right or wrong, and God promises rewards for doing the right and punishment for doing the wrong. With a religious belief in God, you try to do as much as you can to live up to God's rules, and if you do, then you're called old-fashioned. And if you don't, then you should be prepared to pay whatever price comes for not having followed God's rules, for somewhere down the line there is justice, and you pay the price for everything you do."

The sacrifices of the immigrant experience reinforced the belief that nothing came without sweat and toil. A Jewish plumber in his thirties said of his father: "All he knew was he wanted a full refrigerator. He came from Russia when he was fourteen and went to work for a plumber from the same Russian village he came from. Work was his salvation. It came naturally to him. You see, my generation of workers doesn't have the same feeling as their fathers. The young workers are more concerned with themselves as individuals. We want vacations, and we don't like to work like the old guys. We call them Depression plumbers."

The world of scarcity led quite logically to an appreciation for earning; the privations suffered by Canarsians created a need to justify their own sacrifices by accepting struggle as a timeless principle. They often rebuked local teenagers who insisted, "I want to do what I want," and it bewildered and embittered them that their own children, not just ghetto blacks, had succumbed to an ethic of the free and easy life. "Nobody wants to work or wait for anything," complained a Jewish businessman. Had *he* had the luxury of finding a job that fulfilled him? "My old man gave me a handtruck when I was nine, down in the garment district. He said to me 'Here, go to work!'"

And yet there was an element of bad faith in such indignation, for it denied a paradoxical outcome of that immigrant quest for status; had parents not aimed to give their children the abundance they had been denied? Using their children as mirrors of their own achievement, the adults sometimes created an alien set of expectations: "This generation is spoiled silly. It's our own fault. My daughter resents hearing how difficult it was for us, it's a night-and-day difference since I was a girl. Today, the kids have their own stereos and televisions and their own room. You want to give them what you didn't have and kids take it for granted. Kids have this attitude, 'It's coming to me.' They are never satisfied. Kids today haven't had to struggle, they get what they need without paying their dues. I didn't take things for granted, I didn't expect others to do for me."

The disapproval of modern ways is often interpreted as starchy or envious moralism that takes satisfaction in punishing those who enjoy themselves. The celebration of form and duty is seen as a nostalgic flight by repressed personalities into the reassuring myth of constancy. Such verdicts often replace the dogmas of provincialism with a dogma of enlightenment that is as inimical to tolerance and diversity as the moralities it claims to dispel. Resistance to cultural change in Canarsie was often a selective rejection of excesses more than a repudiation of change itself. Tradition itself was dynamic, constantly revitalized through cautious borrowings from the new cultural repertoire. In refusing to absorb new values, the lower middle class was attempting to retain what was meaningful in the past, the worthy values of stoicism, commitment, courage, duty, and balance. When relativism succeeds the firm application of sanctions, social conventions lose their weight of immutability. Individuals, suddenly adrift in a sea of personal choice, are swept back onto their own moral and cognitive resources. If one of the benefits of the relaxation of compulsion is the extension of human possibilities, then Canarsie's traditionalists were right that choice also invents opportunities for derangement and nihilism.

The Family Under Siege

"Everything is changing. Complexes! Complexes!
They use psychology on you . . . If we did wrong,
we would have been smacked."

Of all the changes in lifestyle, nothing chafed traditionalists more than the upheavals in family life. The family was the fount of all value, coherence, virtue, honor, inspiration. As Carlo Levi observed of southern Italians, "It was not that they venerated family relationships as a social, legal or sentimental tie, but rather that they cherished an occult and sacred sense of communality." In the ritualized world of the eastern European shtetl, wrote Irving Howe, "there was little room for individuality as we have come to understand it, since the community was the manifestation of God's covenant with Israel, as the family was the living core of the community."[8]

More than a symptom of diffuse anxieties, the concern with family breakdown was a response to pervasive changes in the cultural environment that touched the family directly. An Italian worker bewailed the difficulty of insulating his family from upsetting messages: "I am not against what they call the sexual revolution. What I am against is pornography. Again, I am mad at something being pushed down my throat. I feel that openness toward sex is good, I should be able to tell my kids about sex, but I don't believe a store should be able to display this trash in the window where my son can look at it. I think a parent should have the right to restrict his children as to what they can look at."

Everywhere they looked, it seemed that the sentries of the culture had relaxed their vigilance. People no longer observed the taboos that once had functioned as voluntary forms of moral coordination. The intrusive powers of law, popular culture, the schools, and news media exposed family space to moral dangers as surely as racial change exposed physical space to physical dangers. The confessional frankness of modern television was not simply upsetting in itself; it contributed to the loosening of parents' ability to "bring their kids up right." As one Italian father put it: "I think they are giving wrong ideas to children of today who look on these programs, because these people like Johnny Carson or David Susskind or Merv Griffin say these things about people living together or homosexuals, and the children believe these people are men who know what they're talking about and if they talk about it nonchalantly, then the kids think there shouldn't be anything wrong with it. By not saying anything, by not condemning it, they are sort of putting an okay on it."

The larger world was a tempting siren as well as a threatening intruder. An Italian traditionalist argued, "Families are disintegrating. Everybody goes off in their own direction. They're indoctrinated with freedom. Girls move out and set up their own apartments. Guys do it automatically. It was unheard of years ago. Everybody was part of the family. There's been a great loss here. You tell me, where did this idea of freedom come from?"

Ideas of freedom captured parents as well as children. "The family is the solid rock of social values," said another Old Canarsie Italian, "but now the mother and father are looking for sexual satisfaction, and they won't devote the time to instilling values and ideals. The family is the center of our community, and if you don't keep it solid and together, you will have educated animals." One Jewish man, the son of a carpenter, compared the family values of his youth in Brownsville with the privatized values of present-day Canarsie. "A lot of this permissiveness is plain selfishness. The parents use feminism and psychology to rationalize their desire to do their own thing after working their ass off for twenty years."

One response to the entrancements of liberty was to redouble efforts to transmit the culture of family. An Italian city worker fought with his daughter who wanted to attend college in another state. "Children are too smart today," he claimed. "The society protects the young, everything is the rights of the young. The times have changed, kids have their own minds, and discipline is way down. As for sex, it's not so taboo. But I still don't allow a great deal of open discussion about it. There is too much freedom and laxness." In small acts of resistance he fought the prevalent tendencies. "Back in the 1960s, everybody was stressing the permissibility of letting teens get their own pads, but it breaks up the home entirely. Children do as they please, they go out on their own. And I don't believe in those coed dorms. My daughter wanted to go away to college, but I put my foot down. They are too liberal at those out-of-state colleges."

Perhaps most frightening to Canarsians was the changing relationship between parents and children, who were showing the same irreverence toward family authority that altar boys displayed toward religious authority. A Jewish housewife blamed the collapse of authority in the household on permissive values. "When I was growing up, I couldn't do certain things for fear of hurting my parents, but today the kids have no shame. They tell you, 'That's the way you feel, that's the way I feel.' They have no respect. They act like animals." The recurring phrases—shame, animals, strictness, permissiveness, looseness—define the unity conjoining protesters against the Vietnam war, families in thrall to progressive child-rearing, lenient sociological judges, shiftless blacks on the dole, and Manhattan voluptuaries: the cult of self, contempt for authority.

The tension between the past and the present determined the traditionalists' conviction that they were in exile. In that context the versatile mantra of law and order took on additional meanings. It gathered all the moral and social dangers into a terse admonition, and at the same time it held out the hope that a semblance of meaning might be restored to a disorderly world, if only by force. "We need more law and order," insisted a Jewish clerical worker, as if the chanted assertion of control was a panacea. "We need law and order in the streets, we need it in the schools. There's been a complete breakdown there. We need law and order in the family. There is no law in the family except me, and my son knows I'll kill him if he talks back to me."

To dominate in intimate life now required effort. A sense of bafflement lay close to the surface of the man's shrill assertions, nudging him toward the inevitable comparisons. "You know, I tried hard to bring the kids up right. I don't know. The world is a lot different today than when I was growing up. The freedoms of today open up insecurities in everything. Back then, during the Depression, it was simpler. You had values. You didn't question. You didn't have these tensions and pressures. The only problem was earning a living."

Italian Americans again were in the vanguard of the counterrevolution in child-rearing. The cult of respect in Italian households was a modern version of the southern Italian adage, "He who disobeys his parents will die like a dog." To those of a psychoanalytic bent, the greater moral and coercive control held by the Italian male over women and children might point to one of the sources of Italian hardness and Jewish softness. As Nathan Glazer has written, "While the Jewish father is often ignored by the mother-son alliance, the Italian father is feared, for great emphasis is placed on male strength, and violent behavior is not unusual."[9]

Many provincial Italian men remembered the harsh discipline of their fathers, and they themselves expected children to comply with commands justified by the superior power, role, or size of the parents rather than by rational explanation or free discussion. One Canarsie salesman told how his "old man" would give him the back of the hand—"He'd lash out at me and punish me"—while his mother dispensed a classical form of ethnic justice—"She'd hit me with a wooden macaroni spoon and I'd go running and slide under the bed."

Some analysts have detected a link between the strict discipline of working-class families and what they see as the authoritarian personalities and politics of many workers. The word *authoritative* captures the spirit of provincial Italian life better than *authoritarian,* which has associations that confuse the emotional quality of family life with the pattern of family authority. One believer in strictness qualified the stern implications of his vision of child-rearing. "But you also need to spend time with children and to show them warmth and express your love to them. Kids need to be reminded they are loved." Unlike the relatively chilly, pyramidal Irish-American family, the traditional Italian-American family tends to be a centralized but supportive regime.[10]

The conventional understanding of the concept of authoritarianism also underplays the philosophic assumptions that recommend strictness. Canarsie traditionalists believed that people would naturally take what they could—property, liberties in sexual encounters, undeserved welfare checks—if restraints on impulse life were lifted. An activist in the Republican party skipped, with virtually no pause, from a demand for the death penalty to a call for reprisals against utility companies that rape the public to a plea for punishing ghetto rioters who run amok. "You need control on some conditions. It's like a child who wants something. If you don't draw the line, they will go for it, they will try and try. But then you slap them on the hand and they get back in line."

The forces of leveling threatened the authority of parents no less than that of God, teachers, police, and priests. An Italian policeman who grew up in Manhattan's Little Italy decried the impact of therapeutic and libertarian values on the traditional *rispettu* accorded the family. "Parents today tell the kid, 'You got your rights,' and one of our big [New York State] Regents professors said, 'Shouldn't children in elementary schools have their rights?' Oh no, I disagree with this, can you imagine a ten-year-old, an eleven-year-old, a twelve-year-old with rights? They got no rights. Their right is me. I am the parent, I will be his right, I will decide what is right or wrong for them!"

The big Regents professor symbolized the apparently growing power of experts and their war against parents' authority and the local wisdom they sought to impart to their children. If the weapons in that battle—rights, self-expression, alienation—were primarily verbal, the issues of justice and authority were no less nettlesome. The therapeutic mindset struck many traditionalists as a kind of special pleading whose disinterested attempts to fathom the whys of disobedient conduct made it impossible to punish infractions of local morality. "Hyperactivity," claimed one Jewish law-and-order civic leader, "is just a fancy term for a bad kid."

An Italian draftsman lamented the way therapeutic discourse disarmed parents. "These days you're afraid to punish the kid or you'll 'alienate' him." Psychology seemed another handcuff on parents' ability to instill the values they deemed worthy without complex rituals of justification. "Common sense is being taken away from us. They send everybody to the psychiatrist these days. It's a crutch. It's another escape. *We've* never gone in for this psychiatry stuff. Don't you see? Everything is changing. Complexes! Complexes! They use psychology on you. The back of the hand doesn't hurt, but you can't do it any more. Right or wrong, back then you knew it. If we did wrong, we would have been smacked."

Therapeutic fashion also burrowed into the culture from within. A leader in the Canarsie Italian-American Civil Rights League was troubled by the leveling within the family, which created odd hybrids of childlike adults and adultlike children. "Too many parents want to have better rapport, they act like teens and they bring themselves down to their children's level. The children say, 'You're not better than I am,' even if you're the mother! They talk about being on the same wavelength, dropping barriers, children even offer them pot. But they aren't equal."

The pediatrician Dr. Spock became a symbol of all the forces challenging the received wisdom. Spock, Canarsians wrongly believed, baldly acclaimed the propriety of getting rid of the old norms of strictness, and he became the sorcerer who was blamed for numerous cultural injuries. A member of the Canarsie Conservative party said, "I have the same discipline my parents did. The iron hand prevailed then, and it should prevail now. There would be less shooting dope and roaming the streets if you used the iron hand. There's too much relaxation by parents. This Spock-type reasoning with the child can only go so far."

Even the public schools, once reliable agents of pedagogical induction, could no longer be trusted to reproduce values consonant with the old homey virtues. One Italian worker lamented, "There's been a total breakdown of the moral values in the schools. There are special classes for girls who are pregnant! We didn't have that thirty years ago! Now these kids wear red bandannas and hair down to their feet." Even more galling, some teachers challenged the received wisdom. "Our educators, and teaching in general, has become so liberal in the last ten years, it scares me. The teachers at Wilson school want fifteen-year-olds to discuss their sex life with the class 'openly.' "

The folk wisdom suggested an effective rejoinder to the forces of indiscipline: firm men who would impose educational law and order. Barry Hurwitz, a strict principal of a Queens high school, became a hero for many traditionalist Jews and Italians by defying the American Civil Liberties Union and their preachments about student rights and expelling a "disrespectful" black student. "Hurwitz is doing right," exulted an Italian leader in the Conservative party. "He's doing all the things he must do, he's a disciplinarian. I'd love to see Barry Hurwitzes all over the school system. Years ago teachers used the hickory stick, and there was nothing wrong with it. We can't get our way anymore."

The mistrust of Piaget-Kohlberg, Dr. Spock, and psychiatry updated a long-standing ethnic suspicion of formal caretakers of all sorts, from welfare bureaucrats to meddlesome professionals to public schools, whose teachings competed with the moral claims of ethnic culture. Traditionalists in Canarsie rightly understood this as a fight to certify appropriate morality. The struggle over curricula involves the state, the schools, and the family in a complicated adversary relationship. Teachers, sex educators, and social scientists have vested interests in keeping their professional monopoly over the definition of reality. Sociolinguists have long argued that teachers in ghetto neighborhoods are the carriers of alien speech and moral codes, and to some degree that is also true of teachers in ethnic neighborhoods. Norms of therapeutic culture and progressive education *do* encourage the criticism of received dogma; experts *do* represent the intrusion of alien meanings into the locale; they *do* undermine the cultural control of parents. One may applaud this trend as enlightenment or decry it as decadence, but the analysis that informs the lament of traditionalists has considerable merit.[11] They were voicing an understanding that feminists and leftist critics of the therapeutic state and professional expertise have been offering for a generation: there is a politics of private life. The sphere of intimate life is not immune to political matters.

The attack on parental authority by experts and children was one facet of a larger political struggle for the control of the culture. A daughter's wish to escape the clutches of a strict Italian father by getting her own "pad" was a break with traditional notions of gender as much as with those of child-rearing. An out-of-state college represented in part a chance to be free from the control traditionally exercised by men over the sexuality of unmarried women in the family. The rights of children, like the growing autonomy of women, reflected the spreading assault on the remnants of the patriarchal family.

"Hybrids and other confusions are abominated," observed Mary Douglas. "Holiness is exemplified by completeness. Holiness requires that individuals shall conform to the class to which they belong. And holiness requires that different classes of things shall not be confused."[12] The early 1970s, then, were the unholiest of times. All the familiar social and sexual classifications that created holiness seemed to blur; the same forces that had obscured the line between children and parents were erasing the differences between men and women.

For traditionalists, the Equal Rights Amendment, presented to the voters of New York State in 1975, would give the government's blessing to sexual confusion. The ERA scored a majority in virtually every precinct of the 39th Assembly District among those who bothered to take a position on the issue. Advocates of women's rights were most numerous in Jewish precincts that had given the most support to the Civilian Review Board in 1966. The ERA carried almost two to one in many Jewish districts, while in other precincts the pro-ERA vote ranged between 50 and 65 percent of the tally. For a Jewish schoolteacher who had grown up "in an environment of thinking people in Williamsburg—that's my liberal background!" advocacy of women's rights was a natural translation of her democratic secular religion. "I support the Equal Rights Amendment but that's not how the Declaration of Independence wrote it. They had a double standard. But men and women are equal. I am not for quotas of any kind, for sex or for race."

The Jefferson Democratic Club represented the more cosmopolitan opinions, but some members were hardly paragons of gracious egalitarianism. In the clubhouse or out on the campaign trail, there was sometimes lots of bawdy, man-to-man camaraderie. "The great residual benefit of politics," claimed one Jefferson Democrat, "is that you get an election district captain with the biggest tits you ever saw." The man kept to a frantic pace of borscht belt commentary. "There's a real let-down after a primary campaign like this; it's like getting laid four times and then meeting Raquel Welch. 'Look, I'd like to, but.' I'm in favor of the ERA. Women should have the right to get ulcers, heart attacks, prostate conditions."

Notwithstanding the locker room banter, the office holders in the club applauded the ERA. Stanley Fink backed the amendment in the State Assembly, a gesture consonant with his steady support for civil liberties. Another Jewish office holder declared, "I am whole-heartedly in favor of a Gay Rights Bill, but we couldn't survive polit-ically if we supported it. Of course I support the ERA! Any other attitude is stupid. It's a holdover from the nineteenth century."

The ERA failed to carry only a half dozen election districts in the 39th Assembly District, and those included the Italian precincts that had repudiated civilian review in 1966 by the greatest margins. The two precincts most opposed to sexual equality voted against the ERA by 62 percent and 54 percent. But Canarsians were not voting only on the ERA on that occasion, and if we count all the voters, in-cluding those who did not vote on the ERA, we get an even better feel for the vigor of sexual traditionalism in Italian Old Canarsie; in one precinct just 30 percent of those who went to the polls supported the ERA.

The disparity between the vote for the ERA and the vote for the Civilian Review Board underlines the importance of separating the racial and moral portions of the social issues. Anxieties about practical danger were less relevant to the ERA vote. While the Civilian Re-view Board went down to defeat in every single Canarsie precinct, the ERA carried almost every precinct. And in many of the Italian precincts, almost half of the residents supported the amendment, despite a grassroots effort by the Knights of Columbus to defeat it.

Visceral sentiment fueled opposition to the ERA. "The woman has lost a great deal by women's lib," surmised an Italian artisan. "Some can hold jobs, but they are getting carried away. I don't feel that I'm the lord and master, but when I say, 'No, this is it,' that's it. Man should have the say in his own home and be able to say, 'This is it, right, wrong, or indifferent.' " Resistance also came from fear that equality would diminish the sharp distinctions between men and women that create form out of chaos. A clerk complained, "The women in those movements are not women, they are not like women in their thinking, they don't act like women. It's like a black emulat-ing a white, it doesn't fit." Sexual equality promised to accomplish the same blurring as the mingling of homosexual teachers and fire-men in normal society. A construction worker merged a variety of negatives about feminism, concluding, "I'm opposed to it. It's too much. There should be a difference. Attraction would be different if they were equal. Women shouldn't work in sewers. They will lose their daintiness."

Some women also took comfort in having a predetermined role. "I'd like to have things left as they are," said a Jewish woman, "with the male dominant and the woman catered to, not as an equal. You get problems and confusion as to who will do what when there are no predefined roles. People like to live by rules." The Madonnalike image of the Italian mother reinforced a pronatalist elevation of the woman's status. Many women enjoyed the minor ceremonial acknowledgment of their being that came from chivalric and romantic displays of solicitude. "I'm against the woman's movement," argued a middle-class Jewish homemaker. "I just saw *Yentl,* and they said, 'A learned woman is a monstrosity,' but that was long ago. Recently women have been recognized. I love being called honey, being used as a sex object, and flirted with. Men have given us so much. We get what we need. And men get the shaft in divorce. Women's liberation is hurting women there."

Women feared that the erasure of the line between the sexes would take away a privileged realm of nurturance. After lambasting "women's libbers," one of the most assertive rightist activists in Canarsie cried, "I'm Mom, not Person," as if a treasured status might be stolen from her. Many Canarsie women—not "little women" who did the bidding of their husbands, but women who chafed at patriarchal control and defied their husbands to pursue PTA work and other activities outside the home—saw feminism as a force that demeaned the values of family and mothering and, instead of offering them a greater sense of esteem, deprived them of dignity. "Feminists say, 'You're a servant, you're the house slave of the man.' That's why a lot of women I know in Canarsie went against the ERA."[13]

Traditional Judaic canon sustained one observant man's antifeminist sentiment. "Women have a special place in life, but the ERA will take it away. The Jewish principle of women puts the mother in the highest position in life. It's the mother who sets the tone of living for the children. The husband is out there observing his religious practice, which he learned at his mother's side, because he spent most of his growing up with his mother, not his father. The ideals were given to him by his mother. Now you take an ERA amendment, the mother's going to go out to work, and the father's going to sit there. That's a detraction from womanhood."[14]

Italian familism and Catholicism also lent support to the maintenance of separate spheres for men and women.[15] The debate at the Canarsie lodge of the Knights of Columbus was a reflective effort to sort out the gains and costs of liberation. Like many Catholic opponents of the ERA, a Knight who took part in that discussion believed that the ERA contained many fine points, which he hoped would be passed in other legislative acts. "I cannot see a woman performing a function being paid less because she's a woman, and I have seen that time and time again." Yet he balanced that belief in fairness against the losses he felt would accrue to women in an egalitarian society:

> I campaigned against the ERA because I thought it would be detrimental to women. Giving them equality really would have made them subservient in many ways. It would have created a responsibility that many women are not equipped to accept. I don't mean the woman who's a businesswoman or an independent person. I'm talking about the woman who's been married for twenty-five years, who's grown up with her husband and her children, and now the children are out of the house and the husband suddenly divorces her. I am more concerned for the privileges of a woman, not equal rights, but better rights, rights which are above men. I'm talking about the woman who's not the liberated kind of woman, she's a woman who's rejected, and it creates problems. I've talked to many career women, women who would use the term "Ms.," and I would say their attitude is that any woman could accomplish if they wanted to. But not every woman wants to. A lot of women enjoy being housewives. I know my wife does. She has her own club, her own particular source of pleasure, she enjoys being a housewife and mother, and she doesn't look forward to a day when she would have to go out and get a job and work. She doesn't look forward to anything but taking care of our children and enjoying the company of our family.

Ultimately, the ERA came to symbolize all the forces that were weakening the bonds of the family, which was already buckling under all manner of inner and outer pressures. "The basic feeling," said a Knights of Columbus officer, "was that it would take away the basic responsibility of a man for his wife to provide for his family, or, for that matter, the *need* of a man to do this. That was really important. It would hurt the family concept, and being a family-minded organization, this was something that could not be supported."

If men and women were truly liberated from their traditional duties, what would bind them to families? And what would hold them together if they could enjoy sexual pleasure without commitment, get divorced without stigma, terminate pregnancies at will? Many Canarsians merged these fears in part because they glimpsed a real unity in all the diversity: the freeing of the self from communal duties. Liberation, they reasoned, could only dim the precious line between nature and culture as surely as did the odd mating practices of ghetto families. As a traditionalist Catholic put it:

> The advent of birth control loosened sex to the point of it being commonplace. Ten years later they legalized abortion. Sex is happening all over the place now. And women want the baby, but not marriage! But marriage is sacred to society. It's gone too far, I tell you, the moral state is eroding. I disapprove of this premarital sex, people living their own way of life. We were raised with certain morals. If you are loose, you revert to animals. You got to hold the line. The dam is breaking all over the place.

Many Catholics in Canarsie, including those with New Deal liberal views on economic issues, felt alienated from a Democratic party that seemed in thrall to the feminist enthusiasms of the upper middle classes. Even those who did not join the Knights of Columbus could agree with the liberal Democratic Grand Knight who defended his "square values" against decadent sophistication. "We have a deep anti-abortion morality, we are obstinate about sexual morality, and we are conservative in our attitude toward pornography and modern films." But the grievances of lonely individuals had little effect unless channeled in some coherent fashion. As the Knights' local campaign to defeat the ERA demonstrated, cultural battles were won or lost by organized collectivities that could mobilize resources.

The Knights played a pedagogical as well as a logistical role, providing a nurturant environment in which networks of moral activists could flourish. Less active members of Catholic lay organizations became exposed to the articulate formulations of more committed moral partisans, who spurred the involvement of the rank and file by invoking ecclesiastical authority.[16] After decrying the permissive influence of the Supreme Court, one Knight activist cited values that were higher than constitutional ones. "Because of our apathy, we let the New York State abortion law slip by, but now we will pull out all stops to outlaw abortion. And we have spoken to the Canarsie movie theaters and told them if they allowed X-rated films to penetrate the community, we would surround them with pickets. We feel that where Peter stands, there stands the church, meaning we follow the Pope." Italian Catholic activists in the Knights and in the Republican and Conservative parties were decidedly not laissez-faire libertarians. They gave priority to family and morality over liberty and the marketplace, and they fought efforts to have the state safeguard the rights of homosexuals and women.

Catholic moral activism was a specialized current in Italian life. The profamily sentiments on which that activism rested faithfully reflected general Catholic anxieties about abortion, premarital sexuality, and feminism, but the rank and file did not all endorse the specific policies of the activists. Opinion polls have shown that the majority of Catholics do not agree with a constitutional amendment that would proscribe abortions. Strong strains in Italian and working-class life support a live-and-let-live attitude on moral matters and the prochoice position on abortion. An Italian mechanic, a self-described conservative, affirmed, "This is a free country. A woman who wants an abortion is not imposing on anyone else's rights." The pagan, anticlerical, and rowdy strains in the plebeian outlook further limited the appeal of religious incursions into private life.

Jewish leaders replied to Catholic moral activism by rejecting the use of state power to enforce communal morality. More positively, they were willing to use the state to expand the sway of individual freedoms. When he was chairman of the Codes Committee of the New York State Assembly in the mid-1970s, Stanley Fink drafted legislation to decriminalize consensual sodomy among adults, hardly a concern that was dear to most of his constituents. An Italian member of the Jefferson Club did not share Fink's enthusiasm for protecting the sexual rights of minorities, and he growled, "What's so damn important about a bill in favor of faggot cock-sucking?"

The prochoice proclamations of Canarsie Jews leaving the polls in 1976 suggest the intensity of the Jewish desire to maintain a strict sphere of individual choice in moral matters. "I don't see where a church or an organization has the right to tell a woman what to do with her body," said a young Jewish woman. "It's not a person until it's born." A Jewish member of the Conservative party argued, "It's up to the man and woman. It's the libertarian position. I still believe in equal rights." Such statements conform to a long pattern of Jewish opposition to prayer in the schools, antiabortion legislation, and blue laws.[17]

Because of their unique ethnic and partisan traditions, Jewish and Italian leaders in Canarsie responded differently to the moral crusading of fundamentalist Protestant forces in the late 1970s. Historically, neither Jewish humanism nor Italian naturalism jibed with the moralistic Christian exhortations emanating from the American heartland. The mobilization of fundamentalists in the 1980 election elicited fear among Jewish Democratic leaders, but Italian Republicans and Conservatives were surprisingly calm. An Italian leader argued, "Those preachers from North Carolina have made inroads. They've gotten publicity, and money and a following. There's nothing wrong with it. I believe in God. This country always has believed in God. The writers of the Constitution included God in it."

The Jewish leaders did not view with equanimity the use of state power to enforce moral virtue. One candidate in the Jefferson Democratic Club avowed, "The Moral Majority are dangerous people. They want to negate the separation of church and state. They want to inject prayer into the schools. They represent the antiabortion, eye-for-an-eye, tooth-for-tooth, pro–death penalty mentality. They would take away the rights of other individuals if they could. They want monolithic thinking rather than diversity. The Jews don't commune with God!" Their nervousness about Baptist, fundamentalist, and southern culture also colored their view of Jimmy Carter. Bible-belt culture seemed to them a general complex of racism, anti-Semitism, and comformism that could easily turn against a vulnerable Jewish remnant. A Jewish official captured the hesitation many of his constituents felt about voting for Carter in 1976. "There is still an overriding fear among Canarsie Jews that they could be next. Liberal and Jewish concerns are not that far apart. They're one and the same. That's why they didn't like Jimmy Carter. They were suspicious of Southern Baptist thinking."

Loyal Americans

"I loved Nixon for loving the country."

In June of 1969, as protest against the Vietnam war mounted, President Nixon warned an audience of college students, "Our fundamental values [are] under bitter and even violent attack." He went on,

"We live in a deeply troubled and profoundly unsettled time. Drugs, crime, campus revolts, racial discord, draft resistance—on every hand we find old standards violated, old values discarded." Nixon had recognized the growing perception among Americans that traditional standards were falling apart in the public as well as the private realm. This moral debate affected the public's perception of domestic dissent against the Vietnam war, of the legitimacy of the war effort, of the character of leaders needed to promote America's global interests.[18]

The diverse sources of Americans' foreign policy views warns against looking for hidden unities behind people's attitudes toward quite different subjects. Canarsians who flinched at the idea of children's rights, for example, did not always balk at granting rights to antiwar demonstrators. This caveat aside, the global issues of the day raised questions similar to the cultural issues. What latitude should be accorded to personal rights rather than to unwavering notions of doing right? How much esteem should be given to values of standing fast versus the values of soft abdication? What immunity from criticism can authority rightly expect?

Italian Old Canarsie, the center of support for manly patriarchy in the conjugal and sexual domain, was also the heartland of the muscular approach to foreign policy. In the early 1970s 48 percent of Jews nationwide fell into the dovish category on the question of withdrawal from Vietnam—22 percent higher than the percentage of dovish Catholic Americans of southern European descent. Italian Americans continually ranked extremely high in hostility to antiwar demonstrators. Their nationalistic enthusiasm, however, was not unmodified. Opinion on the war was highly volatile; as costs and body counts mounted, the proportion of all sorts of Americans who favored getting out also rose. Meade Esposito said in 1970, "If you notice the kids they're sending over there, they still have white spots around their mouths—that's their mother's milk, those kids haven't even been weaned yet. That war is immoral and the sooner we get out of there the better off the whole community will be."[19]

The earthy images of milk, sons, and mothers reflected the irrelevance of ideology to ethnic nationalism. When provincial Italian Americans saw threats to the national security, they would support unflinching action. But when foreign entanglements were justified by noble calls to justice or an abstract crusade against communism, Italians' familism made them draw back from the redemptive mission of helping strangers. Nationalism and isolationism were not contradictory stances; they represented the unchanging value of standing firm under varying environmental conditions.

Canarsians often compartmentalized their opinions, mentally separating doubts about the justice or morality of intervention in Vietnam from a belief in the need to show loyalty to the country. The symbolic appropriation of the American flag by Italian nationalists illustrates the cultural notions of obligation that gave successive administrations the leeway to continue the war. For patriotic Italians, the banner gained in importance precisely as the national accord on its meaning diminished and the nation underwent fission into two hostile tribes, each with its own totem: the hawk and the dove. Just as altar boys mishandled the sacred vessels, some American demonstrators defiled the American flag when they protested against the Vietnam war. Such tactics undermined support for ending the war among working-class citizens who bore its brunt. One Italian veteran of Vietnam wanted either to quit the war or unleash the big guns. "If you had gotten the generals together, the Vietnam situation would have been cleaned up in one year. If you are fighting a war, let's fight and get to it." At the same time he was convinced that "Vietnam was an uncalled-for war. None of us wanted to die. These are brothers, and you're going to send them to die? For what? No one is invading New York City harbor. Industry made a fortune out of this, the guys who made machine guns and rifles."

But desecration of the American flag overwhelmed all doubts about intervention. "It's only a flag, it's only a piece of material, it's got some stripes, it's got some stars on it, but sometimes the kids destroyed their own good solid thoughts. They could have come across with their thoughts in a more professional, I should say intelligent, way. They weren't dummies." He pinpointed the collective harm that a few antiwar activists had brought on the entire movement. "I've got enough sense to say, 'This is one individual,' but a lot of people I know said, 'This is a whole generation,' when it was a few of what we call radicals." The "radicals" seemed to mock patriotism as something base and square and bellicose, while he experienced it as an expression of admirable loyalty. "But the flag is a symbol, it's a feeling you have for this place, it's where I lived my whole life, and someone took a shit in the street and wiped his ass with the flag. That infuriated me!"

Reverence for the flag embodied a style of patriotism sustained less by abstract ideals than by primordial sentiments of belonging to a particular place—"Patriotism should be the first thing in your mind because you were born and raised in this country"—embellished by emotive imagery of blood, kin, and birth—"I'm a man who fought and bled for my country." The respect for loyalty fostered support for service in Vietnam even among those who disputed the wisdom or justice of the involvement in Southeast Asia. "I was against the protesters, they were against all I believed. We're Americans, and if being in Vietnam is what we were supposed to do, then you should do it and support the country. Those protesters shouldn't have been allowed to do what they were doing."

Italian patriotism expressed a moral vision of the state-as-family, which extended to foreign affairs the duty to close ranks against one's enemies. That rendering of loyalty sliced the world into clear ranks of for and against, fidelity and treachery. The starkness of those contrasts did not allow a great deal of room for a loyal opposition or for the ambiguities of dissent in times of war. An Italian Republican leader saw antiwar protesters as traitors:

Their reasons for criticizing America were selfish. They couldn't have cared less about our survival and progress as a nation. It's like when we were talking about the family before. It goes back to the old story. This is where you hang your hat. It's not right to abuse it and talk down the place where you hang your hat. It's like the feeling of family. It goes back to children and the importance of respect and obedience more than anything else. It's the same thing. The respect in the home should be carried to the country you live in.

Personal histories of time-serving persuaded veterans that antiwar demonstrators were trying to evade their obligation. Had they themselves not shouldered the burden of national service in Korea or the European theater? Why, then, should others shirk their duty? Seen in this light, amnesty ratified a distributive injustice. Friendship with those who had gone to fight when called added to Canarsians' identification with the fighting men. One craftsman was working on a skyscraper in the Wall Street area when his fellow workers started throwing concrete down on youths in the street who were protesting Nixon's invasion of Cambodia. In 1976 he reflected back on that time. "Here were these kids, rich kids who could go to college, who didn't have to fight, they are telling you your son died in vain. It makes you feel your whole life is shit, just nothing."

Those whose friends and relatives had died in Vietnam or suffered disability needed to justify their sacrifice as something more than futile suffering. An Italian worker in his thirties told about his ambivalent feelings and the less divided ones of his brothers in the Knights of Columbus. "The men who were really against the Carter pardon for draft dodgers were those with sons who died in Vietnam. We've had three Knights who died in Vietnam. I have strong feelings about that, but I also can look at it with an understanding and ask, 'Did we waste their lives?' They haven't studied it as I have, so they're bitter about those who tried to run from it when their sons got it."

Conventional notions of masculinity sustained the invidious appraisals of antiwar dissenters. In the minds of many, George McGovern's pledge to crawl to Hanoi to secure peace lingered as an unmanly reluctance to defend the national family. An Italian policeman voted for Nixon in 1972 solely because of what he took to be McGovern's humiliating posture of obeisance. The kneeling was not an innocent act, a self-contained lapse, but the enactment of a whole "liberal" way of being in the world. "I didn't particularly care for McGovern's attitude toward the country, I don't believe in going down on your hands and knees, right or wrong, and begging for forgiveness to an outside power."

The reverse of an obsession with honor was the fear of humiliation. Both shaped Canarsians' attitudes toward the Watergate affair and congressional investigations of the Central Intelligence Agency. One hallmark of the recurrent waves of utopian improvement in American life is the focusing of publicity on evil doing. Italian Americans, however, did not share in the tradition of secular revivalism. To the crusaders for redemptive publicity, many Italians replied that it was the courts, the adversary press, and Congress who had betrayed the nation, with all their bleating about wrongdoing. An Italian nurse viewed the exposure of America's blemishes as a besmirching of a great nation: "I didn't like the way McGovern spoke about the Vietnam war, and his whole philosophy, he wanted to pull the boys back without honor to our country. You see, even if McGovern was right in what he said, the way he spoke it went against my grain. Americanism is very important to me, and I don't like my country showing less than what it should be."

Loyalty to Nixon after Watergate affirmed a conception of legitimacy grittier than one based on finicky legalities. When Nixon said he would never accept a peace that dishonored the nation, he spoke to the deepest philosophic promptings in ethnic Americans. Plebeian cynicism suggested that all the perfectionist outrage about law-breaking was a shade naive. A leader in the Italian-American League said:

> Watergate was bullshit, pure and simple. They framed Nixon and killed him politically. I don't care what *he* did. It's disgraceful what *they* did to the country, the press and Congress and the protesters. It's not good to hang your dirty laundry for all to see. That's not greatness. Nixon didn't like Italians, but he loved his country. He's entitled to his likes and dislikes. If I can't yell black bastard or sheeney Jew at home, I can't yell it anywhere. All Americans are prejudiced. I loved Nixon for loving the country.[20]

Out of the patriotic currents of Old Canarsie there developed a strain of nationalism that fed on the provocations of the Vietnam war and the postwar era of lessening American power. Italian nationalism also built on an existing tradition of right-wing reaction, which occasionally displayed an enthusiasm for extreme solutions. An Italian trucker embodied the evolution of America First isolationism "with respect to Europe"—Roosevelt was "negative because he got us into World War II"—into a muscular nationalism "with respect to the Pacific" after World War II: "Goldwater would have won the Vietnam war. We should have had a full-scale war and come out and used the A-bomb. When you are fighting the Commies, it's the only language they understand." Sometimes he spoke the language of the free world. "I don't want communism in America, it's a dictatorial government." At other times he heralded an indigenous variant of Gulag justice: "Can Jane Fonda burn the flag in Russia? She should have been tarred and feathered."

The domestic upheavals of the Vietnam war almost gave this man a chance to act out his repressive wishes. When he came upon a demonstration led by Daniel and Philip Berrigan, left-wing Catholic priests, on the sidewalks of Manhattan, he was angry. "The Berrigan brothers had this sign that made Mother Cabrini look like a slut and a slumlord. I wanted to do a job on them. When people desecrate religion, it reaches a point I don't like. I wanted to slap their faces, and I would have." He spotted a cop and told him, "Hey, take a five-minute walk, and *I'll* end this demonstration!"

The man longed for tribal closure, but he lived in an open society. The essence of pluralism is the clashing of wills, which in practice means the right of citizens to wave red flags, but when a few members of the antiwar movement waved red Vietcong banners, they sparked demonic feelings in patriots like him. The right clothed itself in the imagery of individualism and the slogans of a free world, but its basic impulses were authoritarian.

Notions of duty, betrayal, and loyalty among Jewish leaders in the Jefferson Democratic Club, in the small circle of good-government reformers, and in the PTA hierarchy were at odds with those of their Italian rivals.[21] The gap echoed the contrast between soft Jews and hard Italians that prevailed in racial matters. If Nixon accumulated support among provincial Italians by embodying ideals of personal loyalty and standing fast, he dissipated support among many Jewish civic leaders who exalted due process and accountable power. The defamation of a president's reputation seemed to them a paltry price to pay for the hedged authority of rulers in a liberal democracy. A Jewish Democrat linked benevolent freedom to the protections of an adversary relation between rulers and ruled. Hardly a one-world etherealist, he was a staunch anticommunist who castigated the Soviet Union for the mistreatment of Soviet Jews. Nor did he balk at conceding to the modern state certain geopolitical needs for clandestine intelligence operations. But he balanced that practical need against the sacredness of democratic procedures. "It's great," he averred. "I can tell my senator to go to hell, the rights are mine. I'm proud of a country that can throw out a president. I'm proud of the *Washington Post* and those two reporters. People like that make our country great. It's great that we can investigate the CIA and the FBI. It's great when we wash our dirty laundry in public. Democracy was strengthened by Watergate. It proved the Constitution works. The political system passed the test."

The concern with the abuses of state power attested to the vibrancy of democratic values among Jewish civic and political leaders. A striking tendency to invoke the Constitution, the Bill of Rights, and the Declaration of Independence expressed the Jewish reverence for procedural rules that subordinate personal considerations of loyalty to the less personal realm of law. Jewish Democratic leaders and activists inverted the Italian leaders' definition of danger and betrayal. One of them cited the redemptive charter of the Founders and offered his own notion of Americanism—not loyalty for its own sake, right or wrong, but loyalty to the abstract principles of the Constitution. "We could easily become a totalitarian government," he warned. "You must watch the government, you have to be on their backs at every moment. That's what the Founding Fathers thought. Watergate was a step toward autocracy. The CIA actions and the Ellsburg break-in were threats to democracy and common decency."

Classical Jewish fears tempered support for nationalist binges. To one businessman who had grown up in Germany and had watched the rise of Nazism, America was a promised land that delivered him from terror, and he was grateful. Martin Luther King's criticism of America's involvement in Vietnam made him angry. "I thought, 'How dare that black man criticize our country?' " Yet a primordial hesitation kept him from yielding to the full force of naive celebration. "I've seen stupid patriotisms. I grew up in Germany and I witnessed the Hitler Youth. Stupid patriotism! The Fuhrer! That's why I refuse to say 'under God' in the pledge. That's not anybody's business. The rights are mine."

Their sensitivity to the unholy possibilities of an enraged Americanism separated the Jewish leaders from Republican and Conservative nationalists and marked the same border between two symbolic communities defined by their opposed categories of villains—McCarthyites and fascists for the one, subversives and commies for the other. The Jewish leaders were often strongly anticommunist, but their self-consciousness about threats to civil liberties provided a check on downright intolerance. "I get angry at the communists," one Jewish PTA leader emphasized, "but American communists should have freedom of speech. This is a democracy!"

Demands in the early 1970s to end the Vietnam involvement sparked a physical confrontation between Jewish Democrats and their Italian Conservative and Republican detractors. The bizarre episode began at a "Set the Date for Peace" rally at Canarsie High School. Sponsored by the Jefferson Democratic Club, the rally featured local and national opponents of the war, including Stanley Fink, Paul O'Dwyer, and Cora Weiss. The Club's congressman, Frank Brasco, called for a time limit on American intervention, arguing, "There is no sound reason for us to continue to send our boys to fight in South Vietnam ... We are not regarded as liberators by the people and authorities of South Vietnam."[22]

But the meeting was invaded by counterdemonstrators from the Canarsie Veterans of Foreign Wars, the Canarsie Conservative Club, Catholic War Veterans, local Republicans, and the Silent Majority for a United America Organization. Punches were thrown, and the police made some arrests. One witness glimpsed a connection among the storming of the auditorium by superpatriots, fascist violence, and the Wall Street construction workers' assault on protesting youths. "It occurred to me that this sort of mentality was the same sort of mentality and activity that prepared the way for the debacle in Nazi Germany."[23]

The names of the nationalistic counterdemonstrators give a good flavor of the ethnic base: Russo, Raimondi, Andreassi, Volpe, Fopeano, Tinervia. Andreassi, the Americanism chairman of the local VFW, warned, "Un-American activities in Canarsie and surrounding communities will be opposed with the same patriotic enthusiasm as was displayed" at the counterdemonstration. An Italian Conservative who opposed the breadth of freedom of expression in America said, "There should be an American flag, but in the school auditorium I only saw radical clenched fists and commie solidarity buttons. But our people, the Conservative party and the American Legion, outnumbered them, and we shouted them down at their demonstration." Andreassi implied that freedom of speech was an un-American cover for treachery. "The same individuals who are continuously advocating the overthrow of the U.S. government by their various actions are the very ones who, when confronted by reactions of loyal Americans, are the first to cry foul and invoke the protection of the U.S. Constitution."[24]

The breach between Italian conservative and Jewish progressive leaders over the Vietnam war repeated their disagreements over busing, the Equal Rights Amendment, and child-rearing. Yet the liberalism and conservatism, respectively, of the two groups exaggerated the views of the Jewish and Italian communities. A large contingent of lower-middle-class Jews was no more attracted to left-liberal enthusiams in the realm of foreign policy than in racial or sexual matters. A paraprofessional in the school system decried the protesters who mocked the country that had delivered the Jews from wandering. "I don't like the loss of feeling for flying the American flag, it's part of the whole breakdown of discipline in America. America has so much to give. Too many people take it for granted. All Americans should go to a totalitarian country, come back, and kiss this country's ground. This is my country, right or wrong, don't condemn it and burn the flag. That's not the way to change things. There should be no amnesty for deserters. They have an obligation to serve."

The demand for toughness that had rallied parochial Brooklyn

Jews to Mario Procaccino in the 1969 mayoral race surfaced in the global as well as the municipal arena. A conservative Jewish politician who had applauded Procaccino's pledge to take the handcuffs off the police and put them back on the criminals called for an unambiguous foreign policy. "The government has to take definite action against the oil-producing nations. If oil-producing nations think they can blackmail Israel, then we have to take physical action." He scorned the philosophy that tried to substitute worldly idealism for mettle. "We've been feeding the commies, but as the most powerful country in the world we don't have to beg."

A broader Jewish anxiety about American leaders who vacillated paralleled the Italian respect for men who "stand fast." Decidedly ethnic preoccupations enhanced the geopolitical realism of lower-middle-class Jews. Would American leaders who had cut and run from Vietnam stand by Israel in a world of oil blockades and petrodollars? Jewish pride in the Israeli rescue of a hijacked plane at Entebbe, Uganda, reflected a general disaffection with pacifism. The wife of an insurance clerk argued, "Israel is not my homeland, but they've done a fantastic job. They will survive. Before there will be another Masada, they will blow up the Arabs. Oh yes, I thought [after Entebbe], at last the animals weren't allowed to get their way and hurt our interests. The Palestinian Liberation Organization is worse than the Japanese were during World War II."

One should be careful not to attribute such statements only to right-wing nationalist recoil. Progressive and cosmopolitan Jews in Canarsie shared in the anger over the one-sidedness of détente, in concern about the decline of America's resolve in the post-Vietnam era, and in fears of the rising leverage of the Arab states. Such fears reflected the objective ethnic interests of Jewish Americans as much as obscure psychic insecurities or status anxieties. A Democratic leader declared in 1973, "The Yom Kippur attack by Egypt and Syria will go down in history as a day of infamy, blasphemy, and sacrilege against all peace-loving people." He merged the Arab-Israeli struggle with the larger Cold War: "It was Russian Frog surface-to-surface missiles that bombarded Israeli settlements from the outset of the war; it was Russian SAM missiles that confronted Israeli planes defending their soil; it was Russian tanks that confronted the Israelis in the Sinai and at the Golan Heights."[25]

Zionist concerns caused Canarsie Jews to be wary of public figures who made overtures to terrorist groups intent on Jewish annihilation, and the same concerns warmed their hearts to "friends of the

Jews," like New York Senator Daniel Patrick Moynihan. More than any other figure, Moynihan defined a center of gravity of Jewish opinion in Canarsie on matters global as well as domestic. His position seemed a judicious blend of their diverse political leanings: an economic liberalism impervious to the trendy passions of 1960s reform; a no-nonsense approach to Soviet bullies; and a celebration of American pride encoded in the refusal to bow before third-world diatribes. In the 1976 Democratic senatorial primary Moynihan trounced a crowded field of contenders that included Bella Abzug, Ramsey Clark, Abe Hirschfield, and Paul O'Dwyer. Canarsie Jews leaving the polls declared their affection for their Irish friend: "He spoke his mind at the United Nations, no shilly-shallying"; "As a Jew I like what Moynihan did at the UN"; "He fights for Israel."

Oppositions like pinkish Jews and McCarthyite Italians, or jingoistic parochial Jews and temperate cosmopolitan Jews, do not adequately capture the fluidity of public opinion. They are meant to suggest only that certain relationships obtain when "all things are equal." However much the deep structures of ethnicity and class dispose individuals to certain opinions or types of conduct, history retains its power to modify and embellish opinion.

Although many writers have mourned America's post-Vietnam retreat from the world, isolationist equivocation represented in part the growth of historical wisdom. One can say that a national accord on communist containment had restricted the flow of information and debate for a generation, but a decade of exposure and dissensus broke the control held by official interpreters of reality. Canarsians' opinions shifted; they became more critical of the received wisdom and deferred less instinctively to the claims of government. "I wasn't opposed to the war in the beginning," a Jewish businessman began, "but I came to see that it was patriotic nonsense. As the war progressed, and I saw the brutality, the utter destruction, I began to correct whatever patriotic cocoon I was in. It was inhuman. I began to see that it was unpatriotic to be involved in that kind of war. I started to ask myself, 'Is this a war of aggression or a civil war?' Before, I never addressed myself to those questions. Vietnam wasn't a war to stop communism, I decided."

In one working-class Catholic family, Vietnam incited a feud between mother and son that bordered on burlesque. The mother, a fierce rightist, exalted the American way of life. The son, a Vietnam veteran, defended the safeguards of the Constitution. "Like I said, my mother and I are on completely different ends of the pole. She sees the younger generation voting in communism and not really being worth much and as un-American." He recalled the events surrounding the attack on peace demonstrators on Wall Street by irate construction workers. "At the time, I was having a pretty heavy protest over at Staten Island Community College with the Vietnam Veterans against the War, and the word came down to us what happened down on Wall Street. I got very, very upset about it, right? Because we're all fighting for the same thing, all feeling the same thing, and it was like my brother got hit."

He came home to find his mother watching the television news. "They had the television on with all the construction workers beating the hippies over the head and my mother's sitting there cheering those guys on, 'Hit em, hit those commie bastards, hit those sons of bitches, kill em all.' I walk in and say, 'Ma! How could you say that? That could be me that's getting hit.' " The mother retorted, "I don't want to hear that, you're not going to any of these protests," to which the son replied, "I just came from one over at Staten Island." The mother leaped up, knocked over the chair, and with her fist clenched, "she puts it right up to my chin and with her teeth right together, she says, 'Don't let me ever hear you talk like that again.' " The son replied:

> "I'm not even going to stay in this house and discuss this with you! I think it's ridiculous." Anyway, I run out of the house and slam the door and she's about five foot behind me and as I'm running down the driveway, I hear her yelling in back of me. I might have yelled something like "Shut up," which I never do. I have a lot of respect for my parents, and I just don't talk back to them. I might have said something like "Aw, shut up." She came after me. On her travels going through the driveway, she picks up a lead pipe. I turn around and see her coming toward me with a stick, so I jumped in my Volkswagen, started it up, put it in reverse, burned rubber out of the driveway, and just hauled off down the street, and I left the house for the rest of the day. Like I said, my mother and I are on completely different sides.

Mother and son achieved a measure of accommodation through resigned acceptance laced with humor. They carved out a form of détente, each granting the ineluctable limits of the other's world. "We could sit down now and have a political fight," the son mused.

"But we avoid them because we know how we feel." When Vice President Spiro Agnew resigned in 1973, the son felt an impish impulse. "We walked into the house, and my mother's sitting at the table, and I walk up to her and go, 'Hi, Ma' and she goes, 'Hi,' like she's really sad, so I go, 'How do you like what happened?' So she looks up at me and puts her hand up and goes, 'Son, it's a holiday, let's not talk politics.' So I said, 'Fine Ma, we won't talk politics, but all I can say is this. If you see me standing in the corner giggling, you'll know what I'm thinking about.' So at that point she started laughing."

The tirades against the desecration of the American flag recall the priest's lament over the altar boys' disrespect for the sacred vessels. The parallel suggests only one of the commonalities that appear in many traditionalists' narratives of cultural life. They lashed out at parental, racial, and global appeasement. They fought against limits placed on the prerogatives of rulers in sexual life, family affairs, and foreign policy. They applied adages about family danger and security to national danger and security. They were angered by rights granted to women, children, and protesters.

To the extent that these matters touched underlying primal opinions about self and society, the clash over the benefits of change renewed an ancient battle between tradition and modernity. Edward Shils's apercu on the espionage question in the 1950s is germane to understanding the attitudes of many Canarsie Italians toward congressional probes of CIA improprieties. "As long as the genuine security problem exists, there will be persons whose imagination will be set boiling with excited apprehension." In such cases, "the protection of secrecy and the prevention of subversion have only been pretexts for the continuation of a conflict begun much earlier and quite without relation to the problem of security." As Shils argued, nervousness about national security may be a symptom of diffuse private ills or cultural dangers.[26]

Shils's insight can be applied to all the grievances voiced by Canarsie fundamentalists if we replace "pretext" with "context." Fights over the Eucharist, the Equal Rights Amendment, or law and order defined a symbolic arena in which traditionalists defended their moral security against subversion.

When Canarsians railed against the victory of instinct over obligation, they were in the same corner as many luminaries of high culture who have proclaimed the decadence of contemporary Western culture. About one extreme form of modernism, Lionel Trilling wrote, "The inculpation of society has become with us virtually a category of thought. We understand a priori that the prescriptions of society pervert human existence and destroy its authenticity."[27] In their quest for sexual, moral, and aesthetic law and order, many Canarsians would have turned Trilling's statement upside down: affirming the need for social norms, not questioning their validity, was a category of thought with them. They understood that the prescriptions of society *permit* human existence and *create* authenticity.

Breukelen Houses, low-income city housing

Let's
CARMINE
SPICK'S
AND
NIGGERS
ARE
SHIT
THAT'S
Right
PHIL
DENNIS

Down on Canarsie Pier

Thomas Jefferson Democratic Club, election day 1980

Republican headquarters, election night 1980

Racially changing block, looking north across Flatlands Avenue toward Breukelen Houses

Near Breukelen Houses

part three

Reactions to Threat

6. Striking Back

Exodus and Revolt

*"We're finally rising up, we're striking back,
there will be no more taking it!"*

The people of Canarsie saw themselves as victims of forces that were disrupting life across New York City, but they did not endure that plight forever in silence. Discontent stiffened their resolve to regain control over an unruly social and physical environment. These final chapters explore their attempts to protect themselves, ranging from private measures like flight and vigilantism to more collective measures like the revolt against busing to explicitly political measures like voting. Although reactions to threat cannot be neatly compartmentalized, this chapter arbitrarily focuses on their attempts to resolve the vulnerabilities of physical place.

In this chapter I describe some of the most mean-spirited and violent acts I observed or learned of during my stay in Canarsie. It is doubly important, therefore, to remember that only a tiny fringe of residents participated in these unseemly actions, which were not even typical of the behavior patterns of many of the perpetrators. Although a larger minority of the community approved of, or tolerated, vigilante-style actions, many residents, probably a majority, were only vaguely aware of them.

These qualifications in no way lessen the significance of this dark, demonic underside of Canarsie life. The exception more often than the rule in most societies, collective action is usually the métier of small bands of partisans, and there is no guarantee that activists accurately mirror the thinking of the community as a whole. In Canarsie the cadres of the racially aggrieved had enormous influence beyond their actual numbers and support. The fire-bombing of a black family, for example, although carried out by only two or three residents in a population of 70,000, conveyed a powerful message to minorities in surrounding neighborhoods. Blacks might reasonably decide that they did not wish to test the representativeness of violent attacks. Such acts also influenced outsiders' images of the character of the people who lived in Canarsie. The vast majority of law-abiding citizens were tainted by their militant neighbors.

The striking feature in all the various efforts of Canarsians to exert influence was their increased participation, both inside and outside conventional channels. They resorted to arson, racist ranting, and vigilantism. They engaged in ethnic feuding, formed block associations and crime patrols, and tried civil disobedience to halt busing. They fashioned new concepts of racial pride, middle-class pride, and ethnic pride. They chanted "America, love it or leave it," crafted the slogan, "Canarsie Schools for Canarsie Children," and called for "law and order." And they voted, sometimes with feet, at other times with fists, but especially by deserting the Democratic party, smiling upon the Republican party, and chasing after third parties.

Reaction was a disorderly affair. Backlash contained democratic, populist, conspiratorial, racist, humanistic, pragmatic, and meritocratic impulses. Each moment of insurgency was shaped by notions of justice, calculations of self-interest, and resources of retaliation. Each method of redress had a different price tag, required a greater or lesser investment of time, risk, and knowledge, and held out the hope of different returns of gain or solace.[1]

Jews and Italians exerted influence, punished enemies, and forged alliances in different fashion. Distinct taboos and sensitivities speeded or impeded the mobilization of each group. Their partisan loyalties determined which institutional forms were available to channel discontent. Finally, the two varied in their penchant for settling grudges with fisticuffs, in the strength of their traditions of lawlessness, and in their faith in official channels of remedy. Italians and Jews were "combat ready" in unique ways and in different spheres. Although the two ethnic groups did not achieve a seamless identity, they did move in tandem. Threat blurred ethnic and religious boundaries. Beneath the camouflage of their classical ethnic elements, Jewish reaction and Italian reaction were kindred spirits. Vulnerability underwrote a defensive spirit that spread resistance from the working class to the middle class, from conservative citizens to liberal citizens, from Catholic enclaves to Jewish enclaves.

Mobilization materialized first in local drives to protect neighborhood stability. Canarsians were in agreement on the value of home and children. Their precious, tangible quality contrasted with ambiguous threats from beyond the locale. A conservative analyst of local politics defined the impediments to mobilizing the lower middle classes around abstract, symbolic, or idealistic issues. "You can't organize Canarsie people around ethnicity. And you can't organize them around sex. I don't care if they're pro-gay or anti-gay. There's only one kind of activism you can have in Canarsie: you can organize them around protecting their bucks or their kids." The *Citizens News* described the goad to action as a direct threat to the community. "You cannot oversaturate a middle class community with minority students, without eventually causing revolt or exodus."[2]

Exodus and revolt define the extremes of the spectrum of the means of influence. Albert Hirschman has similarly identified the margin of play in people's responses to dissatisfaction. "To resort to voice, rather than exit, is for the customer or member to make an attempt at changing the practices, policies, and outputs of the firm from which one buys or the organization to which one belongs."[3]

The luxury of exodus, which was perilously dependent on larger movements of credit, housing starts, and interest rates, lay beyond the means of many Canarsians in the late 1970s. High interest rates prevented wholesale white flight, even though blacks had begun moving onto the blocks near the Breukelen project, an influx made possible by the slack white market for homes in that part of Canarsie. On a number of occasions a housing activist who lived a few blocks from the area threatened whites who were known to be showing their houses to blacks. Later, it gave him no small pleasure that in 1980 his block still had no blacks living on it. "It would kill me to go to a closing and sit there across from blacks." Despite his discomfiture with the growing black presence in Canarsie, he had to stay put. "I was never this afraid before. All my friends are saying, 'We can't afford to leave, we can't run this time.' Do you think I'd be here in Canarsie if mortgages were reasonable? Should I go from 5 percent to 14 percent?"

Chance happenings occasionally added to someone's determination to quit the city. An insurance salesman, the morning after his decision to move to Arizona, told of a conflict between his normal restraint and the opposing pull of his frazzled nerves. Sitting in an office in the shadow of the Verrazano Narrows Bridge, conduit of white flight to Staten Island and New Jersey, he stated, "Staying here is going to involve me in trouble. I just can't tolerate it any more. I had my calculator stolen from the office. The 911 police calls go unanswered. There are locks on the windows and gratings and cages on the storefronts. You see, I was brought up poor in Red Hook without gratings on the window."

A few days earlier a carload of Puerto Ricans had pulled up beside him at a light, and a passenger had hurled some chicken bones out the window. "I told them, 'Don't throw garbage.' The guy said, 'Fuck you, everybody drops garbage.' I try to be tolerant, I try to make things look nice. But the chicken bones were the last straw. That was unforgivable. I can't tolerate the abuses of others."

Canarsians, then, did not simply tote up the risks and returns of reaction. While the calculus of exit highlights the shrewdness of backlash, it tends to obscure its passions. The stereotype of the frenzied hardhat, however, captures a plain, if partial, truth. Threat imposed psychic as well as social burdens on the people of Canarsie. A politics of unreason was not their sole response, but it was one of the most unsavory. An effective means of influence, yelling could also be an act of exasperation, recommended chiefly for the cathartic relief it afforded the aggrieved.[4]

The tension between feelings of injury and of impotence fostered an admiration for experts in vituperation who might pay back the minorities in symbolic kind. Spiro Agnew's popularity with resentful Middle Americans stemmed in part from the opportunity he gave them to participate in verbal retaliation against black adversaries. An Italian conservative remembered, "George Wallace sure told them niggers a thing or two!" At Madison Square Garden he had felt joyous that the Alabama governor's voice had silenced the minorities. "Wallace told them, 'Make all the noise you want now, but when I become president, you better watch out.' Wallace wasn't kissing the ass of the blacks to get their votes. He spoke free and told the truth. He was a man who would let them have it." In general, only the most desperate and racist citizens expressed their wish to scream by voting for the Alabama governor in the 1968 presidential race. While Wallace approached the 10 percent mark in the Italian lunchpail districts, he received virtually no Jewish votes. Throughout the North his supporters ranked high on vengefulness, as measured by their agreement with statements like, "Sometimes I have felt that the best thing for our country might be the death of some of our political leaders" or "Some politicians who have had their lives threatened probably deserve it."[5]

The same logic of vicarious revenge can be detected in an Italian bricklayer's gloating: "A black got a beating for stealing a bike the other night. It was the greatest thing I ever heard!" What the aggrieved could not remedy in deed might be resolved figuratively through the barbs of bitter humor; they found solace in the manner of the Eskimo who uses "little, sharp words, like the wooden splinters which I hack off with my ax."[6] "The Department of Health, Education and Welfare is telling us what to do. They're telling us to fill out those forms of the ethnic census." With mock ingenuousness, he advised cooperation. "Okay, I'd put on the form thirty-nine niggers and four spicks." The motive force behind this expressive side of voice was *ressentiment,* a sentiment produced in social milieus that do not permit easy exit. "Revenge," Max Scheler stressed, "tends to be transformed into *ressentiment* the more it is directed against lasting situations which are felt to be 'injurious' but beyond one's control—in other words, the more the injury is experienced as a destiny."[7]

The resentful screams did not occur only in the solitude of a voting booth or in private fantasies of retribution. When rumors of houses being sold to blacks, muggings within Canarsie, rowdiness at a black disco on the edge of the neighborhood, and whispers of the renewal of an ancient busing order unnerved the members of one backlash group, an unemployed glazier divined a coming Armageddon. "The revolution is coming between black and white, we whites have been taking it. But we're finally rising up, we're striking back, there will be no more taking it!" Another Italian man told the group, "I know how these blacks operate. There will be a lot of them when it starts. I saw this when Martin Luther King died. The cops were told not to do anything." Someone cried out, "Why can't we do what the blacks do? Let's firebomb them. We're better than they are. This wouldn't happen in the South." A man dressed in the rough garb of a workman prescribed a hybrid of Italian fascism and the Soviet Gulag. "Mussolini knew what to do. He saw a guy without a job and said, 'Hey you, you're going to Siberia.'" A trucker wailed, "And now they're taking our handguns away from us!"

In the hyberbolic imagination of some of Canarsie's angriest residents, the ordinary errand-going of blacks was converted into an uncanny presence. "They're bringing bad people around here," fretted a woman. "Something's going on! Blacks are walking up and down our streets." Her comrade said, "The niggers aren't bashful. They want Canarsie. They're brazen walking around here. We've got to be on guard, we have to do something about it. It's all slipping away from us." Someone reported, "The niggers are showing their faces around here, but they don't belong here. There is a conspiracy. Someone is trying to panic us." Who was the someone? An unknown nemesis? Blacks? Liberals? Or the people of Canarsie, working themselves into a fit?

In the homey quarters of a civic group, a fringe of the residents flexed their muscles, at least in the free regions of the mind. They envisioned their rebirth as heroic actors who would strut about Brownsville as brazenly as they imagined their black tormentors did when they walked through Canarsie. But the bravado was false. The fear of enemies with diabolical powers was the dominant theme. "They're trying to panic us" was a confession of the speaker's own vulnerability. "It's all slipping away from us" defined the sense of loss beneath the rage.

Most reactionaries preferred, in Shakespeare's image, to speak daggers. A few actually threw them. All the ambiguities of a life played out under the restraint of law then dissolved in the sensuous joys of rough and tumble. One angry right-winger was ever alert for an incident that would ignite his short fuse. Hidden by the curtains near his front door, a shotgun lay close at hand. "I have my gun here, see?" he demonstrated. "The brother of the nigger I got charges against said he'd get me. I saw this light-skinned negro out front, circling the block, so I got my shotgun. I would have killed him if he entered my house." On another occasion he divulged, "I just can't take all these incidents I seen. The niggers took a lady's cigarettes and knocked over a baby carriage." He ran after the suspects, down Rockaway Parkway past Canarsie High School, until he caught up with one of them under the Belt Parkway. "I had to release my feelings. I worked the nigger over real good, I mauled him, I kicked the shit out of him. I seen him later, he says to me, 'Hey, I remember you, you whipped my ass a couple of weeks ago.' Arrogant! You'd think he'd stay out of my community."

The far extreme of local opinion should not lend an exaggerated impression of the irrationality of protest. After a long soliloquy, a woman who had been the victim of black or Hispanic criminals on more than half a dozen occasions turned somber. "When the blacks robbed me, I left all that black-and-white-together stuff." Her assertion reminds us that no matter how demonic were the racist fears of some residents, the people of Canarsie faced real dangers. The strains of place evoked a variety of reasonable attempts, both democratic and authoritarian, to master reality and avert risk.

To forestall attack, Canarsians took a cautious approach to the urban world, replacing expectations of civility from strangers with jaundiced forecasts of danger. They created mental maps and social schedules of good neighborhoods and bad ones, good times and bad times. They transposed stories of past attacks and commonsense notions of "bad-looking" people to pedestrians and situations that bore any faint resemblance to these mental blueprints. They limited their customary rounds to conform with definitions of safe and treacherous zones. Underlying all these maneuvers was a diffuse suspicion of blacks. The remarks of a Jewish woman exemplified their attempts to find clues to likely predators and cues for fighting or fleeing. "I guess I don't really hate the blacks. I hate that they make me look over my shoulder."[8]

However imperfect or superstitious their basis, predictive clues reduce the feeling of risk, and they are often more than consoling fictions. The signs that elicited alarm included race, but not indiscriminately. Young black males, especially in groups, coiffed with Afros or sporting sneakers ("felony footware") triggered apprehension. The wife of a dockworker felt like quite the expert in decoding the intentions of her fellow subway straphangers. The sharp umbrellas and floppy brim hats she associated with black gangs made her vigilant. "These hoodlum blacks act like animals. They act as if the world owed them a living. The way they walk through the train with those long umbrellas and round hats, they try to scare you on purpose. I don't know what their idea is. You got me." On the subway or on the sidewalk a move by a black, like crossing the street or posing an ostensibly innocent question, was searched for hints of evil. Routine travel became an intricate interpretive game.

Canarsians learned to read the environment as well as the tabloids. "Normal appearances," to borrow Erving Goffman's phrase, yielded to the "insanity of place," which exacted a price in costly attentiveness. "Whatever range of risk and opportunity an environment contains," Goffman said, "the individual exposed to these considerations typically comes to terms with them, making what adjustments are necessary in order to routinely withdraw his main attention from them, and get on with other matters." Such a routinization of everyday life has a normative aspect, for "the individual not only anticipates uneventfulness but also feels that he has a moral right to count on it."[9]

Caution did not always suffice to guard against danger. A brawny Italian man worked for a company that placed mesh screens on its trucks to protect the men from the spray of broken bottles that rained down on them from time to time in ghetto areas. Racial conflict diverted labor-management struggles into fights over the workplace, the aim of which was not to secure the men's control over the labor process but to protect them from vandals. The men insisted on two-person crews in the ghettos. "When I work a ghetto area, there's supposed to be a man above and a man below. When I see trouble, I pack the truck and go." Many of the workers, in a posture of defensive caution, armed themselves. "You know how many guys carry things? I got guys right now, I could name names, they carry shotguns under the hoods of their cars."

Vigilance sometimes slid into violence. A white man was working a job in Brownsville when an unkempt black man approached him in what seemed like a menacing manner. Later the black returned with four accomplices. "I seen them coming and got worried, so I reached for my hammer. It's a big five-pound job, with a chisel-like thing on the end. You use it before you drill the holes. Anyway, I was up on the ladder, and they came toward me, so I took a swing at the guy. I got him good, and the others seen me come off the ladder. Now, I'm six feet four, so they started to go, so I just took the hammer and threw it." He paused. "You ever seen a tomahawk go? Well I threw the hammer and got him right in the back."

The teenage sons of Italian workers showed the same penchant for physical action, and a small number of them usurped the police role of detecting, questioning, and punishing blacks they took to be suspiciously out of place.[10] One Canarsie black man attributed his fear of two areas in Canarsie to the vigilante actions of such youthful guardians: "In those Italian areas, I find there is much more animosity to blacks than elsewhere in Canarsie. Years back, even when I was growing up on the Lower East Side of New York, I had to run from the Italians in order to get to school. It was like a track meet, because the local Italian boys, with their garrison belts and spikes, would chase me through the streets. I hate to put the caption of racism on the community as a whole, but there are elements within the Canarsie community which scare the hell out of me."

The man's leery attitude was well advised. In one of the areas of Old Canarsie where he feared to tread, a band of Italian youths spotted a black teenager who seemed to be peering into someone's back yard. "The nigger noticed us watching him, and he took off, so we took off." A wild cowboy-style chase ensued. The black boarded a bus on Ralph Avenue, but he still was not out of danger. "We pulled up in our car, and we got on the bus . . . This nigger didn't know how to act, this nigger was jumpin' and scared." They questioned him. "You were the one in the yard, right?" The black youth replied, "No, man, I didn't mean nothing, I was going to a party." The boys started to beat him. "So we led off with a kick, then I swear to God, rabbit punches to his face, zing, zing, zing. Do you know what would have happened to us in their neighborhood? They would have killed us or something. I almost broke my knuckles. He had a hard head."

Youthful warriors rarely operate without communal permission. The Italian boys formed a proxy police force on behalf of a segment of the Italian community that did not accept the state's exclusive right to the means of violence. Two separate systems of social control struggled for authority. The formal system of law was hedged with rules that sharply delimited discretion; the informal system generated its own notions of justice and remedy. The prevailing practical morality of many Old Canarsie Italians encouraged a preemptive strike; "Do what you gotta do" now, ask questions later.

The milieus of plebeian youths and adults celebrate toughness as a cultural ideal, supply their members with experience in fighting, and reject the sanctity of due process. None of these dispositions, however, accounts for acts and fantasies of self-help. Self-help emerged from a confluence of internal disposition and external conditions. If we hold constant the bent toward vigilantism, features of the environment equally encouraged the decline in trust in the state's ability to detect and punish. Unsurprisingly, a burly hardhat who packed a loaded pistol under the car seat and believed that "commies and others who want to harm us" do not deserve freedom of speech argued, "Citizens have to do something about crime themselves. If I was in my car and I saw a kid mugging an elderly man or woman, I'd stop the car, get my gun, and kill the kid." As the ability of the state to maintain order seemed to dissipate in a web of fiscal, social, and legal constraints, Canarsians of quite different dispositions began to flirt with alternative ways to protect themselves.

One gentle Italian man truly believed in the law and revered due process, but he felt obliged to protect his family from danger. Traumatized by a robbery, he had soured on restraint. "Now," he said, "I have a twelve-gauge shotgun, and I will kill the bastards without thinking." He prized equanimity, but that day, choked with emotion, he saw his sunny bearing vanish. He worried that he might not be able to control his tempestuous impulses. As he told it, respectability was a kind of badge of his arduous climb out of the poverty of immigrant life. His growing passion compromised that cherished, hard-won moral stature.

The drift of pacific Jews and gentle Italians toward fantasies of self-help suggests the power of the environment to weaken faith in due process. Canarsians who wished that criminals could be rehabilitated did not have the luxury of staying off the streets until someone discovered how to accomplish that noble aim. As they walked through the city, they were mindful that felons were copping pleas, exploiting technicalities, and returning to the streets.

Few residents, however, were eager or able to practice self-help; the state had to carry the burden of protection. Michel Foucault has argued that at the midpoint of western cultural development the state replaced private kin-group revenge with its own more majestic vengeance, but the zest for retribution endured as a vital part of the spectacle of the scaffold. Eventually, ferocity underwent the same disenchantment as other aspects of modern culture, and a more dispassionate rationale came to support punishment. "Instead of taking revenge, criminal justice should simply punish."[11]

Could the state even punish, Canarsians wondered, when it was hampered by the sociology of reasons, by finicky worries about rights, or by compassion for the "animals?" An Italian building contractor argued, "Too much is given away to the criminal. They feel sorry for them. It makes me very bitter that people do something wrong and get away with it. I think the punks that commit these crimes should be punished to the fullest extent of the law." A Jewish booster of law and order lambasted procedural "shoulds" that interfered with adaptive responses to risk. "I'm a purist on law and order: I believe you smack heads when you must." In the mid-1960s, 33 percent of white Brooklyn residents believed "unfairness and brutality may have to be tolerated if the welfare of the community is at stake," 63 percent agreed that "any person who hides behind the law when questioned about his activities doesn't deserve much consideration," and 38 percent said that "if the police stuck strictly to the rules and gave every suspect his rights, they would never succeed in convicting criminals."[12]

Like fantasies of self-help, support for strictness was externally induced as well as self-imposed. Physical realities pushed Jewish and

Italian residents who believed in procedural rights in the abstract toward a this-worldly demand for discipline. At a meeting to discuss a rash of burglaries and muggings, a group of neighbors fumed over the apparent helplessness of the police before the forces of lawlessness. One man who was ambivalent warned of the dangers of dictatorship, "Thank God we don't have a police state in America. But"— the voice of clear and present danger—"we do need more police." A victimized resident pleaded with a black policeman, "You know the property is at the headquarters of the gang, can't you recover our property through any means, legal or illegal? I don't care how you do it." The policeman retorted, "You'd better care. We can't violate the Constitution or deprive people of their rights." A lonely voice seconded the thought. "That's right, it's right to preserve our rights. We don't want the police knocking down *our* doors."

Bonds of neighborhood friendship with policemen increased the residents' natural receptivity to police interpretations of reality. In Brooklyn as a whole, although citizens' appraisals of the police did not influence their attitude toward the Civilian Review Board in 1966, Catholics' friendship or kinship with police did have a significant influence. Some 54 percent of Brooklyn Catholics had relatives or close friends on the force, and more than 20 percent of Brooklyn Jews had similarly close ties with law officers.[13]

Police revert to informal standards of "doing justice," wrote Albert J. Reiss, "when their efforts to control are subverted by other organizations in the subsystem."[14] Occasionally, Canarsie police and citizens cut a deal to thwart that subversion. A civic leader and his accomplices wanted to "clean up" a drug-infested playground in Canarsie where white pushers were dealing from the sanctuary of a van. "We were concerned about shooting up drugs and sexual acts in the dark corners of the playgrounds. Me and my buddies beat the shit out of them." The officer told them the laws of search did not permit him to enter the vehicle but gave the green light to their mission. "The officer said, 'Go in the van and beat the shit out of them,' and that's what we did. We did what security requires. There are the great kids who congregate and the animals, the junkies, and we clean out the animals."

The diverse forces encouraging strictness point to a source of the attraction of law-and-order candidates like George Wallace beyond their function as vehicles of cathartic release. Unlike his southern boosters, Wallace's supporters in the North did not show greater hostility to the civil rights movement than those who did not support him. What distinguished them was their endorsement of repressive answers to lawlessness.[15] Wallace personified a style of settling grudges that was legitimized in one portion of the Italian working class by untamed masculine force, by the psychology of deterrent realism, and by indifference to civil liberties. Through words and mien, Wallace pledged to "take care of business" in the same unflinching way vigilantes "did what they had to do" when they "cleaned up an incident" in a neighborhood.

The son of a Neopolitan immigrant who had worked most of his life as a New York sanitationman invoked the images of Wallace the punisher. He was obsessed with the disorders that had swept across America in the 1960s, as well as with the hazards of living in New York City, and he applied the lessons of the strict Italian patriarch to black rioters and ghetto criminals. "I wanted to see Wallace get in there. He was for law and order, and he done his darnest to keep the criminals down, to show them their place. He said, 'No funny stuff,' he was going to punish them. He said if the blacks did wrong, he wasn't going to let them get away with it."

Vigilante actions disclosed the dangers to democracy of informal dispensation of justice. The teenage son of an electrician told how he and his mates had chased some blacks out of Canarsie one night. He had spied three blacks on bikes and yelled, " 'Hey, get the niggers.' One of my friends threw a garbage pail at them and knocked one of them off the bike, but this girl's father protected him from us beating him up. We know we'd get the same treatment in their neighborhood!" As I watched a group of Italian boys storm out of a bagel and bialy shop in hot pursuit of three blacks bicycling down Flatlands Avenue to the barks of "Get the niggers," I felt transported to a world of lynch mobs and magnolia trees. An elderly Jewish woman grabbed hold of my shirt and cried out against such Cossacklike practices in a thick Yiddish accent. "Those black boys didn't even do anything!"

My argument aims only to understand one aspect of white ethnic violence. Canarsie's lawless ones, clustered in the provincial Italian community where traditions of self-help rivaled those of democratic lawfulness, believed they were following the pragmatic form of reasoning cited by Malcolm X in his analysis of just and unjust aggression: "The Bible says there is a time for anger." He was using Judeo-Christian canons to justify black reprisal, but in a universalist jump he recognized a valid condition for white violence. "I feel that if white people were attacked by Negroes—if the forces of law prove unable, or inadequate, or reluctant to protect those whites from those Negroes—then those white people should protect and defend themselves from those Negroes, using arms if necessary."[16]

High School Race Riot

"They go for that eye-for-an-eye stuff . . . they just go after any blacks . . . Tough if it's the wrong one they get."

The game of resistance and accommodation was played out at Canarsie High School by students who alternated the ploys of evasion with the dance of reprisal. Large organizations like schools suffer from unique problems of order that vary with the heterogeneity of their populations, the legitimacy that members accord authorities, and the setting. Institutions partially reflect the social tensions of the larger environment, yet they create dilemmas of their own, or complicate existing ones, by imposing schedules and traffic patterns on mutually antagonistic members. The mixing of black and white teenagers on the neutral ground of the high school made abrasive contact more likely, while rendering ceremonies of avoidance and détente ineffective.[17]

Students avoided or appeased hostile parties by remaining alert in the corridors, skirting zones of transition like dangerous bathrooms, where no agreement on the rules of joint usage prevailed, and herding close to the enclaves where numbers, proximity to authorities, or informal consensus on ownership ensured safety. But the students could not always choreograph their movements with precision or escape involvement in others' fights. A fight in the gym or the lunchroom tended to spill over its original boundaries to entangle networks of allies and enemies.

Disputes between the races revived old rhythms of communal rivalry. Rabbi Alter Landesman, a chronicler of Jewish Brownsville, who lived in Canarsie in the 1970s, told of a fight in the early 1900s between Brownsville Jews and young toughs from Canarsie. On Rosh Hashanah, observant Jews recited the Tashlich prayers at a stream near Rockaway and New Lots avenues. "No sooner did they near the stream than they were set upon with stones by a group of Canarsie hoodlums. Fortunately, the Jews were accompanied by a dog, who saved the day for them."[18]

The origins of racial hostility in the 1970s was blurred in the mists of more recent history. Many Italian boys had cut their teeth on stories of older brothers' vendettas with blacks. An Italian man in his thirties laughed, remembering "my rowdy days as a hitter." To be a hitter in that ancient era of the early 1960s entailed hanging out with rambunctious buddies, sporting a pompadour hairdo, and devoting one's life to "chicks, rock and roll, and fighting." "The last thing I wanted to see was a peaceful year of high school. I was completely ecstatic at the fact we were fighting the blacks. That was my cup of tea."

A decade later racial feuding remained primarily an Italian passion. Alert to slights to their manhood, proficient in fighting, and forbidden to run from trouble by ideals of bravery, Italian working-class boys sometimes found it hard to resist involvement in drawn-out cycles of retaliation. The reluctance of the Jews to get physical puzzled one Italian youth in the mid-1970s. "The only ones fighting around the school that day you were there were Italians. I mean, the Jewish kids crack me up. They don't fight. They actually hid inside the room and locked the doors or ran home. The Italian boys I hang with have less respect for Jews now 'cause they run from something like this. They go to school, and when it comes to protecting what is theirs, they turn around and put their feet in the wind."

That one skirmish outside Canarsie High School in the fall of 1976 tells us a great deal about the larger dynamic of racial polarization. Because I observed much of the action as it unfolded, and knew a number of the participants, I was able to follow the fight closely through its many unusual twists. The episode began in a scuffle between a black and a white youth. What the whites viewed as the violation of proportional retaliation struck the blacks as the rightful completion of a natural cycle of disputing. Up through that enlargement of the dispute, the feud adhered to the conventional back-and-forth rhythm. The spread of the fight from a one-on-one to a struggle between the races is understandable, but unresolved questions remain. Why did a racial fight in the 1970s take a turn so different from a race rumble in the mid-1960s? Why did the idiom used by the community to interpret the controversy owe so much to larger struggles over jobs and political power? Why, that is, did the vendetta become a truly political struggle? To answer these questions will require us to trace the spread of liability and involvement step by step through the mazes of local friendship and politics.[19]

Two earlier fights had preceded the vendetta. "But," an Italian participant puzzled, "they were *fair ones,* that's what got me. The colored kid had beat this white kid, see, but the colored kid says he was coming back with his boys 'cause everybody broke up the fight! He was saying, 'Why you break it up, man? I was kicking his ass!' " Next, when a friend of the black youth bumped into an Italian boy on the handball courts outside Canarsie High School, "He fucked the colored kid up, he gave him a bloody nose, bloody eyes, a bloody mouth. He really had this kid put away!"

The black youth returned with reinforcements. "I seen the colored coming down the driveway," related one white participant in the ensuing fight. "First you only could see twenty of them coming, but after that they had broken into the shop classes and stolen tools and stuff like hammers and screwdrivers." A melee erupted on the playground. "So this short Puerto Rican kid first comes walking by, and he's got his hand like this, I knew he had something in his sleeve. So I turn around and tell my friend, 'Hey, watch out, he's got a pipe,' and then he turns around and swings the pipe at me and hits me in the head . . . I was dazed, I was seeing stars, I was like trying to shake it off, you know, and I just looked up and then I got stabbed."

After the stabbing, which sent the boy to the hospital with a severe injury, a band of the victim's associates prepared to take revenge. A few days later, as we sat in the lunchroom of Canarsie High School, one member of the vengeance squad described their state of mind. "All our boys went crazy. Everybody met with bats and whatever else they had. We just went wild, all the neighborhood boys we hang with. We were screaming, 'Revenge,' 'Kill the niggers,' 'Getting back.' " His black friends told the white boy, "We're staying out of it, man, I'm just going to run home after the school bell rings. I don't want to have anything to do with it. Man, when you white boys start breaking, there's going to be trouble."

White reprisal elicited a black rejoinder, this time away from Canarsie High School with a new set of white and black participants. From the window of her attached rowhouse, the wife of a cabby saw the black raiding party, alleged to be members of a black nationalist youth gang, moving into the white home base near Wilson Junior High. A dozen blacks armed with canes and accompanied by a Doberman pinscher came running from Breukelen Projects through Canarsie and darted into the Wilson playground. "I saw them reach the park and start to attack a youngster who was so viciously being set upon." When the police arrived, the youths streaked from the scene. On their way back to the projects, they spotted an old Italian man on his front porch. "His back was to them. He did not see what was coming. One of the boys jumped up on the fence behind the elderly man, shouting, 'You mother-fucking white man,' and with those words and great force brought the cane down on the eighty-five-year-old man's head, spilling his blood all over his own yard. I screamed."

The black foray into Canarsie set off another wave of violence. Prior to the incursion the cycle had been confined to teenage boys fighting in out-of-the-way places like the handball court. The gratuitous attack on the old man departed from the pattern. The play now fell to the whites, and events began to expand rather than to contain the dispute. At each of several switches, gatekeepers opened new paths of involvement, moving the fight toward a feud. The drama unfolded on three levels simultaneously. First, the victim's circle of "the boys we hang out with" prepared to "break," or engage in self-help. Second, relatives, neighbors, and kin—some of whom had been active in the antibusing crisis—contacted conservative civic leaders with whom they were already acquainted. Third, a number of political leaders entered the fray on their own initiative, sought out complainants, and improvised a role as third parties.

The duty to strike back devolved on the running buddies of the injured boy and the young male relatives of his girl friend. They formed a clique of mainly Italian boys who for years had resented the special treatment they believed black students exacted from cowering white teachers. The mother of one overheard the boys plotting strategy. "I told him he should make sure he don't get in trouble, but I got the usual 'Don't worry.'" The ethics of the street, with its literal calibration of injury and reply, preempted the procedures of law: "They go for that eye-for-an-eye stuff. They might get the wrong one that did it, but they just go after any blacks. When the boy got hurt two days before, they got all riled up. 'Cause their friend got hurt, they got to get revenge on anyone. I told them it makes no sense to get the ones who weren't there, who weren't the right ones that did it, but they said, 'Our two were innocent!' They just wanted anyone to pay for what happened. It's the street rules. Tough if it's the wrong one they get."

The scope of the fighting widened at this point, branching outward to implicate adult residents, civic groups, and political operatives. The local leaders mobilized by the incident did not represent a random draw. The patrons of the Italian boys included the Canarsie Conservative party, the Concerned Citizens of Canarsie, and local

Republican leaders. The absence of Jefferson Club Democrats, who preempted a key role on all public issues, showed how resistant such volatile grievances were to settlement through patronage politics. It also revealed the lack of ties between the Democratic establishment and the bedrock community of backlash, and the "tacit coordination" that matched audiences and leaders who served each other's mutual interests.[20]

Apprehension over the playground incident prompted a night meeting of concerned residents, a loose network of Jewish and Italian backlash activists outside the establishment civic groups, that had formed during the antibusing crisis of 1972. Instead of diverting the avengers into peaceful channels, they pushed the aggrieved youths to the brink of violence. One man harangued the audience. "The blacks split open the head of one of our boys, and nobody will tell the kids to arm themselves. But as a parent, I will tell my kid to arm himself." A member of the Conservative party equated physical reprisal with freedom of expression. "It's our right to dissent." The wife of a craftsman lamented the special advantages she claimed blacks enjoyed in martial prowess. "Face it, there's not a cop in the precinct who can catch the fattest of the niggers . . . Now I'm not calling for retaliation. Just a little deterrence." A civic leader with many friends in the local precinct relayed a message of support: "A lot of the cops are saying, 'Good luck, do what you gotta do.' "

A discussion of the right to bear arms interrupted the meeting. A civic leader admitted, "I carry a weapon. I've no license for it, but at least I'll be alive." The wife of a construction worker advised, "Carry something. Don't be a jerk." Another woman retorted, "Learn their ways. Do what the niggers do. They bury butcher knives in the weeds." Another woman decried the ultimate in black special advantages: "The black girls have knives in their Afros, but I got to go into my handbag."

The kids in the room took the adult passion as a license for action. An Italian youth broke into the elders' back-and-forth, "If they're armed, then we have to be armed." A teenager who later played a prominent role in the retaliation sloughed off the stance of appeasement. "I've been hiding in a corner for eighteen years of my life. I've been facing niggers and Puerto Ricans with their switchblades. But I've got a .32 automatic now." One of the adults told him, "You have to make a stand. Get the dirty wash under the rug."

The convocation shows the correspondence between teenage street bands and the shock troops of militant backlash. Beyond the cunning of political hustlers in search of a clientele, beyond the coincidence of acquaintanceship, the youthful champions of self-help and their adult backers were joined by a moral affinity. Both were loose cliques whose members adhered to the parochial codes of local knowledge and folk remedy. Both accepted that canon of plebeian manliness, "Do what you gotta do." Both felt alienated from respectable channels of civic and political influence.

Early the next morning, on an overcast fall day, members of the clique of white avengers provoked blacks entering Canarsie High School, and one of them barked, "The niggers are beating up my friends, you niggers go home." With studied expertise, a policeman separated the races, but the white boy, a sash of metal chain around his waist, insisted, "We'll take care of this our own way."

As tempers flared on the street, a meeting of student representatives, school officials, and community groups inside began to discuss the grievances of white youths who were boycotting classes to protest lax school security. The gathering, a caricature of interest-group pluralism, included leaders of the aggrieved white students, the black head of the student government, a district leader of the Jefferson Democrats, delegates from the Italian-American Civil Rights League, Alan Erlichman of the Concerned Citizens of Canarsie, and officials from the security unit of New York City high schools, from the offices of minority representatives of Brownsville, and from the Board of Education.

Violent action in the streets and protest politics in the school were tandem responses to the same adaptive dilemmas. The student council president presented the following petition to the school administration, marking the political import of geopolitical struggle.

WE THE STUDENTS OF CANARSIE HIGH SCHOOL BOYCOTTED FOR THESE REASONS:

WE *ALL* THE STUDENTS OF CANARSIE HIGH SCHOOL MAKE THE FOLLOWING DEMANDS TO INSURE OUR SAFETY WHILE ATTENDING SCHOOL:

1. A realistic plan for effective security in bathrooms.

2. Strictly enforced traffic controls in all corridors prohibiting gangs or groups from collecting in hallways—program cards must be checked.

3. Preventing groups of strangers from loitering on the outside of school grounds during the school day.

4. Absolutely no weapons allowed in the school—this includes all implements which might be used as weapons such as canes, umbrellas, sticks, chains, etc.

5. All lockers to be locked with only school locks—unannounced inspection of lockers at irregular intervals must be conducted by school officials.

6. All entrances must be controlled so as to insure that only students and authorized persons are admitted to the school.

7. A grievance procedure must be instituted to process apparent violations of the school safety rules.

8. A security force sensitive to and reflecting the racial makeup of the student body of the school. Increased to a size capable of enforcing all of the above.

The petition's emphasis on security contrasts with the movement for student rights that appeared in some high schools in the 1960s. Students in Canarsie did not ask for the freedoms of the open classroom. Instead, they commanded officials to expand surveillance, to deprive students of rights of access and movement, to search and seize property. Just as the parents asked the state to provide more order and less liberty, students asked the educational state to secure premises rather than rights. Students and parents alike viewed civil liberties as an impediment to acquiring a more fulfilling life. Their identification with the victims made it hard for them to imagine that they might lose something from an authoritative state. A convergence took place between the codes of lower-middle-class life, which devalue abstract conceptions of rights, and the environment in which Canarsians carried out their tasks, which suggested democracy might be too dangerous in a volatile plural society.

The fight in the high school was part of a larger movement of ethnic succession. The final demand on the petition made this more politicized meaning of the rumble explicit: "A security force sensitive to and reflecting the racial makeup of the student body. Increased to a size capable of enforcing all of the above [demands]."

The white plea for racial sensitivity fulfilled an unspoken desire: to hoist the minorities with their own petard. Had not blacks claimed in 1968 that white teachers could not relate to black students? White students now said black security guards could not give whites a fair shake. More than a rhetorical contrivance, the grievance was deeply felt and long-standing. Around the time of the rumble, one white student complained about the dual system of justice in the high school. "Well, in Canarsie High School, you could say, the security guards are all niggers, so whenever the black chicks are cutting out, the guards hang with the nigger chicks in the hallway, and they don't like to hassle them. It's ridiculous. Like if you had white guards in the school, you wouldn't have all these niggers in the hallways."

The black head of security for New York City schools bravely tried to calm the tensions. "This meeting is not about blacks or whites but about *students'* demands for more security guards. We are as concerned with security as you are, but we lost one-half of our people in the budget cutbacks at the office of security . . . That's why Canarsie has the small number of guards it has. That's what you got and you got to live with it." An Italian student broke in, "I feel people are beating around the bush. We're concerned about having only black security guards. We want some of 'ours' we can go to." The official replied, "I have a predominantly minority force. I lived in the ghetto and grew up with white police, and I am thankful for police whether they are green or not." The student shot back, "You are making this a racial thing." The head of the Concerned Citizens of Canarsie interjected, "They come out of a predominantly white community and they want white guards to reflect this . . . Why not transfer a white guard in? We want an integrated staff so the kids can relate to him." A black woman quickly rejoined, "That's dangerous!"

The white demand for quotas effected a ritual counterclaim from the blacks. "If you follow that principle," said a spokesman for a black state senator from Brownsville, "then get the correct percentages of black teachers and supervisors. Now it's not reflective of the minority percentage in the school." The head of security summed up the fateful consequences of relying on quotas to redress injuries: "If you make it racial in one area, it's hard to keep racial percentages out of the others."

As the exasperated white youths listened to black adults argue for a color-blind norm of merit and the white adults laud the merits of quotas, they gave up on the powwow. "People come from Brownsville and stabbed one of our boys," cried a white youth. Another pronounced, "If it be we have to protect ourselves and carry something, we will carry something. We're not going to take these things." A black woman yelled, "Bring more black teachers to Canarsie."

Suddenly a staccato of pounding feet and screaming voices broke up the impasse of the meeting. Hundreds of students were running through the corridors of the school yelling, "Riot, riot, riot." The blood feud was moving toward its dénouement.

The precise sequence of events remains cloudy, for the brief battle was over by the time I reached the street. But one youth later told me, "Some of us white kids went over by the niggers and some words got started. Those niggers said something about there was three of them, and three of us should fight, make it even or something like that. And then I said something about how come fifteen guys beat up one guy." According to the white boys, a black youth threw a bottle, they took off after him, and he "ran into someone's fist." When he turned to flee, another white boy said, "I gave him my share of whatever," and cracked him across the head with a chain. "I didn't feel good that I was defending myself. It's just that what's the point of fifteen guys ganging up on one guy? Everybody was talking about having these stupid meetings, but it turns out you can't do it that way. Like the only way you can get 'em back is by doing like that." His companion felt more joy in violence. "I hit one on the legs with a thick stick. I said, 'Good, he won't run any more, he won't be able to walk any more probably, at least for a while, and stop beatin' up on white people.' "

The arrest of two white boys and a show of police force put a stop to the fighting. In the days that followed, a group of conservative activists took up the cause of the arrested youths and formed a Canarsie Two Defense Fund. The arrest of the whites struck them as evidence of a social order that pampered blacks and deprived whites of justice.

Canarsie's young warriors were like a ritual band bonded by the promise of blood vengeance. As the ethnographer of a fearsome Latin American tribe wrote, "The Jibaro certainly first of all wants to take revenge on the person who committed the crime, but if he cannot be caught it may instead be directed against some one of his relatives."[21] Such collective definitions of guilt may have a predictive value in urban settings, yet if it was reasonable, in some limited sense, for the whites to generalize revenge, their shortcircuiting of the lawful means of protection only encouraged blacks to use private methods of vindication.

At one point during the riot an angry mob of black youths swirled around the school grounds and surrounded me and an Italian man. One black exclaimed, "Hey, the honky chained a brother. We got to get a honky back." The man struggled to personalize the collective notion of liability. "That wasn't *all* white kids, but *one* dumb honky fuck, and we'll take care of him. Ask the kids, I'm for all of you, white and black, and I say now go inside or go on home." A black youth drained the tension from the encounter. "I know Sal, that's right, he's for all the kids." Another black youth shook his head. "Damn! These honkies are crazy. They're taking us down."

His words, "These honkies are crazy," seemed a fitting epitaph for a crazy day. It rescues us from the bias of looking at the blood feud only through Canarsie's eyes. Many of the blacks, or at least their parents, knew the taunts of "Niggers go home" that had greeted blacks when Canarsie High School opened its door in 1964. One of the white boys who participated in the fighting later admitted the ambiguities of private dispute settlement, especially its tendency to involve innocent bystanders:

> There's a problem, 'cause there are niggers that are all right, which is pretty much the majority of them, they don't hassle or anything, but there are the ones that are still in that crowd that are hassling, and you're beatin' up on the ones who didn't do anything and, you know, occasionally you get the ones who do something. I've thought about it a lot. Wow, what if this guy didn't even do anything, he's just got beat up for nothing. But then I start thinking of our friend, I mean what he do, he didn't do anything either.

The contradictions of the feud replicated those engendered by all forms of racial polarization, whether in the political arena or in the school yard. The cycle of vengeance was never completed. Instead of being self-cancelling, the feud set in motion a train of events that created new debts. One attack obliged another to even the score. "Private revenge," wrote Giovanni Lorenzoni, a turn-of-the-century student of the Sicilian Mafia, "increased murders because, if the offense is remedied by the state, the cycle closes; but if it is remedied by the individual, a new cycle is opened."[22]

Revenge may have had a short-term logic, but it diverted resources from solving the basic problems that had created the fighting in the first place. And it led to larger instabilities that detracted from the system's ability to survive, create, and produce. Feuding brought education to a temporary halt in Canarsie High School, just as racial polarization throughout New York City impeded the ability of the polity to serve the public good. Both in Canarsie and in the nation, the system choked on its conflicts.

Maintaining the Neighborhood

"I won't let them ruin Canarsie. I'll join a terror squad to keep them out."

In his analysis of the social foundations of economic behavior, Max Weber argued that "the economic source of 'receipts' (in a natural economy) generally lies in the monopolistic appropriation of opportunities to exploit property or services for a return. The underpinning of all these incomes is nothing but the *possibility* of violence in the defense of appropriated advantages. Predatory incomes [booty] and related modes of acquisition are the return on *actual* violence."[23]

The resort to violence against blacks was only one of the methods by which Canarsians protected their privileges in the housing market. The public triumph of protectionism stemmed in part from the stilling of integrationist voices, since home-owner and political groups tended to give a forum to a self-selected sample of defensive opinion, and integrationist factions had few incentives or opportunities for countering racial anxiety. More fundamentally, protectionism was inherent in an environment at risk. When property and security were threatened, invitations based on trust were replaced by wary exclusion; the open market yielded to the closure of racial monopoly, the universalism of law gave way before the particularism of property, and a resolve to control the unknown succeeded the acceptance of spontaneity. The cumulative effect of these developments was the creation of a two-tiered reality: on the surface a fictitious open market for purposes of impression management, and backstage a clandestine market in homes.

Canarsie's declining ability to replenish its white population, and the willingness of a growing black middle class to pay premium prices for desirable housing, gradually overcame the resistance of white home owners to sell to blacks. The home owners' shaky position modified the usual hierarchy of desirable and unwanted buyers. The terms of acceptability were renegotiated in line with current demographic realities, ethnic boundaries were stretched and altered, and certain kinds of nonwhites were bumped ahead of blacks as priority buyers. "I love the Orientals," said an Italian trucker in 1980, "because they mind their own business, they respect you as an individual, and their morals are good. They're a clean, family people. Race is really unimportant to me. The Koreans, the Filipinos, and the Chinese are decent people. It's the garbage I hate. I'd be happier if life was not this way, but it's a gamble I can't make. I'd prefer it if Canarsie turned into a Chinatown rather than seeing it become a Harlem."

Praying that the "right kind" of buyer would stumble upon the neighborhood struck many housing activists as a dangerous tempting of fate. Keeping information about vacancies out of circulation in the *New York Times,* where minorities might spot them, seemed inadequate. "We have to replace the whites who are leaving or getting old," a civic leader warned at an unofficial meeting of Canarsie's leadership. "Let's advertise in the Jewish, Italian, and Chinese papers. We've gotten good results from *Il Progresso.*" Yet the strategy of diffuse enticement also failed to turn around the inauspicious ratio of white to black demand. Like employers in need of scarce workers, the community now began to search for the objects of their ardent desire.[24]

The strategy shifted from excluding blacks to recruiting whites, in particular the windfall of emigré Jews who arrived from the Soviet Union in the 1970s. The Russian Jews were especially attractive candidates for that role. Significant numbers of them already resided in Brooklyn. They were not scattered randomly through the borough and lived well within the reach of the connections of the Canarsie Jewish community. A Jewish leader who was active in the effort to bring the Russians to Canarsie described the cynical motives behind the manufacture of ethnic demand. "We use the feeder pattern. The repatriation organization knows where the Russian Jews are placed in Brooklyn, so we know how to find them. They are especially concentrated in Brighton Beach—we call it Odessa by the Sea. We use the Russian Jews as pawns to fill up the Canarsie spaces with whites." A related gambit involved busing Russian Jewish children into the Canarsie public schools to compensate for declining white enrollments, which residents feared would intensify pressures to bus in black children. The links between the Jefferson Democratic Club, the school system, and Russian Jewish organizations facilitated placing a boroughwide Russian language program in Canarsie's public schools.

Hauling the Russians halfway across Brooklyn belied the standard white arguments against busing. A Canarsie black man seethed that the whites were playing "dirty pool." "How can they say they are against busing blacks, but then they bus the Russian Jewish kids from all the way out in District 23? Israel talks about Zionism and the promised land, and they protest when the United Nations equates Zionism and racism, but look what they do right here in Canarsie. They practice another form of racism!"

Neighborhood buying services provided another way to replace the uncertainties of the market with the assurances of recruitment. One home finder's service in the northwest quadrant of Canarsie operated out of a synagogue. Interested residents, captains in the Democratic Club, and members of civic groups spread the word to sellers, "We'll get the buyers for you," pressured them not to put up "for sale" signs, and advertised for prospective buyers in other temples and through word of mouth.

The insertion of external interested parties into the selling process altered the balance of power among sellers, realtors, and buyers. "When a homeowner wants to put his house up for sale," observed the *Canarsie Courier,* "the first agency contacted would be this [home-buying] service and they, being a group of interested, conscientious homeowners themselves, would see that the sale is put into the right hands. As one community resident put it, 'The blockbuster can't get hold of a house unless you give it to him.' " Home finder's services had at least two critical consquences. First, the requirement that realtors consult with the community before selling reduced their autonomy, but vulnerability to local boycotts gave them incentives to comply. Second, the pyramiding of resources— the linking of the home finder's organization with synagogues outside the community—relieved Canarsians of the need to discriminate; they could achieve their intent by limiting the ability of blacks even to acquire information about openings in the marketplace. Widening the gap between uninformed and knowledgeable shoppers left minority buyers in the dark.[25]

Ethnic recruitment did not always purchase white solidarity. Jewish groups tended to beckon Jewish buyers and renters, which created tension between Jews and Italians. In the late 1970s the Italians' resentment of the growing presence of Orthodox Jews in one corner of Canarsie gave birth to a new form of reactive ethnicity virtually overnight. The Orthodox had constructed a ritual fence of wire, which was coiled around the telephone poles. When the fence was unrolled on the Sabbath, certain religious prescriptions could be lifted, thereby permitting observant women to move freely with their baby carriages from one house to the next. That visible ethnic presence bothered an Italian man, who favored the ideal of white purity over ethnic pride, and he decried Jewish clannishness. "It aggravates me, because the Orthodox list homes in their home-buying services but will they allow Italians to sit on the board to see who's coming into the neighborhood? The Orthodox say, 'No, we want to bring in Jews to keep the synagogues full and steer blacks out.' I felt it was a disservice to the Italians. And they won't use Italian or Christian pork stores! The rabbi said no. It's the dominance of one group over another."

This man respected the Jewish Defense League and loved to repeat the statement of its one-time leader, Rabbi Meir Kahane, "A .22 for every Jew." "The JDL are tough boys, they're good to have around in a pinch, but don't use Jewishness against me. Now the Jews and the Italians are battling, and the Christians want to put crucifixes on their door and on the telephone poles for their identity purposes. But the rabbi said that anyone with that idea is an anti-Semite. I say, don't use that one on me. As soon as things don't go their way, they pull that thing about anti-Semitism."

The tensions between an Italian watchdog and tribal Jews defined the limits of racial brotherhood in Canarsie. Some residents saw a need to regulate the housing market, because the spontaneous decisions of separate individuals acting on their own might not serve the communal goal of racial stability. Institutions, presumably, would supply what private decisions failed to ante up. But the dissensus among whites, obscured by their common fear of racial tipping, impeded the search for a joint strategy, for groups in Canarsie did not agree on what was right or advantageous any more than did the individuals for whom they claimed to speak. Without a federation to regulate the maneuvers of its member groups, each group was free to go its own way.

Intercession by civic groups in the selling process ranged from reaction to complaints brought by individuals to initiation of proactive conduct on their own behalf. A leader of an Italian home owners' group described how the third-party role created a medium for reminders of obligation. "This guy has an argument with his neighbor, he wants to get back, so he says, 'I have no second thoughts about selling to a black.' He says, 'I'll fix your ass when the times comes to sell. I know who I'm going to sell to.' So we watch for these quarrels and convince them they're not just hurting the one individual but friends and neighbors of fifteen years."[26]

In ambiguous situations a civic group's initiative could catapult the group into the limelight. When rumors that a Manhattan broker had offered an inflated price for a home in central Canarsie touched off fears of blockbusting, representatives of one conservative civic group took the lead in convening a meeting to form a block association. One man took the podium and described the task before them. "We must teach technology. People don't know how to sell their houses. We will remove signs from public display." Another speaker urged, "Break the law and sell to whom you want. It's your obligation to one another to break laws. Do for your particular block. Individuality is important. You must develop a nationalistic feeling on the block. Retain the individuality of your part of the community. It's psychological: you feel part of an organization if it's smaller."

Block associations were not inherently racist. The heads of some groups invited the few blacks on the block to participate, gingerly defining the task as underwriting the class level or racial stability rather than the racial purity of the street. In 1980, afraid that a spate of sales to American-born blacks was threatening the caliber of their Canarsie block, some West Indian blacks took the lead in fomenting resistance to the newcomers.

The block associations rightly grasped the limits of private decision making in attaining communal goals. By creating the impression that residents could master their own fate, such organizations helped to prevent the wholesale panic that would only reinstate a de facto state of segregation. The existence of a nominal authority created a mechanism for channeling violence into more peaceful forms of action. One block president learned to cool out the hotheads on his street. "You see, I don't believe in vigilantes, I try to talk to them, they are angry people who won't see what they are doing." The sale of a home to a black family touched off wild talk of bombing among a few people on the block. "I told them, 'No bombs. The house is attached. Is it the child's fault? Do you have a guarantee the bomb won't hurt the neighbor's house?' You try to deflect panic."

Leaders of block associations found themselves the objects as well as the initiators of suasion. Racist and fearful residents tended to be overrepresented, and that skewed pattern of participation worked against democratic ideals. The president of one group, subjected to intense pressure by a cadre of racist neighbors, was cool to a new black resident. "What can I tell you?" he said to me. "You go with the majority. I work with blacks, but I won't socialize with them in my house, because if it gets like that, people will say 'He's a black-lover.' "

Ethnic recruitment, block associations, and home-finder's services were improvised solutions to social needs unfilfilled by established bodies. They symbolized the general advantage of organization over the marketplace: the regulation of private acts that might hurt the interests of the most vocal, determined segment of the neighborhood. Voluntary groups served as clearing houses for knowledge and complaints, as schools offering the lessons needed to straddle the line between legality and transgression, and as instruments of surveillance that expanded the quality of information about sellers. They served as early warning systems, which permitted compensatory action by factions wishing to reverse a sale, and they refined guesswork about the likely conduct of neighbors. Residents who did not join a block association were marked off as risky mavericks to be watched more carefully.

In the case of an absentee owner who was ready to sell, distance from the active minority who tried to seize the power to define the block's interests through force, self-promotion, or organization was spatial. Closeness made sellers susceptible to sanctions; distance reduced the impact of gossip or reprisal, widened the chasm created by the incongruous financial perspectives of stayers and movers, and increased the community's fear of a literal and figurative sell-out. One Italian man played a key role in relaying the community's nervousness to an absentee owner. "Four or five black families put money together to buy the house. The person who owned the house happened to live next to a few of them [blacks] on Long Island. I call her, I says, 'You live next to the black people that you know, but those blacks you got down there are different from the people coming from the ghetto here.' They wanted to have a big spiel about it. So we ended up not selling the house. The house went to a Jewish family."

The distance between movers and stayers was more often financial than physical. A mover's primary interest was in getting a good price for the house, which created liability for those remaining. Appeals to a seller's loyalty helped regulate the temptations of that murky status during the transition from insider to outsider. The power of the appeal, however, depended on the seller's receptivity.

The final form of distance was thus social. Residents who were not involved with neighbors could go about the business of selling without the pressures generated by social entanglements. In one extreme case the seller's isolation from people on the block led a vigilante to cross ethnic lines to restore the flow of community suasion:

> There was this Jewish refugee, see, and he was showing his house to blacks, so I got my Jewish friend and I told him, "We better visit the refugee before it's too late." The refugee thought I was a troublemaker from the Mafia, he starts crying, "You're here to threaten me." So my friend spoke to him in Jewish, which related to his feelings. So I got in the door to explain the way things are, right? Now it was an effective thing, 'cause the refugee came from a German concentration camp. I said to him, "What you are doing, selling to blacks and screwing your own people, is no different than what happened to the Jews in Germany." He choked on it. He didn't know what to say.

While most housing activists relied on gentle sanctions, a few did not shrink from retributive ones. "We had an incident on my block," said a conservative politician, "but we used what you might call a little persuasion to call that sale off." A civic leader told an audience in the same veiled language, "I see people being *made* to understand. They're realizing their sins." Few of those present doubted his precise meaning. Through such euphemisms the speakers were owning up to what was common knowledge: reprisals were available to chastise sinful sellers and unwanted buyers.

"It is disconcerting to discover," William Gamson concluded from his study of American protest groups, "that restraint is not rewarded with success." A look at the historical record convinced Gamson that "those who use more unruly tactics escape misfortune because they are clever enough to use these tactics primarily in situations where public sentiment neutralizes the normal deviance of the action."[27] The practitioners of firebombing relied on that passive tolerance of violence. "You heard about the firebombing of the black family the other day?" a Jewish member of a backlash group asked me. "Well, I'm against violence, but they're jeopardizing my home and children, and I will bomb to protect them."

One Jewish carpenter had voted for George McGovern for president in 1972, when many of his colleagues were deserting the Democrats. "I would have voted for a prairie chicken over Nixon. Attorney General [John] Mitchell was the most dangerous man in the country. He was a threat to our civil liberties."

But his progressivism vanished in the heat of racial threat. Many of his workmates in the building trades had lost their heavily mortgaged homes in the construction depression of the mid-1970s. As a child, he had never lived in a private house, so the move to Canarsie was a substantial accomplishment. "It felt good owning my home, it felt real good." He showed off the front lawn, then the back yard, saying, "The rich liberals, they look down on my little piece of the American dream, my little back yard with the barbecue here. Underneath this veneer of sophistication, though, I want to keep mine and fuck everyone else. Those niggers are the marauders of Brownsville. They ruined Brownsville, but I won't let them ruin Canarsie. I'll join a terror squad to keep them out. The liberals and the press look down on hardhats like me, but we've invested everything we have in this house and neighborhood." He paused for a moment, then asserted his self-regard: "I can be a good father and a nice guy and still say, 'Fuck those niggers.'" His convoluted attempts at self-justification perhaps betrayed ambivalence in some region of his consciousness, suggesting that people paid a price for giving in to viciousness. Speculation aside, however, the image of marauders at the portals reminds us of the precariousness of democratic values under conditions of intense fear.

The self-appointed guardians sometimes aimed their wrath at whites. The firebombing of a house owned by a white who had "sold black" reminded others to include the possibility of violence in their closing costs. One woman defended a firebombing: "It will be a warning to anyone else who is thinking of selling to blacks." Reprisals were also punishment for violating local segregationist norms. In the words of a Brooklyn realtor, "You see, in the Italian areas they do it themselves. They burn the house down. They do it to the white who sells, not the black who moves in. It's really a form of retaliation: the white who sells is the betrayer of the community. It goes back years. Italians like to be with their own kind. They have this feeling that it's their little community."

A guerrilla raid by a band of Italian boys embodied the anarchic streak in Italian provincial communities. More than youthful passion, their acts ministered to popular adult wishes to preserve racial purity. A Puerto Rican family had moved onto a block near Rockaway Parkway inhabited by many working-class Italians. When a rash of burglaries hit the small storefronts lining the commercial strip nearby, the community attributed them to the new residents. There was much angry talk about the unkempt appearance of the house and its inhabitants. One member of the raiding party who ousted the Puerto Ricans claimed: "They were the filthiest family you ever seen, right out of Brownsville. We got them out of Canarsie. We ran right into the house and kicked the shit out of every one of them. Put it like this. Say we moved into Harlem, how we gonna get wanted? What's gonna happen? What they do to us? We'd catch a beating and one of us be killed within a month. Those niggers go a little bit crazy. They go out for blood. So that's how we feel!"

The violence of a small minority of the Italian community outraged one Jewish civic leader: "They threaten people who are selling their homes, they threaten to follow them where they move, and they blow things up. Many Jewish residents have to sell, but there are no white buyers. What can they do? They are fearful of Italian roughnecks and their strong-arm people."

Resistance to integration declined in the late 1970s, in part because the areas of incursion were mainly Jewish. But when a resident of Italian Old Canarsie placed his home with an "outside" broker who brought many blacks to see the property, the North Canarsie community convened what turned out to be a wild meeting. Leaders from the Jefferson Democratic Club advised taking a lawful course of action, but the volatile home owners were in no mood for such niceties. An Italian man who was at the meeting observed, "We almost had a lynching party the other night. It got so explosive, all the people were screaming, 'We don't want them niggers here.' They didn't want to hear 'My husband is a pacifist.' They wanted to hear, 'He's going to break some heads.' " The community resorted to informal methods to resolve the incident. "The house had been sold already," said a politician close to the situation, "but they got the broker to stop the sale. They went to him, seven or eight strong, and said, 'If you can't turn this around, then we will take care of it.' After that, the broker was more than willing to give the house up."

Bombings were rarely acts of passion but were governed by shrewd calculations. A neighbor said, "I was standing outside, see, and the people were ready to bomb the house. The guy had a bomb in his car. He wanted to throw it in the house. 'Don't you dare!' I says. 'Upstairs, you got a white tenant and her two little babies. It's not practical. You gonna hurt the tenants. Do it the right way, not the wrong way.' They wanted to knock off the house. He says, 'Let's bomb the house right now.' They thought the people who owned the house were upstairs."

Another time a planned bombing collapsed when the group that was to perform the deed decided the time for effective deterrence had already passed. A woman described that ambiguous point of racial transition on her block. "It's dumb, but it all comes down to money. That scares them. I knew college grads with no common sense, professionals, like nurses and teachers, who were threatening the bombing. 'Aren't you worried about your real estate going down?' they'd ask me. It cost them $2,000 to get the bomb, but it fell through. [The people in charge of the bombing] told them they didn't want to have anything to do with it, they were going too far, it was senseless to bomb because it was beyond the point where things on the block could be stopped. It was too late." The number of blacks on the block determined the likely impact of the bombing, and thus the effectiveness of violence.

Vengeance disclosed the hollow rhetoric of community and revealed the private temptation beneath the professions of harmony. The ethos of best return verifies Max Weber's anatomy of neighborliness as "that somber economic brotherhood practiced in case of need."[28] Canarsie's definition of brotherhood denied the noble vision advanced by the civil rights movement, as well as the faith in humanity retained by a dwindling remnant of Jewish humanists. Brotherhood in Brooklyn had come to mean the gift of freedom from reprisal, which had to be forfeited when property divided the true-hearted from the once faithful.

Violence sent a tragic message to proud, striving blacks who sought the good life whites tried to hoard for themselves. Every ploy of a realtor, block association, or school board confessed that equality was a lie in the Canarsies of the nation. Could it hearten blacks that all the preachments about ambition and merit rationalized a system of plunder that ensured the spoils would go to the established? What did the terror practiced by a few enemies of quotas enforce but a racial guarantee for whites?

7. Canarsie Schools for Canarsie Children

The Canarsie Busing Crisis

"This is a Warsaw ghetto mentality in Canarsie. It's an uprising like the Masada."

Vigilance and fire-bombing lay midway between communal fight and the private surrender of flight. Each of those answers to threat had unique drawbacks, but the larger problem was that Canarsians were asking the wrong questions. They were trying to resolve problems caused by forces of economics, politics, and culture that were remote from the ken and control of the neighborhood. Their cure demanded systematic kinds of intercession that were the province of higher levels of organization and interpretation.

The collective form of action analyzed in this chapter, the anti-busing movement of 1972–73, disclosed the same promise and pitfalls as less organized endeavors to transcend private strategies of protection. Protest had a semblance of group purposefulness, but its main effect was to raise the level of conflict. In place of the anarchy of individuals, small bands, and associations fighting for their own interests, there now appeared an anarchy of larger groups fighting for vindication—Jews, Italians, taxpayers, whites, sanitationmen, school districts, home owners, teachers, neighborhoods. The city moved no closer to a vision of communal harmony.

Comparing their right-tilted radicalism to the compensatory swing of the pendulum, many residents described how, in a virtually instinctive recoil, the parries of the left had sent them reeling from a preferred position at the political center. "I became more militant because the other side polarized things," claimed an Italian Republican. "Twenty years ago, I was a middle-of-the-roader. But I saw the threat of the left and the liberals during the 1960s. The pushes of the liberals pushed me to the right." But the environment of threat did not automatically select out resistance; an intellecutal process hastened and validated political retaliation.

Canarsians used the metaphor of noise to represent the resourcefulness of blacks and their own relegation to the status of a class without influence. Ghetto riots amplified their impression that protest was a resource of coercion held in repose by minorities, readily available if they could not get their way through politics. According to a Canarsie rabbi, "The black man is the low man on the totem pole, and he is screaming loud because he figures he has nothing to lose, so he might as well scream his head off. I think the government favors the group which makes the most amount of noise, and middle-income people make the least amount of noise. The high echelons of society make a lot of noise because they have big clout. The little man in Canarsie gets caught in the middle of the ladder. He's afraid to scream and doesn't have the clout, so out of necessity he gets to feel, 'Everybody's picking on me,' even though nobody is really picking on him."

In the second, activist phase of the interpretive process, the silent majority tried to find its voice. The revised appraisal of the merits and defects of silence and screaming aimed to clear away restraints on more vocal modes of participation. It began to dawn on increasing numbers of residents that pressure and organization were essential ways to gain one's ends.

In 1976 a convocation of backlash groups from all across New York City crackled with the speechifying of rightists, including some from Canarsie. A large sign on the wall of the catering hall admonished, "DEMOCRATIC NATIONAL CONVENTION BEWARE, We'll be there . . . at Madison Square Garden." A civic leader told the audience to bring its belligerence out of the closet and to voice publicly the feelings of resentment normally confined to family, to tavern buddies, to workmates. "The key to our success," he boasted, "is that we don't skirt the issues. We talk the truth. You must speak the truth and the ideas you express in your own kitchen."

Speaker after speaker tried to loosen the chokehold of respectability that strangled middle-class voices. They called on whites to refrain from apathetic collusion in their own disenfranchisement.

"The problem lies with the white, not the black, communities," one man argued. "The ethnic politicians are afraid to get up and fight for the ethnics. The black leaders get together and nobody condemns them when they say black power. It's exalted. It's about time we demanded that our politicians represent white ethnic rights." Another speaker complained that white middle-income people "don't give a damn until the kid is bused or the wife is raped. They had a march in Selma, and people came from California. 'They' organize, but your damn neighbor is home watching TV . . . I'm sick of being treated like a second-class citizen. We don't holler enough . . . why are we so quiet?"

The rafters really shook when a New York City radio talk show host preached to the Bensonhurst believers as if they were under the tent of a religious revival, not at an Italian catering hall. "Let's be heard, we will be heard, we were meant to be heard. This is a government for the people. We are the people. America is opposed to busing. Why do we have it, then?" He celebrated average ethnic Americans, heroic in their ordinary virtue. "You are the maligned, hard-working backbone of the nation. The media is against you. They tell you you are Archie Bunkers. You are not Archie Bunkers. You are great Americans. The people from Europe, *our* people, didn't have bilingual programs and model cities programs, but they worked hard to learn, they didn't have professions, but they learned and worked." His voice rose to a stirring pitch. "They came from Romania, from Italy, from Poland, from Ireland." Invoking the power of Italian anarchism, he told the audiences of the gains to be had from stubborn refusal and of the enslavement conferred by respectable silence. "The one area Judge Garrity wouldn't touch in Boston was the North End, because the people are Italians and they wouldn't stand for busing." He then berated them, as if the contrast between their heroic possibility and humiliating dispossession would stir them to action. "The squeaky wheel gets the grease, and you people don't squeak. You are supine, a bunch of slobs, quiet."

And he led them toward action. "You are a great majority, this is still a democracy, majority rule is still in effect. A new wind is blowing across the land of America, Americans of common sense are tired of this crazy social experiment . . . You are the working people, you raise families, you have responsibilities and obligations, you don't collect welfare and show up at an ACLU or NAACP demonstration—*they* know how to exert pressure. Germany in the 1930s showed that a dedicated minority can rule a disorganized, dissolute majority . . .

But declare yourself, you must make your voice heard, you must not surrender to this madness."

A new reckoning of the appropriate ways of settling disputes was taking place in more temperate forms closer to the ideological center of gravity of Canarsie politics. After lamenting the Jewish fear of acting tough and fierce, a conservative Jewish civic leader called for redressing the one-sided exchange of benefits that was liberalism: "We came to a new understanding. When you run, you turn your back to get stabbed in the back. If you don't run, but don't fight back when someone is fighting with you, you get your race smashed, so there comes a time when you have to stand up and fight back."

A risky environment set in motion a search for models that might legitimate a muscular Jewish stance. One side of that process was a growing respect for the adaptive traditions of other collectivities.[1] This was reflected in an admiration for Italian muscle, which began to qualify the furtively whispered condemnation of roughneck Italians. A rabbi from a Conservative temple attributed the resurgence of Jewish pride to the Holocaust and the struggle for Israel's territorial integrity, but he added, "And the last few years we've learned from the blacks. You see it especially with the Hasidic Jews, they've become strong fighters for their rights. They demand their share of federal funds. The Hasidim even took their case all the way to the Supreme Court. And you see more Jews wearing yarmulkas. They are saying, 'It's my world as much as others'.' "

A second facet was the rediscovery of latent and shadow themes in the Jewish experience. Zionist assertion offered a proud example to be emulated. The Israeli victory over the Arabs in 1967 was a momentous event for Brooklyn Jews, including the Canarsie antibusing activist who complained that Jews were still not "warlike" enough to suit her. "The Jew is not as militant as the black minority. We wouldn't be led to the ovens this time, but we still are too passive." Yet victory in war heartened her. "Since the 1967 war, I've felt that the Jews are a stronger people and I've been more proud to be a Jew."

Ethnic precedents further back in history lent themselves to contemporary purposes. A conventional Democrat, who marked his political change of heart with the busing crisis in 1972, retrieved the ancestral image of a Jewish warrior tradition. "This is a Warsaw ghetto mentality in Canarsie," he explained. "It's an uprising like the Masada. When you can't do anything, when you're pushed to the wall, you fight back. The Jews fought back, even though they knew they would be dying."

The Canarsie school crisis of 1972 translated these sentiments into action. As a bit of street theater, the revolt had a certain fascination, although the events of the crisis were not sufficiently illuminating to justify a blow-by-blow description. Nonetheless, a passing knowledge of the episode is required to permit a more nuanced understanding of its meaning.[2]

The revolt began with the predicament of black children who lived in the Tilden Homes project in the southern tip of Brownsville. Since the early 1960s, they had been zoned into Meyer Levin Junior High, a predominantly white school in white East Flatbush. This placement did not change even after the Ocean Hill–Brownsville school crisis, when the decentralization law divided the city into local school districts. Although the Tilden children lived in District 23 (Brownsville), they continued to attend Meyer Levin in District 18 (Canarsie/East Flatbush). But as East Flatbush suffered rapid white flight in the late 1960s, and the black enrollment at Meyer Levin approached the 50 percent mark, the integrationist rationales for keeping the Brownsville children in District 18 were undercut by East Flatbush fears of racial tipping. Parents at Meyer Levin, black as well as white, dug in their heels and demanded that the Tilden kids go elsewhere. "Under no circumstances," the Canarsie/East Flatbush local school board told School Chancellor Charles Scribner in April of 1971, "will we give consideration to accommodating these children who live outside our district." On the opening day of the 1972 school year the parents at Meyer Levin physically prevented the Tilden kids from entering the school.

There now ensued a game of complex gambits and shifting alliances among Canarsie, East Flatbush, and Brownsville. The agreement on rejecting the Tilden children had united the District 18 local school board, which was split five to four between the white Canarsie majority and the black and white East Flatbush minority. The two sides now began to jockey for position. The Canarsie members voted to send the Tilden children to an all-black school in East Flatbush, the East Flatbush contingent favored sending them to Canarsie, and the courts ruled that the children belonged in the district. The compromise that was hammered out placed the Tilden children back at Meyer Levin, except for thirty-one whom no school in the district would accept. At this juncture Chancellor Scribner suspended the Canarsie/Flatbush local board and assigned the "Tilden 31" to John Wilson Junior High in Canarsie. It was there, wrote *New York Times* reporter Iver Peterson, that "he ran into the Canarsie housewives."[3]

Canarsie's riposte was swift and kinetic. About a hundred residents occupied the school while their neighbors thronged in the streets. Each morning for three days a jeering crowd greeted Reverend Wilbert Miller, the leader of the Tilden 31, as he led the children to the school. The minister summarized the situation: "They're tired of running, and we're tired of being pushed around, and there you have the impasse."[4] The threat of a court order finally induced the parents to leave on Thursday, October 19.

Pressed on one side by East Flatbush and on the other by white Canarsie, the chancellor now demanded on October 23 that the Tilden children be sent to Bildersee Junior High (JHS 68), also in Canarsie, which Deputy Chancellor Irving Anker had dubbed one of the ten most segregated schools in New York City. In contrast to Wilson, which had close to one-third minority students, Bildersee was 97 percent white. One Canarsie PTA leader worked valiantly on that compromise. "We tried to prepare the Canarsie people for the Tilden children to go to Bildersee. We held meetings in the community to get them ready, and they would have accepted it. We decided to roll out the red carpet for those Tilden kids." The woman traveled with a group of Canarsie PTA leaders to Brownsville to meet with the Tilden parents. "We went to their church on a Sunday morning, and we told them, 'We are offering your kids the best possible education your youngsters can get.' They accused us of hate. It was an unbelievable morning. We had gone honorably and they didn't trust us. They thought we were pulling the wool over their eyes." Rebuffed by the black parents, the whites felt betrayed.

In accusing the white delegation, the Tilden parents were simply employing the same logic the residents of Canarsie used in all their encounters with blacks. The black parents had probable cause for nervousness. Their children had already been traumatized by howling Canarsie mobs. Could they be expected to separate the good element of whites from the bad, when the whites claimed it was impossible to separate good blacks and bad? The *New Yorker* wrote, "As the parents of the J.H.S. 68 children were busy enumerating for reporters the dangers of exposing their children to the invaders from the high-crime area of Brownsville, word came that the black parents had rejected the proposal, indicating that *they* feared for the safety of *their* children in the 'hostile' environment of J.H.S. 68."[5]

Bildersee was not destined to play the role of racial equalizer. The central school board reversed Scribner's ruling and ordered the Tilden kids back to Wilson, declaring, "We believe it would be a mistake to use these particular 31 children, who have already been the victims of traumatic rejection, as a battering ram for the integration of JHS 68." Another wave of resistance spread through Canarsie, and the combined PTAs of Canarsie spearheaded a boycott of the elementary and junior highs that kept 90 percent of the students out of school for almost two weeks.[6]

On the first day of the boycott, a Friday, Chancellor Scribner escorted the Tilden children to the Wilson School through a gauntlet of howling residents. The theater of the streets moved indoors to a movie theater over the weekend, where two thousand residents heard community leaders decry the chancellor's orders. An Orthodox rabbi told the buzzing crowd, "Tomorrow we must have every single person out there in front of [John] Wilson to demonstrate to the powers that we want the decentralization law upheld . . . What's good for the goose is good for the gander." The president of the Canarsie Jewish Community Council declared, "We have built the swamps of Canarsie into a beautiful community, and no one is going to take it from us."[7]

The revivalist spirit of the meeting was a portent. Civic leaders had now given Canarsians permission to indulge in the popular mood of defiance. At seven A.M. Monday morning, October 31, 1,500 residents turned out in front of the Wilson School to protest the arrival of the Tilden children, who became the targets of racist invective and the mantra, "Canarsie Schools for Canarsie Children." Out of a school enrollment of more than 9,500 students, only 477, most of them black, showed up for school that day, and the boycott stayed at the 90 percent level for most of the week.

What did black children experience as they heard the jeers? A teacher at Wilson Junior High noted their suffering. "There's a lot more touching, hanging on to teachers. Kids have a tendency to be more physical when they're frightened."[8] One can only imagine the thoughts of redneck lynch mobs flashing through the minds of the black parents who stormed past the cat-calling whites. The black poet Wilfred Cartey discerned the ghoulishness of a silent majority no longer content to remain silent:

Canarsie is the end of the line.
They break their silence there
the silent majority.
White eyes spit skeletons
from blood red faces
once powdery white—
white powder of a skull.
They rend the silence
the silent majority
screeching white-powdered
hatred
on the backs of little
black children.
Only the filth of their garlicked
insides stinks more than the filth
from their mouths.
Only last night Madonna and child
Lull-a-bying a bawling baby
white with the powdery whitness of the skull.
They crack the silence, the silent majority
Spaghetti insides turn to fat white worms that
hook upon the unsuspecting feet of small black children.
Connivance of a broken silence,
the emissions of the promises broken
in a white White House.
Even the wind of the typhoon
cannot outblast the breaking wind
of hatred
Oh Madonna of the garlicked insides, prey on black sinners
Now and at the hour of your death . . . . . . Jesus!
There in Canarsie break the silence,
you silent majority,
white hatred splitting from your garlicked insides
Canarsie is the end of the line:
that is where they break their silence,
the silent majority.[9]

Roving bands of Italian and black toughs flaunted iron pipes, heavy chains, and sticks with protruding spikes. At one point some black gangs, twenty to fifty strong, roamed the neighborhood in search of excitement and faced down their white counterparts.

When asked if race was the issue, four white youths laughed, and one of them said, "I hate niggers. I've been fighting them all my life. I enjoy it."[10]

The Italian-American Civil Rights League achieved publicity for its efforts to mediate the racial quarreling among the young. The newspapers became enamored of one league captain, a husky long-shoreman who tried to cool out the gangs. After he strode into a crowd of black youths and advised them to "keep cool," Reverend Miller declared, "I want to rap with that man. He makes sense." The Peacemaker, as the *New York Post* dubbed him, asked rhetorically, "Why should kids who used to be friends suddenly be enemies? Why should kids on the same basketball team be standing on the opposite sides of the street throwing rocks at each other? They shouldn't be."[11]

Alarmed by the specter of impending violence, the PTAs asked residents to refrain from the raucous protests while the boycott continued. By Wednesday, November 1, the demonstrators had dwindled to a hard core of 150, many of whom sported Italian League or Conservative party buttons. One member harrangued the group, "I say that if we don't keep our stand, they'll take over the whole place and then where will we be?" A man raised his fist and urged, "Defend, defend, defend."[12]

Negotiations between the local board and the school board effected a temporary resolution on November 7. District 18 agreed to submit in ninety days a plan to equalize racial proportions in Meyer Levin, John Wilson, and Bildersee. The Tilden kids were to remain in the district. Scribner had all but won his initial package of demands. The PTA leadership, in urging an end to the boycott, knew they had not assuaged the community's anxiety. They consoled it with a pledge. "The combined PTAs of Canarsie will demand that no Canarsie children will leave Canarsie in this rezoning." A PTA leader reminded the audience at a community meeting that the local board would pursue its cause through litigation. Hundreds of residents opposed the apparent capitulation to Scribner. "In the ensuing hubbub, speakers wrestled for control of the microphone and bull horn; a newsman was hustled out of the auditorium . . . The cry went up, 'No school Wednesday—We are one!' "[13]

The cry of sell-out, marking the breach between a die-hard remnant and the official leadership, anticipated the second boycott the following spring. When it began in early March, it no longer enjoyed the stamp of respectability, and neither the PTA leadership nor the political establishment would condone the protest. Hidden by the agreement on the need for racial stability during the first boycott, the division of Canarsie into warring factions could not be obscured during the second.

The local school board, hampered by the Canarsie/East Flatbush split, worked through November to redraw the racial map to satisfy the chancellor. The plan envisioned a modest shift in racial percentages by 1975, phased out the Tilden kids, and precluded any busing from Canarsie to East Flatbush. Rabbi Joseph Frankel, one of the four East Flatbush members of the local board, decried the numbers as unduly generous to Canarsie. "We don't see near equalization in the plan . . . What we're looking for is as close to parity as possible." The East Flatbush counterproposal called for busing Canarsie students into East Flatbush, and Alan Erlichman, president of a new militant antibusing group, the Concerned Citizens of Canarsie, insisted that the one nonnegotiable demand was that "no Canarsie children will ever leave a Canarsie school."[14]

Scribner's rejection of the Canarsie-tilted plan renewed the showdown. He accepted the first-year ratios but spurned the phaseout of the Tilden children. The compromise was Solomonic, with something to sour everyone. It disappointed the whites and blacks of East Flatbush who hoped that busing would relieve racial pressure in its schools, infuriated Canarsie militants who insisted on the removal of the Tilden children, and opened up the breach between the antibusing rejectionists and the political and educational establishment, which opposed any more civic disorder. In February the Canarsie organizations, in a rafter-shaking meeting at the Jefferson Democratic Club, voted against another boycott by twenty-seven organizations to six.

Having lost the tally, the Italian-American Civil Rights League, the Concerned Citizens of Canarsie, and the Jewish Defense League took their case to the people. They revived the politics of exhortation and heated the community to its boiling point. One antibusing activist later recalled that only two of Canarsie's rabbis had supported them, and one rabbi had said he didn't want to see a Baptist church down on Rockaway Parkway. "During the second boycott, Rabbi Strizower said we had to live with our brothers, but we ignored the religious leaders, we ignored the politicians, and we ignored the Jefferson Club vote when it went against us. And we ran those commies [from Youth against War and Fascism] out of Canarsie."

On February 28, parents at five of Canarsie's eight elementary and junior high schools voted in favor of a second boycott. According to a *Village Voice* reporter at one school, in response to a PTA leader who argued that a second boycott would harm the legal appeal of Scribner's decision, "the room erupted in shouts and cries of 'Boycott! Boycott!' 'The only favorable changes we're going to get is if the Brownsville kids are phased out *faster* than we want,' somebody yelled." At the Wilson School, which voted against another boycott, an impassioned woman screamed, "Support your neighborhood, 211. Your neighborhood supported you." And a man shouted, "Your school should burn down."[15]

The second boycott began in a bruised Canarsie. The PTA leadership pressured families to send their kids to school. The Italian-American Civil Rights League, mindful of the reputation for militance it had earned during the first boycott, said, "There will be no violence, just a boycott." The Concerned Citizens of Canarsie and the league pledged not to prevent students and teachers from attending school. By April the passions of rebellion were spent, and the boycott petered out. When Chancellor Scribner resigned, the Board of Education lost its combination point man and fall guy. The Jefferson Club continued to press for a compromise. After a month of lost class time, parents grew increasingly anxious about their children's education, and the boycott dwindled. Holding to its policy of cautious accommodation, the Board of Education found the midpoint between the Scribner position and that of the Canarsie militants: a gradual phaseout of the Tilden House kids. The community overwhelmingly endorsed the compromise. The NAACP appealed to State Commissioner Nyquist on behalf of the Brownsville children, but the Canarsie school crisis was over, for the moment.

The rebellion against busing had profound aftershocks. Whatever reasons had moved the residents to take the plunge into activism, commitment changed the way they thought and acted.[16] Participation brought strangers together and heightened the residents' receptivity to new learning. Picketing in front of a school, protesting a judicial decree, seizing a school, canvassing door to door, and riding in motorcades—these heady acts did not drain alienation but intensified it. The boycott made one Jewish businessman, born on the Lower East Side to an abiding love of Franklin Roosevelt, move from a boosterish faith in the democratic promise of American life to a deep and bitter cynicism:

I was on the barricades in front of John Wilson Junior High School. I got hit with eggs. The city government was cramming busing down my throat. They were pushing me to do something I didn't want. They were taking me for granted when I pay my taxes, so I decided to stand up like a man for my rights. I got hit by police with clubs for breaking through the barricades. I was lowered to this standard. I'm not against blacks. We didn't want non-Canarsie blacks in. You see what happens? I still get tears when I think of the boycott.

Commitment expanded the resources of the aggrieved. They now belonged to a ramifying network of the disaffected, which grew by a process of spontaneous generation. Linked through the organizations that gathered them in the same room for consciousness-raising sessions, the protesters became part of a communal effort to find an idiom and an organization to express their needs.

Ordinary, hard-working family people learned to trade knowledge, replay scenarios, and coordinate strategy. The crisis left in its wake combat-tested residents adept in occupying a school, mobilizing a community, defying a school board. Two Jewish activists in the Italian-American Civil Rights League reminisced, "Before the boycott, I was just your average, go-to-work, come-home, and watch-the-tube kind of guy. I didn't know a thing about organizations in Canarsie." The school crisis changed all that. "The middle class became professional activists. We had knowledge and experience by the end of this busing situation." His buddy told a story of the deepening of his skills as an agitator, which he used to help another nearby community. "In August 1973 there was some racial trouble in the Flatlands section. All these frightened little Jewish girls came to the Italian League because the women wanted to lock themselves in. They needed a pro, and I was a pro then, I knew how to lock in a school."

The revolt against busing reflected the demise of the apathetic electorate of the 1950s, and the rise of a feistier brand of citizen. The American of the 1970s held a more jaundiced view of political authority. William Gamson observed that those with scant trust in formal systems of adjudication tend to rely on constraints, or force and protest, as a form of influence. "Such a group . . . has little to lose by constraints. Since the probability of favorable outcomes is already very low in the absence of influence, it is hardly necessary to worry about resentment."[17]

It might be argued that having little to lose, the residents who sparked the school crisis had indulged in a desperate flailing against all reason. The fall of Masada, Marvin Harris has pointed out, did not end the Jewish military-messianic lifestyle. Two thousand years later it was revived in Canarsie in the revolt against busing. But, whether as the fight against the Romans or the repudiation by Canarsie Jews and Romans of the liberal state in Brooklyn, was the Masada a last-ditch stand of a lower middle class that refused to face facts? "History," Harris continued, "shows that the Jewish military-messianic lifestyle was an adaptive failure. It did not succeed in restoring David's kingdom; rather, it resulted in the complete loss of the territorial integrity of the Jewish state . . . Does this mean that military messianism was a capricious, impractical, even maniacal lifestyle?"[18]

Harris answered his question in the negative. The argument for the practicality of the rebellion in Canarsie is even stronger. Canarsie gained more control over its development than would have been possible otherwise. The stories of civic action, and the corporate organizations that were its legacy, suggest a net gain in the neighborhood's capacity to direct its fate, whether for democratic or tribal ends. Yet to fully explain the enigmatic cunning in backlash, we need to take a second look at the school crisis, this time with the aim of understanding the diverse kinds of voice that became audible during it.

Middle-Class Militants

"They were afraid of losing everything.
They rendered to Caesar the ten bucks
for self-protection."

The liberal community, the chancellor of schools, and minority leaders viewed the insurgency against busing as an outpouring of racist mania. Kenneth Clark, the black social psychologist on the New York State Board of Regents whose scholarship had been incorporated into the legal briefs in the Supreme Court's 1954 decision on *Brown* v. *Board of Education,* attributed the "crime in Canarsie" to racism, "conscious or unconscious," and deemed the scene in front of the Wilson School a "reflection of profound sickness in this nation."[19]

Pete Hamill caught the more ambiguous reality of the uprising in his *New York Post* column, entitled "School Bus Named Desire," of November 1, 1972. "And again, even here, in Canarsie, New York, in the North, in the heart of it all, there are children: 31 of them still unformed, driven by the desire to unlock the mysteries of books and learning, and arriving at a place of learning to discover what is usually only between the lines of all those civics books, to walk again into the poisoned memory that makes up the dirty little secret of our history." What was the secret? "Go back, go beyond JHS 211, go back beyond Ocean Hill–Brownsville, and the heart of it was a crime. It was the crime that one group of humans inflicted upon another group of humans by making them slaves." Hamill did not sling accusations promiscuously:

> The people of Canarsie did not commit that crime; no, it was their people, their fathers and grandfathers who were the victims of crimes, the victims of pogroms in Eastern Europe, the victims of feudal thugs called kings and bishops in Italy. To blame Canarsie for the initial crime of slavery is to be a racist, to blame *all* whites for the crimes of a few . . . But all of us—liberals as well as conservatives—have to begin to understand what they are afraid of. They are not afraid of black people or Puerto Ricans *per se*. They *are* afraid of what happens when racial balance is tipped in a school.

The rising up of a placid community, the breaking of lawful and routine patterns of making wishes known, is an event of remarkable singularity that demands explanation. The transformation of private residents into public citizens was part of a revolutionary surge that shook ordinary politics, toppled the local dons, and forged a culture of resistance in the streets.

The revolt against busing was deferred white vengeance for the New York school crisis of 1968. An Italian resident bristled, remembering that time. "The blacks wanted decentralization at Ocean Hill–Brownsville. They fired white teachers and put in black teachers. Now that might be a good idea, maybe blacks could teach black history better. But then 80 percent of the fired Ocean Hill–Brownsville teachers came to Canarsie, and now the blacks want to come here! They want the white teachers back!"

The suspension of the Canarsie local board in 1972 bolstered the residents' belief that blacks were double dealers who wanted everything played their way, blithely shifting from community control to integration as it suited them. A Jewish activist decried the sundering of a norm of reciprocity: "Any kind of equity has to be a two-way street or it's a no-way street. If you want equality for you, you damn well better be prepared to give that same kind of equality to me. Don't you dare try to control your district and then try to control mine too."

While sophisticated members of the PTA circles were preoccupied with the issue of decentralization, for most residents the issue remained the impact of the denial of the local board's formal power: the busing of children into or out of Canarsie. A Jewish boycott leader dressed down a young McGovernite liberal: "You and the god-damned liberals, you screamed along with the blacks in 1968 for community control. You made concessions at Ocean Hill–Brownsville, and now whites want what the blacks have, and you say we can't have it. How come they can do it and we can't? And so you call us racists!" As the progressive deciphered the conversation, "The leaders were smart enough to see the loophole decentralization gave them. They could say, 'This isn't about niggers, it's about decentralization.' " She exaggerated the extent to which community control was a bald masquerade, but she understood that the cry "Canarsie Schools for Canarsie Children, Black or White" conferred magical powers of legitimation.

The crude words, offered by a democrat recoiling from the crudeness of some of the protesters, touched to the quick the primitivism of the crisis. She was not wrong that an abstract fight over the merits of decentralization would not alone have engaged the passions of the average Canarsian. Rather, the command to bus turned thirty-one children into a harbinger of all the social and physical threats that surely would follow, as Canarsians saw it.

The restraints of a resource-lean environment, in which the scarce resources were white children, set the axis of conflict. A disprivileged, white-poor East Flatbush tried to export blacks and borrow whites from a Canarsie rich in whites. An activist in school matters described the triadic exchange involved in the shuffle. "The whites in East Flatbush don't have the money to move. They can't sell their houses if the buyer is white and finds out his kid has to go to Meyer Levin Junior High. So the Flatbush parents want to get Canarsie whites in their schools to stabilize things. But there aren't enough whites to go around."

Canarsie declined the trade. The newsletter of the Concerned Citizens of Canarsie countered, "East Flatbush is demanding the destruction of Canarsie, as the only solution to their ever mounting integration problems ... Canarsie must meet and solve all of its school problems only with the resources of our own community, and ... no child will leave Canarsie schools to 'whiten' East Flatbush."[20]

The busing crisis gave a new twist to a classical problem of human ecology. In an era of judicial activism, the forces that regulate the composition of a territory's population are political as well as natural. Communities sought help from the courts and bureaucrats to effect through command what the marketplace and spontaneous movement of people did not provide.

The fear of loss explains the readiness to mobilize, but discontent encourages flight or gallows humor as often as it summons rebellion. Jewish resistance represented little more than fatigue with running and a revised estimate of the gains to be won from standing fast or from putting one's foot to the wind. A member of the Jewish Defense League who joined the busing insurgency defined the diminishing marginal return on exodus that gave birth to protest:

> We had seen what happened in Bedford Stuyvesant, which was a Jewish community, and in Brownsville, which was a Jewish community, and in East New York, which was a Jewish community. The same thing happened in East Flatbush, a former Jewish community. Many of the people here in Canarsie are the same Jews who left those communities and moved to Canarsie and said, 'Hey, where do we go from here? We've seen what happens. Are we going to abandon it again? For what? When do we get? We have worked for this area, we're not going to allow it to be taken away from us. We're not going to allow our kids to be jeopardized and terrorized in the schools the way they were where we came from. We ran away from that once, we're not running again. Never again!

Discontent could have been channeled through existing communal institutions. Compared to other neighborhoods, Canarsie had a lively organizational life. The neighborhood might have kept the faith in the Jefferson Democratic Club's quiet efforts to bargain with the courts, the school board, the State Assembly. Why did a powerful political machine lose its monopoly over the means of influence? To answer these questions, one must understand the organizations that channeled the passions of the rebellion.[21]

The success of the rowdies was first and foremost an organizational response to seductive opportunities created by an environment in flux. However much the established leaders tried to contain popular volatility, however much alienated activists tried to capitalize on it, the deliberations of the powerful and the pretenders alike began from a spontaneous surge of outrage. The established leaders did not satisfy the rising demand for action, in part because the respectable Jews had limited influence over the most uproarious elements in the community, such as the tough Italian youngsters aching for a fight with black youths. Ethical restraints also limited the leadership's powers of suasion. The official rulers—the PTA leadership, the Jefferson Democrats, the local school board, most of the civic and religious institutions—had little taste for the antics of the demonstrators. "The Jefferson Club," one strategist recalled, "took the position of no boycott. We used delaying tactics and lawsuits to buy time, to try to keep everyone from getting hot. The school boards subscribed to this philosophy too."

In sum, the pressures from below, the inhibitions of the established leaders, and the vacuum created by their apparent abdication formed an open invitation to crafty operators. The Italian-American Civil Rights League, later the Concerned Citizens of Canarsie, and to a lesser extent the Jewish Defense League became the voice of militant dissent by default. The Italian League was able to step into the breach because it happened to be at the scene. Its role in the game of backlash came from the members' combat readiness as an organization already in place in Canarsie, the lack of a clear function or constituency in the boroughs before the boycott, and a willingness to parlay a flair for braggadocio into a broker role. "At first," one Italian League activist recalled, "the PTAs took the lead. But the situation was disorganized. Those first two weeks there was name-calling, and people were throwing rocks, and the police had to use their clubs. The whole thing was crazy. But then the community came to the Italian League. They were panicky, and we were asked to take care of the situation. Only when the people came to us did we take over." A year earlier, at a rally at Columbus Circle in Manhattan, 100,000 New Yorkers had heard backlash leader Anthony Imperiale tell the crowd, "The blood of Roman gladiators flows in your veins."

But after Mafia sachem Joe Columbo was gunned down, the league never achieved a clear purpose. Now in Canarsie the league found itself in the forefront of the action. At the height of the boycott 40 percent of its dues-paying members were Jewish residents. In the most elemental organizational terms, the wildness was good for the Italian group.

True to its southern Italian heritage, the league excelled in clandestine maneuvering behind the scenes, skirting bureaucratic rules in favor of personal forms of intercession. They negotiated directly with Reverend Miller, they presided over powwows between black and white youths. Breaking up fights, containing intemperate residents, and maintaining order, the league provided a paramilitary force to secure peace.

According to local gossip, the league's posture of respectability aimed to counter rumors of alleged ties to organized crime. An activist in the Italian League grinningly scoffed at the accusations but confirmed the informal governmental role. "The newspapers reported that Lindsay had the Mafia cooling racial tensions, but it was really just four or five of us local guys. The league found a way out. We cooled out irresponsible people and sent one really explosive captain away. We were ready for action and civil disobedience if necessary, but we weren't the Mafia. We were pussycats."

Ethnic suspicions made the task of coalition building difficult.[22] Speculation about the league's connections to organized crime in part reflected a lingering Jewish mistrust of *prost* Italians, which limited the league's ability to develop a broad market for defiance. During the vote on a second boycott, as Italian League loudspeakers broadcast the warnings "Okay [JHS] 211, you're getting twenty more kids from Brownsville tomorrow," a Jewish woman muttered aloud, "My God, we got taken over by the coloreds in Brownsville and now we're getting taken over by the Mafia. What's going to happen to us?"

The need to allay Jewish fears spawned the Concerned Citizens of Canarsie and boosted its leader, Alan Erlichman, into the public limelight. At the outset the CCC was little more than a front for the Italian League, designed to veil the Italian image of the antibusing radicals. An Italian League official recalled the merger. "At the time of the busing crisis, Alan Erlichman was a member of Chapter Eight of the Italian League. He thought he could get more Jews into the situation by opening a second organization so it would look more impressive. He was a good speaker. We called him 'The Voice.' He took the show away from the league and got the Jews who were afraid of the league."

The activists were the shock troops of Middle America, always out in front directing and cajoling the community. If taken literally, however, the vanguard image is misleading; the willingness of the militants to assuage Jewish anxiety shows that they responded to wants as well as shaped them. But they reveled in the populist image of redeemers of the people. Viewing themselves as challengers to an encrusted ruling class, the Italian League and the Concerned Citizens saw the established leaders as privileged traitors who used their offices for personal advantage. "The PTA people and the entire community leadership," claimed one league official, "are linked to the Jefferson Club. The unactives, the passive majority, were non-club people. All the PTA ladies and the activists on the executive boards of civic organizations get to be teachers' aides, or their husband's business needs the club, and many of them are substitute teachers."

Leaders of the CCC and the Italian League pictured themselves as rebels, uncowed by a need for respectability. They pointed to the purity of their character as opposed to the tainted motives of PTA officials and the Jefferson Club liberals. One activist argued that the league "was the only organization with the guts to stand up to the conspiracy of government, courts, and judges to do what was expedient at the expense of the middle class. The Board of Education attempts to pacify black militants and integrationists, and there was the Italian League, we were pissed off at the political system for letting this happen. The Italian League was the only one that represented the people."

Pride in guts marked the exuberance of the plebeian who had launched a strike against powerful interests. Guts joined the maverick leaders and the citizens in a mysterious unity, which they contrasted with the distancing elitism of diploma holders. One league official came back from a meeting at the central Board of Education smarting from the insults he discerned. "I attended the secret Board of Education meetings and there were all these important people there. But I said, 'No secret meetings.' They figured they could con me and pacify us with their diplomas and schooling. They think we're stupid. But we were waiting for any dealings or conniving. It was underhanded dealings going on, plain shit."

The radicals claimed to translate the people's will directly. Since the established organizations were filters on popular demands rather than robust conduits of the people's will, the militants appealed to their neighbors directly over the heads of the civic groups. Guiding this strategy was the theory that a majority needed deliverance or awakening. "Ninety-nine percent of the people in Canarsie," insisted one of the antibusing leaders, "belongs to an organization and never goes to a meeting." In his view the local liberal ruling class suppressed the wishes of a silent, hidden, or apathetic majority. Such a reading was a rational adjustment to reality. The radicals were alienated outsiders with incentives to take it to the people. They could not compete in the more crowded organizational terrain. "We controlled the people and the streets," the activist continued. "During the second boycott all the organizations went against us: the Jefferson Club, the local school board, and the PTAs. But the end result was that we won with the people."

The crisis swelled the ranks of regular participants in civic life with residents who were normally apathetic. The self-propelling force of panic, and the tentacles of influence that reached from the militant leaders to their friends and neighbors, encouraged involvement by the most fearful and resentful residents. A PTA leader was upset by the chasm between her values and those of the new, aggrieved rank and file. "I don't want my children to be bigots. I told my daughter, if she loved a black man and wanted to marry him and was aware of the difficulties, that's OK. I would accept it if he was a good and kind person." She glimpsed a different sensibility during the crisis. "Most of them were bigoted. They felt, 'No Jews ever stood up and fought back,' and now they were standing up and fighting back. That's how they felt. I'd say my school is the most bigoted in the community."

The radicals' task was to elicit the voice of quiescent citizens, but where to find them? How to evoke the stilled voice of the famed silent majority? To tap the vein of uncontaminated opinion, the insurgents bypassed organized Canarsie and looked for a mandate in the sound and fury of protest. The contrast of open streets and closed organizations symbolized the opposed political ecologies of moderates and radicals.

The Jefferson Democrats worked quietly through official channels to reverse the Scribner ruling. They maneuvered in settings away from the hustings, encouraging a spirit of talk, lawfulness, and compromise. In the fall of 1972 Assemblyman Stanley Fink had briefed housewives occupying Wilson Junior High on the progress of negotiations. His photograph appeared in news stories that reported him heading to Albany to meet with the state commissioner of education and exploiting the breadth and reach of the club's social ties to officials. Fink's opponent in the upcoming Assembly race, Dominick Andreassi, a conservative Republican from Old Canarsie, joined the protesters at Wilson. *New York Times* reporter Maurice Carroll observed, "Behind the police barricades that separated protesting white parents from the boycotted schools last week was an occasional shout of, 'Where's Fink?' 'I'll tell you where Fink was,' Mr. Fink said yesterday. 'Fink was at the central board of education trying to resolve this.' Early in the squabble Mr. Andreassi spent a night with parents who had barricaded themselves inside the school."[23]

American politicians of widely differing sympathies have appropriated the language of populism. Did the radicals truly speak for the people? Did the establishment sell out the people? Or did the rowdies overpower a disorganized majority with a dedicated minority? The Italian League and the CCC undeniably gained an impassioned following, whose entrance into the political arena, suddenly rendered permeable by the force of popular outrage, diluted the power of the Jefferson Democrats and their allies in the PTA hierarchy. But that is all one can say with any precision. The radicals' estimates of their support gave them wild discretion to fathom signs of acclamation. Fifteen hundred citizens protested in front of Wilson Junior High in the early days of the crisis, but that group was an eclectic bunch. When the PTAs pleaded for calm, the number of die-hard rejectionists shrank to a score.

Yet the currents of support for the radicals tell us little about the quality of the consent that formed it. The turn out at mass meetings was a self-selected flock of panicky residents in their most panicky moments, hardly more representative of the community than the civic groups were. The frenzy of the mass meetings excited the senses more than they informed the mind. Frenzy, however, was more than a quirk of ecology. The tactics of the radicals enhanced popular receptivity to the most apocalyptic appeals. One civic leader spoke a considerable truth when he said, "The militants need commotion and upheaval. They are masters of the mob. They feed on energy that is fed them from the environment. But they generate nothing by themselves. A few people were permitted to excite the residents and scare them during the school crisis." One of the most successful boycott organizers unflinchingly conceded his rival's analysis, depicting his philosophy of mobilization in a terse staccato.

"We have to get the adrenalin flowing, we have to plant the idea of losing Canarsie, we have to motivate people from a negative viewpoint. We are troublemakers."

The febrile appeals succeeded, not because the residents were infinitely suggestible but because the radicals played to their fears. An Italian-American unionist condemned that reinforcement of the received, and divisive, wisdom. "Whites have been fed, and are still receiving, the same kind of news about blacks. The trouble with the Italian League and the CCC is that they have not really given themselves a chance to go out and be objective about it. They gave the people the old information, that by bringing blacks in you're going to destroy the neighborhood, by bringing blacks in, the values of the property will go down, by bringing blacks in you have destroyed any kind of decent living. This is the thing that was drilled into people."

A useful approach is to ask what specific needs the militant leaders satisfied in a particular time and place. A savvy leader in the Democratic Club who despised the methods of "the crazies" described what they offered their anxious clientele:

The militants speak to the ordinary frightened citizens who allow themselves to be led. The people are acting out of fear. But the fear is rational. It's not irrational. It's the fear of mortgaged homes. They need solace. The rabbis and the churches are mortgaged to the hilt too. There are the economic concerns, like selling houses. They're in trouble, they can't run. And there's the physical fear. Blacks come in and there's violence, maybe not because they're black, but the influx creates crime and this is a legitimate fear. They feel they don't have a vehicle. The crazies say what they're thinking and feeling. The legitimate leadership and the bureaucracies of the nation don't care about their legitimate economic problems. They're concerned with not being labeled bigots. So the people have nowhere else to go.

The risks made Canarsians loath to gamble. All their scenarios during the crisis may be seen as an adjustment to a fear of betting. They acted as if the crisis where a game of "deep play," Jeremy Bentham's concept, as explained by Clifford Geertz: "He means play in which the stakes are so high that it is, from his utilitarian standpoint, irrational for men to engage in it at all."[24] The residents had to make a whole series of guesses for which adequate information did not exist. Were the Tilden 31 just the opening wedge for all of Brownsville? Would a tipped Wilson Junior High repeat the fate of Meyer Levin Junior High? Would busing blacks from Brownsville to darken Canarsie end with busing Canarsie children to whiten East Flatbush? Could the courts, the school board, or the chancellor be trusted? Did Canarsians dare commit themselves to accepting the verdict of law? Would conceding the loss of the local school board's autonomy lower the threshold for future overrides, which the growing black population of Brooklyn made likely? These and a dozen other questions focused all their fears about vulnerable social and physical places in a heated moment of anxiety.

The pronouncements of the boycott demonstrated the worst-case scenarios being played out in the mind's eye. "We've run once," cried the residents, like haunted people, "we've seen what happens." The deputy chancellor of schools conceded the truth of the protesters' disquiet. "They know the basic population changes are against them, but there's nothing they can do about it," except, he added, "to stop panicking." Chancellor Scribner scornfully came out against "any compromise in Canarsie that would give white parents assurance that the percentage of blacks and Puerto Ricans in Wilson Junior High would be limited."[25]

The radicals, then, did not invent the mood of apocalypse. They embodied and inflamed it. One resident recalled the warnings of the militants in the Italian League and the Concerned Citizens. "They would say, 'If one black comes into Canarsie, they'll take over the neighborhood.' " The flyers spoke just as bluntly to those fears. "If we lose our schools, we will lose Canarsie. Boycott!!" A school board member, begging the audience to be patient, reminded them that Scribner would no longer be chancellor after April 1 and asked them to postpone a second boycott: "So if you'll just be patient." A radical leader ran to the front of the room: "Wait until April 1, should we? Well, I know what April 1 is. It's April Fool's Day. Don't be fooled by this kind of talk. Boycot now is the only answer."

The essence of the radicals' appeal was the wager they offered. The betting strategy of the moderates was patience, repectability, and compromise, all of which raised the quotient of risk. And they required a greater outlay of trust in official remedies, a kind of side bet that removing the action from the locale to distant jurisdictions—accepting the verdict of law, national bureaucracies, the Supreme Court—would not deliver Canarsie to strangers and increase the odds for a sellout once public surveillance was relaxed. The militants' betting strategy demanded no such faith. The warning against April Fools emphasized the chanciness of intemperate optimism. The radicals affirmed a fearsome vision of the world that, in a situation of murky confusion, had a pleasing definiteness.

As in most economic transactions, everything depended on limited information and therefore on ill-formed hunches about the community's ability to ward off tipping. Nobody could be certain where the mysterious point lay beyond which it would be too late to intervene. Taking the unequivocal position that the busing order must be nullified seemed to remove the need to contemplate that possibility. The elaborate theater of the radicals said that under no conditions would they stand for raising the level of gamble. "Under no conditions" was both a threat and a promise. The militants developed popularity in a second way, then, by implying that they would use any methods to achieve the goal of a risk-free—which for many demonstrators translated into a black-free—Canarsie.

The mark of the radicals was their free-wheeling style of exerting influence, suggesting a tacit pledge to try racist or unlawful means to gain their ends. "They swaggered around like soldiers," complained a school official, who saw in that martial strutting echoes of neo-fascism. A group of activists in one antibusing group exulted in their contempt for effete respectability. "We are troublemakers. We make demands. We make the school board know we aren't pacifists and we will fight back. I was proud to be called a militant during the school crisis."

Their brashness was not just a gratuitous expressiveness whose function was purely cathartic. The radicals encoded, in words and bearing, a determination to stand fast that maximized their ability to accomplish ultimate goals. Means and ends were thus not strictly separable. Pragmatics and dramatics fused together in lower-middle-class radicalism.

Some protesters translated the language of hints into actual screams, the shrillest form of literal voice. A schoolteacher whose car was run off the road by local right-wingers remembered, "Aside from the actual violent acts, there was psychologically oriented violence: the fear and the panic and the propaganda. They would say, 'If one black comes in, they'll take over the neighborhood.' Or they would say, 'If you send your kids to school and don't go along with the [second] boycott, we'll beat you up.' " One of the most unsavory tactics used by a few boycott enforcers involved yelling "Your mother doesn't love you" at children whose parents had sent them to school. The memory of that atmosphere of violence lingered for years in the mind of one bitter Canarsie man. "I was called a nigger lover. People told me, 'Get out of Canarsie, or else.' And there was a fire-bombing. I still get nasty mail and comments. The kids in the neighborhood say, 'Hey, there goes that nigger lover.' "

A few of the protesters made good on their threats. Two Jewish activists exploded in fury against picketers from the Youth against War and Fascism. "We went after them and punched them out in front of Wilson Junior High. And my buddy bit one of them commies on the neck real good." Such actions prompted the *New York Times,* in its editorial of October 25, 1972, to condemn vicious groups that "aroused passions of which a civilized community can only be ashamed." On election day, a week later, as Canarsians voted for McGovern or Nixon, the *Times* urged "the community's forces of good will to dispel irrational fear and counter vicious rumors."[26]

The *Times* later seemed to concede the effectiveness of militance: To abandon integration "because of a grapevine of local threats," the paper argued, would be "a surrender to racism." The notion of a grapevine of intimidation unwittingly moved the *Times* closer to William Gamson's claim that "rebellion ... is simply politics by other means. It is not some kind of irrational expression but is as instrumental in its nature as a lobbyist trying to get special favors for his group."[27]

The radicals engaged in militance with cool deliberation. The imagery of showdowns and standoffs reflected their awareness of the utility of rowdiness, spurred by other events of the times. A moderate PTA leader put the Canarsie rebellion in the larger perspective: "We thought the boycotts during the Ocean Hill–Brownsville crisis were terrible, but we whites learned from the black militance. It all goes back to 1968 and the days of Sonny Carson," she noted, citing a black nationalist leader. "Yelling at people for crossing a picket line," said one activist in the Italian League, "is not really intimidation. It's just like labor actions."[28]

The militants' sleight of hand enhanced their apparent popularity. In one of the most perverse instances of fakery, some captains in the Concerned Citizens of Canarsie pointed cameras at parents who broke through the picket lines to send their children to school. The cameras lacked film, but the ersatz surveillance was as effective as the real thing. A leader laughed, remembering the false props. "We used the cameras without film to pretend we were observing who broke the boycott. It was a good scare tactic, but that one got us into trouble."

The radicals were painfully aware that their boasts of support did not translate into supporters on the street. To compensate, a small core of zealots adeptly manipulated the media and inflated the impression of their numbers by shuttling the same protesters from school to school. "You remember," said one of the most important boycott leaders, "ninety percent of the community did not care last time. We mobilized them only for a short time. I mean, there were only twenty-five or thirty people you could really count on, the committed people. Most Canarsians weren't that sympathetic with us. We had the same people running back and forth from school to school. We closed the schools last time with only one hundred people."

The ambiguous bonds forged by a small band of militant leaders and the larger swirl of their eclectic followers point to a more formal understanding of the surge of Jews into the Italian-American Civil Rights League in the earliest days of the school crisis. The tradition of restraint, the fear of demagoguery, and the lack of militaristic local leaders forced anxious Jewish residents to rely on patrons of militance. The militants' nerviness compensated for the followers' failure of nerve, embarrassment with hooliganism, or plain lack of know-how. In contrast to the Jefferson Democratic Club, the hard-liners delivered not perquisites but a pledge to run around formal channels when necessary.[29]

A Jewish official in the Jefferson Club grudgingly conceded the effectiveness of the militants. "The Italian-American Civil Rights League mainly brings security to the Canarsie community . . . Their value is psychology. Italians will stand fast to fight. They stand firm. They are our muscles, the muscles for the Jews." A member of the Jewish Community Council of Canarsie highlighted the classical nature of the Italians acting as stand-ins. "The Jews in Canarsie have always looked on the Italians as their *shabbos goy*," he argued, using the Yiddish phrase for a gentile agent hired to perform physical duties forbidden on the Sabbath. "We have always wanted the Italians to do our fighting for us."

Although they were uncomfortable with the racist language and *prost* behavior of some militants, many residents delegated responsibility to the less squeamish for acts they deemed not kosher but necessary. The militants, primarily right-wing Republicans and backlash Democrats, enticed a thousand families from all partisan and social spheres to give ten dollars each to the Concerned Citizens of Canarsie. The Italian League and the CCC, an Italian politician observed, "mainly recruited from those with less education, but they also attracted some of those with more education. They didn't like the league or the CCC, but they stuck with them because they were afraid of losing everything. They rendered to Caesar the ten bucks for self-protection."

The nuances of the man's remarks qualify the inherently ethnic nature of the relation between anxious Jews and Italian protectors. He was a humane Italian democrat; decrying the invective of the militants, he included Jewish activists in the category of Caesars. Although Caesarism appeared more frequently among one ethnic group than another, he saw it as a tendency within all human beings.

Residents who enlisted in the ranks of the militants received more than they may have bargained for. They mortgaged their sympathy and imagination to political creditors who inflamed the passions of the community, some from conviction, some from a desire to promote their own fortune, some from the panic they shared with their neighbors. Their worries about property values threw the market for Canarsie homes into the doldrums and stained the name of the community. A minority of the militants acted unconscionably toward innocent children and families exercising their legal rights to an education. The radical leaders shouted for law and order, but their disorder encouraged lawlessness. The militants' threats cast doubt on their boast that they represented a silent majority. If the majority sided with them, why did they have to perform the dance of bravado to produce it? While some leaders said they were anxious about the future quality of education in Canarsie, local educators believed the commotion set back race relations and educational performance in the schools a year or more. One administrator asked: "When are they going to stop this and let me get back to work? Without the Italian League and the Concerned Citizens of Canarsie, there would have been no crisis. The crisis made race relations in the schools worse. I spent one year breaking up fighting between blacks and whites. I'm an educator. Let me educate!"

Mayhem scared off many would-be adherents of the radicals. The militants' efforts to suppress their most "enthusiastic" members reflected an awareness of the penalties of unruliness. Containment became most urgent when a loose band of wildly swinging rebels decided to become an organization with a mandate to speak for the community. In 1976, when Alan Erlichman tried to seize Stanley

Fink's Assembly seat, a CCC member warned at a meeting, "We got into a lot of trouble last time when we used the cameras to see who was breaking the boycott. We cannot act prematurely this time. The whole ball game in activism and civics is timing. We'll bury ourselves if we act hastily."

The disagreement was more about seemly methods of disputing than about the goal of racial stability.[30] Rival attitudes toward roughhouse defined membership in distinct political communities. The respectable and the radical factions of the movement against busing each claimed its own leaders, bases of support, and political sympathies. Although many Jews and Italians did not conform to the stereotypes of cosmopolitan democrats and populist rebels, the moderate and the militant leadership formed the nuclei around which people gathered in varying degrees of affection, antagonism, and ambivalence. Behind the rallying cry "Canarsie Schools for Canarsie Children" was not a real solidarity. Chanting was an attempt to will it into being with a slogan. Hidden by the unified resistance to busing, the heterogeneity of the crowd mocked the chant of the Italian League, "We Are One."

Mainstream civic, political, and PTA leaders, including those who supported the first boycott, viewed the wild side of insurgency as an outburst from the most nativist segments of the neighborhood. An Italian Democrat decried the protofascist promptings he discerned among many antibusing militants. "They were prepared to use the community for their own ends. They were demagogues without integrity. I hold them in utter contempt. They play to people's need to rationalize that the other guy is fucking them over. The activists are hate-mongers who should retreat to their holes." A Jewish PTA leader contrasted practical fears about tipping with the distasteful racism of some of her neighbors. "The bigots are lower, ignorant, less educated people. The problem is with the vocal bigots, and their fear and insecurity. But I say, black or white, we're basically the same. We should have brotherhood."

Partisan differences as well as mutual disapproval created a gap between the Democratic establishment and many of the militants. When the combined PTAs called for a halt to raucous demonstrations early in the school crisis, the 150 rejectionists who remained in the streets wore buttons favoring Nixon, Agnew, and Dominick Andreassi, the Assembly candidate of the Conservative and Republican parties. Many of the Italian activists were registered Republicans and Conservatives, with a history of support for nationalist rightwingers. The ties of the militant leaders to civic and political organizations also show a right-wing character. Alan Erlichman worked at the borough level in Procaccino's campaign against Lindsay. Andreassi ran in 1972 on the Nixon-Agnew ticket, was endorsed by Procaccino, and claimed the title of Americanism chairman of the Canarsie American Legion. Officers and candidates of the Conservative party were active in the militant organizations, as were members of the Jewish Defense League.

Little snippets of life history signal the link between militant backlash in the neighborhood and populist conservatism in national elections. An Italian woman in the forefront of the protests refused to socialize with blacks because of "their loose morals." She had voted Republican since Truman broke General MacArthur, and she was a defender of Joseph McCarthy. An admirer of Barry Goldwater with a history of participating in local vigilante actions discerned a conspiracy of "liberals who are infiltrating us." He applauded Wallace's stand in the schoolhouse door. The shock troops of the antibusing radicals included the man who suggested renaming Wilson Junior High for Martin Luther King's assassin, the vigilante who beat the black man under the Belt Parkway, and the woman who told the white youths at Canarsie High School to "do what you gotta do." The rank and file that swarmed to the militants was diverse; at its center the antibusing mob contained the cadres of right-wing reaction.

The rebellion against busing, then, was more than a movement of unaffiliated masses. The cause of radical dissent energized a second, shadow set of local activists in civic, political, and ethnic organizations. Their connections formed a loose-knit network, one that was less ramified and powerful than that of the rival Jefferson Democrats and their allies in religious and educational institutions. Insurgency was thus not separate from ordinary politics. The radicals weighed their every move, considering the impact on the Democratic establishment, and every failure of the establishment created new temptations for the insurgents. Maurice Carroll identified the political spillover of the busing crisis in his *New York Times* story of November 5, whose title read "Canarsie School Crisis Expected to Hurt Democratic Incumbent [Stanley Fink]." The prediction was accurate. In 1970 Fink beat Andreassi by an almost four-to-one margin; his margin over Andreassi in November 1972 was less than two to one. The busing rebellion also launched new political careers. Alan Erlichman would use the organizational base he developed in

1972–1973 as a springboard to challenge Fink in the Democratic primary of 1976.

The busing brouhaha enacted in the streets the same theatrics that were unfolding politically across the nation. It marked the breakdown of legitimate authority effected by racial conflict and the wild movements outside traditional forms that were released by the breakdown. The rise of a culture of resistance, the flurry of political initiatives outside customary channels, and the rising fortunes of right-wing demagogues echoed the dominant mood of backlash in America in the late 1960s and early 1970s. If the insurgency against busing was a revival of community, the crisis equally revealed the friction beneath the surface of Canarsie. The local cracking apart of a rickety confederation into radical and respectable wings of dissent, like the splitting apart of Jewish opinion into its provincial and enlightened streams, symbolized the division in the nation of resistance to liberal reform into its plebeian and genteel factions.

The prickly tension between the temperate and the unruly recurrently promised to divide Canarsie into warring parties. The entente between them was always provisional, full of tense ambivalence and disapproval. The breach over the legitimacy of self-help was only the most telling division, heavily weighted on the side of the law-abiding. Clashes erupted as well in local and national elections. "Even though the neighborhood is the typical locus of brotherhood, neighbors do not necessarily maintain 'brotherly' relations," Max Weber admonished. "On the contrary: Wherever popularly prescribed behavior is vitiated by personal enmity and conflicting interests, hostility tends to be extreme and lasting."[31]

8. The Trials of Liberalism

Democrats Divided

*"Fink wins big against the radicals ... They want
the radicals only during something frightening
like the busing issue. But then they want them to
disappear when they feel safe again."*

Brooklyn residents focused on the ordinary elements of life when
they judged the risks of integration or the rights of criminals; no one
could afford to forget about personal security, subsistence, or survival. Practical reality forced all citizens to take heed.

A distinctive politics of space formed around the need to assuage
concerns about busing, tipping neighborhoods, crime in the streets,
scatter-site low-income housing, judicial leniency, the safety of
schools, white flight, and the death penalty. None of these issues fit
neatly into the familiar categories of the New Deal party system.
Nor was it even clear what the national leadership might do about
the dilemmas of place. The origins of many of those problems lay in
national migration flows and regional patterns of economic growth
and disinvestment. Their local consequences could be only partly
controlled or, at best, exported from one neighborhood or state to
the next. As a result, the felt needs of countless urban dwellers were
not met by the prevailing leadership.

A new breed of political entrepreneurs who were more comfortable in the familiar niches of the neighborhood emerged on the wave
of anxiety and outrage. The politics they developed was essentially

the geopolitics of local community. Deterrence, counterforce, holding ground, securing borders, flanking maneuvers, and standing fast formed its central organizing concepts. One strident Italian reactionary from a Brooklyn civic association outside of Canarsie told a crowd of the danger of falling dominoes. Pointing to the south shore communities of Canarsie, Bensonhurst, and Bay Ridge, the speaker warned, "We are the last decent neighborhoods left. If we all had come out like this twelve years ago, we'd have had a Little Rock in the North." He referred to the civil rights bills of years ago and "all this talk about minorities. Now our children are the minorities in the schools. We are no longer the majority. And today it's the schools, tomorrow it's your home and community and business."

The Italians had an edge on the Jews in politically responding to threats to locale, but their readiness did not spring forth full blown. The absence of a liberal, socialist, or labor tradition among Italians, Nathan Glazer has observed, left a vacuum "filled by the ideological outlook of small homeowners, which many Italian-Americans were or aspired to be; this involved opposition to high taxes, welfare programs, and the like . . . Views on the general problems of the city . . . are hardly necessary when one's major concern is the neighborhood and its home owners."[1]

This portrait is apt, but it needs updating. The Wagner years were relatively calm, before racial lines were sharply drawn during the 1960s and 1970s. Glazer captured the peaceful, inward-turning side of the politics of neighborhood. But challenge quickly brought to the fore a more muscular spirit. For Italians, the ever-present obligation was, in Richard Gambino's words, *"agire da maschio,* to act in a manly fashion." Manliness involved "protecting one's blood and advancing family security and power. One did this not by being noble, but by being clever, foxy, shrewd." Gambino qualified the stereotype of docile but volatile Italian men. "They will tolerate a great deal as long as it is not viewed as a threat to *l'ordine della famiglia.*"[2] Tough talkers like Mario Procaccino in New York City, Frank Rizzo in Philadelphia, and Tony Imperiale in Newark bore a striking resemblance to that classical ideal. When it came to defending their neighborhoods, they would not let genteel scruples stand in the way of their mission. They perfected a domestic brand of *realpolitik.*

Italian Canarsie fielded a flock of backlash candidates recruited from local Republican circles, the American Legion, the Conservative party, and North Canarsie civic groups. Italians of populist conservative stripe recurrently challenged Jewish Democrats in councilmanic and assembly races, but they could not win election. The Italians were at a numerical disadvantage, and they did not participate as vigorously as the Jews, which created resentment of Jewish clout. One Knights of Columbus leader reflected, "We felt we needed more Christian influence and representation in Canarsie. After all, we are 45 percent of the community. An imbalance existed due to our own apathy. But the Christian people in Canarsie should have a voice."

The ultimate power of the Democrats was based on their incumbency and an ample resource base. At one o'clock in the morning following the election, Vito Battista, the conservative avatar of the city's home owners, discussed his 1975 defeat at the hands of the Jefferson Club's Councilman Herbert Berman. As the elevated trains rumbled past his headquarters at Ozone Park, Queens, he reflected, "I fight with a beanshooter and they have an atomic bomb. They have high-paid patronage workers, judges, the payroll. The Jefferson Club pulled out their buses from the unions, they had twenty-three busloads—Truckers, the Seafarers' Union, the Longshoremen's Union, and the Butchers' Union. The Democrats have the grips on them. It's Meade Esposito."

The Italian electorate could not determine Canarsie's destiny; whatever chance backlash candidates had depended on Jewish voters and Jewish leaders. While the Jews historically did not match the Italians in their penchant for geopolitics, the vulnerabilities of place worked on them in similar fashion. An Italian policeman depicted the imperatives that united a wandering people with a pagan Mediterranean people whose sense of communality flowed from attachment to place. "The Italian people are not going to run. Italians stand fast. And the Jewish people? They are tired of running. They've given it all up. That's how they lost Brownsville and Crown Heights and East New York. They're tired of that shit."

The canard that craven Jews lost East New York resembles that old *j'accuse* of the jingoist, "Who lost China?" The accusation of surrender was not simply a case of misplaced concreteness or the musing of a paranoid mentality. As New York City was stripped of the restraints that allow hostile groups to coexist in a plural society, the aptness of Italian realism forced Jewish idealism to give ground. Threat prompted increasing Jewish calls for someone to do something, whether constitutional or not. Vulnerability expanded the Jewish audience for geopolitics.

Yet private wants require organizational channels to become audible. Institutional arrangements may silence some kinds of speech and broadcast others. The Jewish leaders who controlled Canarsie politics, and their Jewish and Italian allies in the interlocked network of civic institutions, worked to keep racial invective from spilling over into public conversation. The Jefferson Democratic Club was first and foremost an electoral machine with vested interests in incumbency. The anxieties of place, however, mobilized new participants around the volatile issue of race, diluted the power of the club's controlled electorate of 3,000 dues-paying members and beholden captains, and introduced uncertainty into the political environment. Moreover, the club labored under a burden of loyalties that did not restrict Italian Republicans and Conservatives. Tightly coupled to a borough organization that spanned black and Hispanic assembly districts, the club was not an autonomous unit free to go its own way. A conservative Jewish businessman voiced a popular lament over the demise of the local Democratic party as a conduit of white influence. "The establishment Democrats kiss the asses of the black vote, and Stanley Steingut has lots of blacks in his district. Meade Esposito knows the black politicians are significant in city and statewide influence."

Ethical inhibitions reinforced the Jefferson Club's reluctance to exploit racial passion. The precinct captains were a diverse lot, but the officials and their personal coterie belonged to a more cosmopolitan segment of the middle class. Ideologically, they were centrist and progressive Democrats with enduring New Deal commitments. Both Italians and Jews in the inner circles of the club embraced a self-image of respectability that led them to condemn racist irrationality. An officer of the club lambasted the forces of right-wing reaction that surfaced during the school crisis of 1972. "Nothing is accomplished by racist ranting and raving. The school boycott was a danger to civil rights. It's your right to go to school."

The Jews of Canarsie lacked the Italians' head start in backlash. The handicap was organizational as much as cultural. But if they did not possess a ready-made instrument of parochial reaction, the Jews would play catch-up and invent their own vehicles. A decade of jeopardy produced a sprinkling of Jewish leaders cast in the mold of Procaccino and the others. As Irving Howe noted, "One result was the rise within Jewish neighborhoods of demagogic types like Jerry Birbach, who inflamed every sensitive Jewish nerve in a 1972 struggle over integrated housing in Queens."[3]

The dominance of the Jefferson Democrats meant that the conflicts played out elsewhere as wrangling between Democrats and Republicans erupted in Canarsie as fights inside the Democratic party. Because of the explosiveness of the racial issues in the 1970s, the entrenched leadership was less able to insulate party primaries from right-wing challengers. Alan Erlichman's primary run in 1976 against Assemblyman Stanley Fink epitomized the power of geopolitics to disturb politics as usual. On December 18, 1975, the state commissioner of education, Ewald Nyquist, handed down a decision, later withdrawn, ordering the New York City Board of Education to ensure "that the racial composition of the student body of [Meyer Levin Junior High in East Flatbush] will reflect the pupil population within the district." To achieve such a distribution would require the busing of Canarsie children to East Flatbush, and that prospect revived all the old anxieties of 1972–73. One PTA leader said Nyquist should "climb down from his 'ivory tower' and face the reality that there just aren't enough of us 'endangered species' left in the city . . . to stop the segregation in the East Flatbush schools." This was the situation in which Erlichman decided to run for state office.

It would be hard to find two more perfect symbols of the impulses at war in the Brooklyn Jewish psyche. Fink's admirers liked to boast that he, a graduate of New York University Law School, was "a real brainy guy." Erlichman had first gained recognition as a leader of the militant forces during the antibusing insurgency of 1972–73; a large, brawny man sporting a bushy Fu Manchu mustache, he exuded a tough, kinetic air that earned him, in Yiddish, the epithet "the bear" from an elderly woman who disapproved of his "roughneck" ways.

Whatever their differences in style, the ideological gulf between the two men was even wider. A bright star in the Jefferson galaxy, Fink was by 1976 chairman of the Assembly's Codes Committee. A graduate of the spoils system overseen by Meade Esposito, he shared the regulars' mistrust of the moralistic rhetoric of good government crusaders; he unabashedly defended one assembly appropriation of $40,000: " 'What the hell is the Canarsie Health Station?' he said with a straight face. 'The Canarsie Health Station is a good old-fashioned piece of pork barrel.' "[4] The regulars admired practical pols, "mechanics" who did not wear visionary ideals on their sleeves. Esposito liked to tweak the Manhattan reform group called the New Democratic Coalition (NDC) by claiming the initials meant November Don't Count.

While no Jefferson Democrat gave short shrift to serving "the Jefferson team," Fink was not a machine hack. He championed legislation protecting the rights of consumers, prisoners, and homosexuals. In a display of great courage, he voted against an antibusing bill that he deemed unconstitutional. A *New York Times* profile concluded, "What Mr. Fink has is a keen intelligence, an ideological commitment to civil liberties that has given him one of the most liberal voting records in the assembly and—especially since he joined the leadership—a nicely developed sense of who needs what and when."[5]

While Fink balanced service to the district with broad human concerns, Erlichman narrowed the discussion down to the issue of middle-class survival. He represented a form of politics hitherto unfamiliar in Jewish circles, having as one of its hallmarks the unembarrassed singling out of blacks as arch-rivals. Around the time of the primary, Erlichman told a meeting of backlash groups, "The racist hates blindly. I hate anyone taking what's mine, no matter what their color ... The blacks don't want to improve Brownsville, but they want to take what we have built." He unblinkingly defended the propriety of racial exclusion. "When they [blacks] have learned respect for law and order, then maybe they won't bring crime into our schools. When my nine-year-old can walk through Harlem safely, then I'll consider integration."

Erlichman gave his clientele license to dwell on their own suffering, cutting through all the frustrating mediations represented by Fink's concern for the rights of citizens in the abstract. He had no squeamishness about playing hardball. His analysis of ghetto insurgency as political blackmail suggested a manly course of action at odds with the Jefferson Club's equivocation, emphasis on policy, and respectability. As Erlichman saw it, blacks used the threat of violence as leverage. They held officialdom, liberal sympathizers, and politicians hostage to veiled hints of retaliatory unrest. Liberals lacked "the intestinal fortitude" needed to "take action against these 'free-loaders' [for it] would be political suicide, and would cause 'unrest' in the 'welfare community.' " Yet, he continued, "should this 'unrest' turn into the usually threatened riots and looting, these very same liberals would 'tie' the hands of the police and allow the unlawfulness to prevail in the name of 'fair play.' "[6]

The campaigns were studies in contrast. Fink's campaigners had a relaxed, joshing air as they strolled about the community and worked the crowds at the supermarkets. They avoided controversial issues, citing instead their service to the community. In speech sprinkled with Yiddish, a precinct captain approached an elderly lady shopper in front of Waldbaum's supermarket and gently led her over to Fink as if he were a prodigal Jewish son: "Come meet our Stanley, he's one of our own."

The Erlichman retinue tapped gamier passions. One campaign worker warned potential voters, "Don't vote for the Jefferson Club. They're nigger lovers. When Erlichman is elected, we'll drive all the niggers out of Canarsie." Making the rounds with the candidate, another man asked, "So what if middle-class blacks are deprived of their rights? Democracy is doing what the majority wants." At a school board meeting a black man accused the Canarsie majority on the local school board of segregationist intent. The recent busing order, he argued, "recognizes the inescapable conclusion that separate but equal is not equal ... You ladies and gentlemen are attempting to turn back the clock prior to the Supreme Court decision of 1954." At that juncture an Erlichman volunteer broke in, "You can go back South." The black man replied, "You better try and send me back there, baby," and he concluded, "I beseech the parents of both East Flatbush and Canarsie, with the exception of loud-mouth here, to fight against this resolution ... because it supports a dogma which if carried to its ultimate conclusion will only perpetuate a generation of hate-mongers among our children, and eventually the United States of America too will face what all other racist societies face, because they too became all-consuming in their hate."

The hostility between the Fink and Erlichman factions was unstinting. An Erlichman aide, called a liar by one Jefferson Club campaigner, warned, "After this election, I know somebody I'm going to rip apart." The club reciprocated the hostility. "I see Erlichman and his henchmen and I see the swastika. He is a prime fascist. He is a demagogue with no integrity. He and his people are hate-mongers." Reaching for a way to capture what he saw as pandering to the fear of the residents, the man dubbed such backlash antics "crotch politics."

When the votes were tallied, the voters returned Fink to Albany. The power of the machine, popular mistrust of establishment politicians, and the friends-and-neighbors effect of any local election complicate the attempt to interpret the voting. Yet from one angle, the surprise is how well Erlichman did against the Jefferson dynasty. From the start he conceded the club its strongholds in the ten precincts of the assembly district outside Canarsie—Bergen Beach, Mill Basin, and Flatlands—where Fink's majorities climbed past 80 percent. In the forty-odd election districts of the Canarsie portion, how-

ever, the strength of the Jefferson Club dropped noticeably. Erlichman beat Fink in four precincts (two of them Italian), held him to
less than 55 percent in another six, and to less than 60 percent in another nine.

The infusion of ideology and passion into an Assembly primary
race was portentous. The appearance of occasional Jewish rebels as
fierce defenders of the neighborhood dramatized the elasticity of
classical Jewish restraints under the pressures of an altered material
environment. The Jewish electorate split into its provincial and cosmopolitan constituent parts. It would be mistaken, however, to take
Fink and Erlichman as personifications of stable impulses within the
Jewish, or even the middle-class, psyche. The relative balance of the
two impulses has varied widely in the course of history and under
differing conditions. To some extent, the primary challenge was
prompted by the fluke of the renewal of the busing order. The election brought to the surface emotions that had been dormant in Canarsie since the crisis of 1972. In a reprise of his earlier fight against
Jefferson Club moderation, Erlichman was waving the banner of antibusing insurgency.

At the time of the 1980 presidential election, one Jefferson Club
official thought back to the fight between Stanley Fink and Alan Erlichman four years earlier. "The problem with the militant groups is
that they were one-issue organizations. All they knew was antiblack
and antibusing. They had a limited scope, and once the threat of
busing disappeared, and as integration in Canarsie has been increasing naturally in the schools and in the neighborhood, they lost their
function. We don't have those bitter primaries like we used to in the
middle 1970s. The conservatives were disheartened by the loss in
1976. The Thomas Jefferson Club has an even stronger monopoly
than it used to."

As the fleetingness of "crotch politics" indicates, right-wing insurgency was a response to conditions that changed over time. A Canarsie lawyer defined the labile relationship between threat and
preference that characterized Canarsians' reaction in all realms of
culture and politics. Under conditions of "normal politics," he argued, most Canarsians preferred leaders like Fink, but fear of risk
suspended normal inhibitions. "The people of Canarsie have been
traumatized. They prefer a leader like Stanley Fink to represent
them to the radical approach. Fink wins big against the radicals. I
am convinced that they want the radicals only during something
frightening like the busing issue. But then they want them to disap-

pear when they feel safe again." Such a judgment is inevitably distorted by partisan bias, but it does rightly point to the different settings in which resentment politics fades and flourishes. And to grasp that moment of middle-class radicalism at the local level is to understand much about the crisis that shook the national Democratic party in 1972 and that remained unresolved for many years thereafter.

The Democratic Party in Decline

*"Canarsie people are basically the old-fashioned
type of liberals in their ideals . . . That's where
their hearts are until they're personally
threatened. Underneath it all the average
Canarsian has the heart of a garment worker."*

The upheaval in local politics was unusual, at least in one respect. Among old-style Democratic constituencies, the social issues of race, Vietnam, and lifestyle tended to affect national elections more than local ones. Many social scientists have noted the functional virtues of this splitting of the polity into a two-tier system. It permitted the "old" bread-and-butter liberalism to endure in pragmatic votes for state and congressional elections, while presidential contests became the focus of heated spiritual struggle over the "new" liberalism. But if the Fink-Erlichman contest reversed the more general pattern, it remained something of an aberration. More often the Jefferson Democrats retained their hold on local office without serious worry. The national Democrats were not so lucky with Canarsians.

Rebellion in the streets of Canarsie evolved along with national, no less than local, politics. During the 1972 presidential race, many conservative activists stole a few moments from the busing protest to campaign against McGovern because they deemed that prairie populist an apostle of "forced busing." More than a few shrewd Canarsie-watchers believed that Nixon reaped a sizable portion of the Jewish vote because the election came at the apex of the antibusing agitation. With the urgent events unfolding on the streets in front of Wilson Junior High, the national election seemed somewhat remote. A McGovern campaign worker pinpointed those contrary pulls of community and society. "Meade Eposito liked McGovern, but he hated the punks who ran the campaign, the outsiders who went to New Hampshire, the out-of-state bureaucrats and technocrats. The national McGovern people were totally unconcerned with busing, but local busing was the only important thing in the election in Canarsie."

The state's efforts to reach down into the locales to redress racial injustice boomeranged; eventually the communities tried to even the score against an intrusive judiciary, the bureaucracies, the state. The emotions of outrage, vengeance, and humiliation spilled over into the political arena. They drowned some candidates in a sea of indignation, carried others away on a tidal wave of victory. Ultimately, national politics was the realm in which grievances were inflamed or arbitrated, conflicts stoked or resolved, legitimacy accumulated or dissipated.

Elections in the late 1960s often seemed like cockfights or slugfests; the voters affirmed not the goal of corrective equilibrium but their own irreconcilable desires. Everett Ladd's description of blue-collar restiveness with the Democratic party as neopopulist retaliation against the party's liberal wing captures the power of electoral revenge to alter political fortunes.[7] The upheavals of the party system reached their apogee in the presidential elections of 1968 and 1972. The elections before 1968 formed a prelude, with hints of convulsions not yet manifest.

In 1968 the country was racked by antiwar protest, political assassination, and urban conflagration. Garry Wills evoked the demons that had been let loose in that stormy year. "There was a sense everywhere, in 1968, that things were giving. That man had not merely lost control of his history, but might never regain it. That palliatives would not serve, and nothing but palliatives could be found. That we had slipped gears somewhere, and a train of mismeshings was chewing the machinery up." Since, as Wills observed, every election year is a revelation, "it was precisely this period of self-revelation that some men feared as we entered upon 1968. What would the mirror show? There was slim hope we could avoid trouble in the cities, on the campus, in Washington, in Vietnam, during the fevered time of primaries and convention and campaign and election. The democratic process itself was considered dangerous, offering as it does so many opportunities for demagogy and demonstration, riot and assassination."[8]

The election offered a choice of Hubert Humphrey, a liberal Democrat of New Deal vintage; Richard Nixon, a Republican plumbing the waters of southern strategy; and George Wallace, a reactionary punisher committed to the defense of Southern tribalism. In Italian Canarsie the power of ethnic conservatism manifested itself in the collapse of any viable Democratic candidacy. Humphrey received a third of the vote, Nixon took between 50 and 60 percent, and George Wallace gained the remainder. A police detective embodied the nonauthoritarian conservatism that nourished the vote for Nixon. The man had turned against the New Deal when Roosevelt tried to pack the Supreme Court. He had favored Goldwater in 1964 because he was "an honest and candid man who made no beans about" what he was planning to do in Vietnam. And he voted for Nixon because "he was a conservative, yet cognizant of the needs of the country, and he would put the brakes on free government spending." Drawn to Nixon's pledge to "shape up crime" and to his attacks on busing, the policeman felt that "George Wallace is abhorrent to the average individual. I didn't like his dyed-in-the-wool southern philosophy."

Nixon's appeal was pure simplicity. He heralded a less malevolent version of Wallace's crusade against 1960s liberalism. Wallace offered rollback; Nixon promised containment. While 44 percent of Wallace supporters believed that "Negro progress" was too fast, only 22 percent of Nixon supporters agreed with that view. Richard Scammon and Ben Wattenberg observed that Nixon was the only candidate of the three running in 1968 whose supporters wanted to maintain Negro progress at its current level rather than slow it down or speed it up.[9]

George Wallace, the true talisman of the parties of order, received about 8 percent of the vote in Canarsie's Italian blue-collar precincts. Many Italians who liked the way he voiced their fiscal and racial fears, however, backed off from voting for him because he struck them as racist, polarizing, or demagogic. A dockworker toyed with the idea, "but there was no way I could vote for him. He would have caused too much resentment among blacks and split the nation in half. I don't like having second-class citizens. I could never have voted for Lester Maddox either."

Some resentful Canarsians would have voted for Wallace except that they saw endorsing a long-shot as a waste of the franchise. Why indulge in cathartic gestures when more practical backlash alternatives lay close at hand? Even those who voted for Wallace were spread along a spectrum of racist opinion. One worker voted for him "as a protest, because of what he said, 'Get rid of this liberalism and stay in the middle.' But I personally didn't like him. I didn't like the way he stood up to John Kennedy at the University of Alabama. The coloreds are entitled to go to schools if they want."

To his most fervent adherents, Wallace represented the gamiest of racist sensibilities. An Italian truck driver who voted for Wallace felt revulsion at the mere thought of racial intermarriage. "I'm totally against it. Did you ever see a mongrel kid, a white kid with Negro features? It's a bad mix. I can't see it." Men like Nixon, McCarthy, and Reagan, he believed, spoke to little people like him and did not promiscuously give their sympathy to minorities or third-world nations. Yet Wallace, more than the others, personified his kind of rough-and-tumble solutions. "I liked him for standing up in front of the school door [at the University of Alabama]. He wouldn't tolerate a mongrel race. He said, 'Let's protect middle-class rights.' " Such sentiments did not express the dominant strain of conservative opinion in the Italian community, yet Wallace's support from precinct to precinct did carve out the zone of susceptibility to authoritarian forms of reaction. Wallace approached 10 percent in the Italian working-class districts that defeated the Civilian Review Board by margins of nine to one, rejected the Equal Rights Amendment in 1975, and had given Barry Goldwater his most respectable showing in 1964.

If the restraints of Jewish politics did not preclude support for candidates like Procaccino, would it choke off the movement toward the forms of reprisal associated with Wallace? After all, civility and restraint are not frozen attributes of personality or culture. Despite the factors that nurtured resentment among Canarsie Jews, however, no audience for Wallace developed in Jewish precincts. His backing there fluctuated between 1 and 3 percent, and non-Jewish voters most likely accounted for those votes. The Jews' imperviousness to Wallace defined the limits of elasticity of Jewish political culture in the face of threat.

Vulnerable Jews were resentful of blacks, but their tradition prevented translating the resentment into racist crusading. What calls for attention is not the visible decision but the hidden one, which occurred when angry Jews who had voted for Procaccino or Nixon begged off from Wallace. The anonymity of electoral returns masked the cultural forces that discouraged a Wallace vote among Jews. While many of the Italians in one backlash group voted for Wallace or applauded him without embarrassment, historical memory kept resentful Jewish members from an incautious flirtation with him. A Jewish woman described her ideal politician as a strange hybrid—

part Truman, part Roosevelt, and "a part of Wallace." What struck her fancy about Wallace was "where he talks about the blacks getting too much. But the rest scared me. Being Jewish, I was afraid he'd get me next. He was too much like Hitler, and we don't need another Nazi Germany." The eccentricity of the times, not of the voters, encouraged such thoughts. Another woman in the antibusing movement drew the line at Wallace "because he's too strong, too antiblack, too anti-Semitic. I want someone who will calm the blacks down, but not someone who will go too far, not someone who's too overpowering, someone who'll come down on the Jews."

A distinctively Jewish brand of bigotry emerged from racial resentment. A Jewish backlash leader once told a group of antibusing activists, "The middle class is gagging on all of this. Why are we afraid to admit we are bigots? A bigot is only the derogatory form of sensible. A bigot hates without basis, but we have reasons to hate the niggers. It's not blind unreason. I hate them with my eyes open." Most aggrieved lower-middle-class Jews avoided such Talmudic convolutions, and for many the prominent emotion directed at blacks was fear rather than hatred, but others tried to classify bigotry. "I was afraid of Mr. Wallace," said a clerk. "His kind of bigotry could turn against me or anyone else. He might move against the Jews next. I thought there were some good things in what he did to the blacks, but there was some bad too. His is a blind, inbred kind of bigotry."

The weakness of Wallace's candidacy attests to continuities in Jewish politics. More striking than the occasional Jewish flirtation with Nixon in 1968 was the resilience of Democratic loyalty in Canarsie. Adlai Stevenson in 1956 had received a combined Liberal/Democratic tally of 85 percent. The level of support for Humphrey in 1968 was only five to ten points lower. What was Humphrey's appeal for the Jews? "I don't say Humphrey's a complete liberal," claimed one man, "but he's a middle-of-the-road liberal."

Dressed in the familiar garb of the New Deal, Humphrey spoke the homey language of the common man, not the New Politics lingo of the upper middle classes. He earned kudos from centrist and liberal Jews alike for his efforts to tear down an abhorrent racial caste system in the South. Humphrey thus provided an ample outlet for conventional Democratic partisanship and progressive New Deal-inspired sentiment. A teacher placed Humphrey in a natural line of liberal Democratic succession. "I associate the Republicans, you see, with conservative, American flag-waving, authoritarian politics.

They lack respect for average people other than those who are like themselves." Men like Humphrey, Roosevelt, and Kennedy, by contrast, reflected the Democratic faith, which she saw as "humanism in broad terms, social programs, the decentralization of large corporations, and the creation of a broader tax base."

An Italian attorney hinted at the enduring, if wounded, liberal spirit embedded in the hefty size of the Humphrey vote. At heart, he claimed in 1976, the Jews remained faithful to their former ideological leanings.

> It is true that Canarsie is more vocal about its conservatism, like during the busing crisis. That's one kind of conservatism. They're supersensitive about the schools. And fiscally, they're more conservative. But Canarsie people are basically the old-fashioned type of liberals in their ideals, but to the extent the ideals have hurt them, they have given up those ideals. They're the kind of people who participated in trade union concepts that implanted the liberal ideology in their heads, so they could claim to be entitled. That's where their hearts are until they're personally threatened. Underneath it all the average Canarsian has the heart of a garment worker.

The 1972 election did not dispel the urgency of race and Vietnam. In four years the Democratic party had moved to the left. The oddities of the nominating process produced a candidate who had come to personify all the forces that were anathema to the ideals and the interests of the lower middle classes. At times it seemed to them as if George McGovern had been conjured up by a nightmarish fantasy, so perfectly did he represent the denial of everything they held dear. To Republican and Conservative local activists, McGovern loomed as a wild-eyed bolshevik whose free-spending ways would far surpass even those of John Lindsay. Canarsians were especially sensitive to his support for busing just when the Canarsie school crisis had brought to a boil all their fears of loss.

In Italian Old Canarsie, Nixon improved his 1968 showing, and the Democrats' candidate dropped down ten points as McGovern received only a fourth of the vote. One nationalistic stalwart described the reinforcing effect of push and pull that produced a Nixon victory in 1972. "I admired Nixon for appointing a pro–capital punishment court, and he tried to destroy the Douglas court and restore middle-class rights . . . McGovern scared the living hell out of me. He would have pulled out on an ally! He would have run from South Vietnam."

Voters of diverse political affections, not only right-wing nationalists, recoiled from that impression of appeasement. McGovern alienated countless loyal Americans who did not think that patriotism was tantamount to jingoism. An Italian unionist who believed that "the banks grew rich on New York City, they made money on those bonds, and the little people got hurt" was a great believer in détente between the Soviet Union and the United States, as well as between blacks and whites, and he condemned racists "who feed the community negative news about blacks. They never give themselves a chance to be objective." In 1977 he judged his earlier support of American involvement in Vietnam the result of succumbing to propaganda:

> Communism is something I was indoctrinated about. I have to be frank. Communism to me is terrible. I was brought up in the era of World War II, and I believed sincerely, "This is my country," and maybe because I had that kind of attitude of gung-ho, where I would go to war for the United States of America, because it was an unblemished country, that the U.S. was right, that it was wrong to question us because they are doing everything for me. This attitude has changed. The United States, which I love dearly, has blemished itself. It has been shown that they have interfered in other countries, and one of the things I feel now that I didn't feel then was that they tried to impose their will on Vietnam.

That skepticism came late; in 1972 the gentle unionist was in the forefront of those proclaiming that peace must come with honor. "I felt so strongly for the MIAs [soldiers missing in action], I believed we should not stop the war until we got our prisoners back, because I was a fighting man in Korea." He voted for Nixon in 1972, his first defection from the Democrats, when "McGovern made that statement which to me was un-American: that he would get down on his hands and knees if he had to to stop the war." He defined a contrary ideal of character: never cut and run, do not kneel in self-abasement, stand firm and proud. "I was so strong for the American ideal that we would never do such a thing and Americans would stand up and be counted because this is our country, you're in it, our country right or wrong, like the gentleman said."

What did Canarsie Jews make of the quixotic McGovern—a Democrat, true, but a strange and unsettling breed of Democrat. "I call it the Judeo-Democratic party," said one Canarsie man. The exasperated hyperbole was only slight overstatement. Partisan loyalty plus residual liberalism held the Jews in place in 1968 and kept them from bolting to right-wing punishers or Republican conservatives. Similarly, they had reviled the limousine liberalism of John Lindsay, but in voting for Procaccino, after all, many Jews were simply reaffirming the immemorial prescriptions of a Democratic tradition. McGovern, though, was a Democrat *and* a limousine liberal.

1972 proclaimed the elasticity of Jewish politics. McGovern's Jewish support was double his Italian support, but Jewish defections dropped the Democratic vote to a historic low. The normal Jewish vote for the Democratic ticket, which had barely wavered from 1928 through 1968, fell precipitously in Canarsie by more than 25 percent, substantially higher than the national fall-off in the Jewish vote.[10] Out of forty-six election districts in Canarsie, forty predominantly Jewish, McGovern won only nine, and four of those were by razor-thin pluralities. In most Jewish precincts McGovern received only between 40 and 49 percent of the vote.

Law-and-order Jews saw in McGovern a more loathsome version of Lindsay, and countless Zionists, for whose affections Nixon made a great play in 1972, echoed the opinion of the Conservative rabbi who voted for Nixon "for Zionist reasons, because McGovern made anti-Israel statements." The remnant of progressive Democrats remained loyal to the party, including most of those in the highest echelons of the Jefferson Democratic Club. Many Jews had to swallow hard to pull that Republican lever.

Years later, liberal and moderate Jews described their feelings of guilt, of betrayal and self-betrayal, and of foolishness over the lapse from ancestral tradition. A PTA leader who had voted for Lindsay in 1969 because she thought Procaccino was a racist sighed, "I'll never live down that vote for Nixon. My relatives will never let me forget it. It was difficult for me. I didn't want to vote for McGovern. I shouldn't have voted at all. My father voted Democratic his whole life!"

Samuel Lubell's soundings of public opinion in that presidential year "revealed more torment and indecision among Jews than in any other voting group in the nation."[11] One member of the United Federation of Teachers distinguished between the situational conservatism created by the new agenda of the 1960s and an earlier ideological conservatism. She separated herself from "those who are conservative because of what they've been through," and she included backlash Jews who had been run out of East Flatbush. "They are tired of the threats, year in and year out." She considered herself "an average Jewish liberal, I guess. You know, I lived in the South, and I just couldn't see blacks in the back of the bus. It was terrible. People living in shacks, it was shocking that blacks couldn't use public accommodations. The civil rights movement was a great thing, it was a movement for human beings. People are people." But what did it mean to call oneself a liberal when the times had played havoc with all the comfortable meanings of the word? She defined a liberal as a mensch, "someone who feels more for the underdog than a conservative does. I am still a liberal, maybe." Like many others who carried the residue of their Brownsville upbringing, she retained a global appreciation for the qualities of decency that liberalism suggested, even if it lacked ideological content: "A liberal cares more for people, while a conservative only thinks about how they are affected by the issues. They have less heart."

Her heart was not so large that it could extend to the black militants she had done battle with over Ocean Hill–Brownsville. "I didn't feel for the militants, but there are militants who are white too. It's not a racial thing." The passions of the late 1960s changed her, in at least one sense:

I guess you'd say I became more conservative. In voting against McGovern in favor of Nixon, I came down to the level of my community. It was during the phase of the rioting and the uprisings. I don't stand for militance of any kind, black or white. And as time passed, Lindsay was handing the city over to the most militant groups to benefit himself. You know, I loved Adlai Stevenson. Just listening to him was a joy. He was a liberal, but not an ultra-liberal. I guess you could say that we didn't relate to the 1960s issues then.

In hindsight one can see that 1972 signaled the peaking of the furies unleashed by the 1960s and the waning of the passions of race and Vietnam, which had divided the nation for a decade. The next election suggested something of the calming powers of the electoral ritual. Presidential elections could dampen conflict as well as sharpen it, revitalizing the morale of a nation reeling from the pain of change and longing to be told of its essential wholeness, its goodness, its innocence. Countless students of the party system saw in the frenzies of 1968 and 1972 a major realignment of American politics that would dethrone the Democratic majority installed by the New Deal with a Republican one lauding the virtues of Middle America. Some of those same pundits credited Watergate with preventing a "natural" movement toward the installation of a populist right-wing regime. Whether Watergate derailed that realignment or merely postponed it, leaving it for Ronald Reagan to add the finishing touches in 1980, became a matter of spirited controversy among academics and partisans alike. About the profound effects of Watergate on the American people, however, there can be little doubt.

A mistrust of the political process lingered in Canarsie through the middle 1970s. If among the provincial that sensibility was evident in a free-floating suspiciousness, among the sophisticated it took a more principled form. A liberal Democratic Jewish teacher exclaimed, "After Watergate, it's crazy to have trust in politicians. I'm totally cynical, skeptical. Whether it's a question of power or influence, it's who you know at all levels. Nixon said he was the sovereign! Can you believe that? I was indignant. Someone should have told him that this is a democracy, not a monarchy."

America's humiliation by the emboldened third-world oil powers drove home most forcefully the arrival of a new era in American life, a time when the government was unable to enforce the global prerogatives that once had guaranteed the nation's economic growth, and fears about economic survival returned. The rise of foreign economic rivals made the position of the middle classes even shakier. A businessman in the garment industry, squeezed tighter and tighter by Japanese and Taiwanese competition, suffered a brief but demoralizing mental breakdown.

> I was afraid of things being out of my control. What is happening to the middle classes? Con Ed bills go up, the telephone bills go up, taxes go up, but I can't increase my business! In New York City, the market is shrinking. I can't see the equity in it. I don't understand the system anymore. The coats which Alexander's sells are foreign made—I resent that. Burlington Mills buys from the Japanese. The small man like me can't market his product in a fair, equitable exchange. People on this block are losing their jobs. It's a tragedy.

The easing of racial tensions across the nation allowed the middle classes to focus on the spread of economic privation and uncertainty. A moderate Jewish Democrat, a merchant with a great fear of crime in the streets, returned to his political moorings. Convinced that "the Republicans are out for big money," he described a temporary dulling of his liberal awareness. "I used to be a fanatic liberal, but then I became a deep conservative during the 1960s, but now I would say I am a liberal conservative. The black people made me into a terrible conservative, a reactionary. The black was encroaching, I feared him, the militance of his actions scared me. I shrank from it. I became conservative in my thoughts about what to do in race relations. But I've swung back now, with the relaxation of militance in racial problems."

One melancholy craftsman, laid off in the mid-1970s downswing of the housing industry, refused to accept work at wages below his skilled status. His wife winced as she told of his dispirited mood. "He won't take a three-dollar-an-hour job. He's been a plumber for eighteen years, and his father was a plumber too. He's afraid and he's lost his confidence." The man compared the frenzy of the 1960s and his present hard times with the apparent simplicity of the 1950s. "There were values back then. It was black and white, with no grays, you knew the side you were on." The Bensonhurst of his youth, where he hung out with his buddies, "was a different kind of society then. I still see those guys. I have happy memories of fun. I loved rock and roll, and went to see Little Richard at the Brooklyn Paramount. People were dancing in the aisles."

But in the 1960s, "John and Bobby Kennedy were killed, and the violence and assassinations took over from the rational approach. I thought society was coming apart." The civil rights movement, with its threats to job and home, and later Vietnam pushed him and his workmates hard to the right. As he told it, the shift was a momentary response to unsettling distractions, which induced many class-conscious workers to vote for business-oriented Republicans who ministered to the social and racial fears of bewildered Middle Americans. "We forgot our places a few years ago, you see. I mean we weren't like the old guys, the Depression plumbers. We were making ten dollars an hour, and we bought houses and Cadillacs, and we had it good. But then the hippies were cursing and the blacks were threatening everything we had. We forgot we were workers and voted against our interests."

The economic climate of the 1970s was a graphic reminder, and many of his friends pulled back hard from the Republicans in 1976. "All my friends in their thirties, their ideas are changing. We're all disenchanted now, we're finding ourselves down, just working to pay the bills. The inflation makes you feel you're shoveling shit against the tide. You're losing things you had as a kid. We're losing our homes and our Cadillacs." He echoed the feelings of many in Canarsie as they looked at the frenzied decade behind them and the new uncertainties ahead. "We're just trying to find a place for ourselves in this crazy world."

The contest between Jimmy Carter and the incumbent Gerald Ford took place against that backdrop of worry. The cues given by the candidates were as diffuse as the issues were novel. Unlike Nixon, Ford was a Republican without a sharp ideological persona. Nor did Carter, masking ideological diffuseness with appeals to goodness and renewal, offer an easily classifiable identity. As a result, the electorate was left floating, unfocused.[12] As the campaign progressed, suspicions grew that Carter lacked backbone and that he waffled on issues. Conservative activists in Canarsie became convinced that he would not stand up to liberals and big spenders, despite the fiscal conservatism of his program. "Carter was saying different things to different people, but I thought he'd give it all away to the minorities."

Many Old Canarsie Italians thought Nixon had been railroaded, but Ford's pardon of Nixon did not sit well with others. And Ford had rebuffed New York City at the lowest ebb of its fiscal crisis. The *New York Post*'s famous banner headline had read, "Ford to City: Drop Dead New York." An occasional voter leaving the polls in 1976 grumbled about the pardon, but Italians and Jews, conservatives and liberals alike, complained about Ford's affront to the city. "I voted for Carter," recalled one Catholic messenger. "I didn't go for that 'Drop Dead New York' business."

Jewish nervousness about Carter's southern Baptist culture offset the fears that Ford was prejudiced against New Yorkers. Carter's preachy affirmations of moral renewal did not jibe with the sardonic style of provincial Italians, and they prompted more explicit worries among Jews. "I hear Carter," one Jewish progressive confessed, "and I see the lynch mob." Or as a New Dealer put it, "I couldn't stand his smile, but I was really afraid he'd have a revival meeting on the White House lawn, and his mother would be out there shaking the tambourine."

The pressures of economic crisis, of moral revitalization, and of party loyalty yielded a Democratic victory. In the absence of a populist-style right-wing alternative, the Republican vote plunged in the Italian precincts toward its Goldwater nadir; Carter squeaked by with a shade more than 50 percent of the vote. The Democrats' bounce-back in Jewish Canarsie was just as striking. Carter returned the Jewish vote to its Humphrey levels of between 74 and 85 percent.

Did Jimmy Carter reassemble a once-proud Democratic majority? Perhaps the semblance of familiarity is misleading. In some elections pressing wants and ideological preferences are driven underground. In others, hitherto latent considerations of class, of ethnicity, of morality, and a host of other concerns that vary in their enduring significance, are brought into the open. Carter's disavowal of classical New Deal themes warns against overinterpreting the return of ethnic Democrats to their ancestral moorings.

In truth, the Democrats were living off a mortgaged and ever fickle loyalty. In 1976 Jewish Democratic support nationally remained below its customary levels. And Italians had not suddenly forsaken their responsiveness to conservative Republican nationalists or their partisan mutability. As New Right theories have long maintained, a conventional Republican like Ford reactivates lower-middle-class suspicions of Republicans as the party of big business and the country club set. Only right-wing "populists" in the Wallace/Agnew/Reagan mold could excite the Catholic grassroots. Given the pall of Watergate, the floundering economy, and Ford's "Drop Dead New York" message, Canarsie Jews and Italians fell back on the inertia of old partisan loyalties and patterns. The true signature of the election was the halting, even grudging mood in which Canarsians voted.

The meaning of the election was self-contained, a temporary response to the corruption and uncertainties of the preceding years. The odd milieu and new issues imposed something novel on top of the New Deal axis and the 1960s alignments. Carter's winning coalition, Gary Orren observed, "was composed of something old, something borrowed, and something new."[13]

A strange interlude, the 1976 election continued a pattern of drift that had become apparent in a succession of short-term, four-year electoral partnerships lacking the cohesion to last even to the next election: not a rolling realignment, then, or a nostalgic restoration, but something closer to a roller coaster: up one year, down the next. Waiting and seeing, partially cast adrift from their old electoral moorings, the voters of Canarsie were in a holding pattern.

The Carter victory was a redemptive time-out from Democratic decline, but revivalism is only a stopgap. Even if voters are willing to trust stirring moralism or intimations of freshness, the ability of an incumbent president to use rhetoric to cover gaps in performance is decidedly limited. The 1980 election would vividly demonstrate the limits of revitalization.

Election Day, 1980

"Carter said in 1976, 'Trust me, trust me, trust me.' So I trusted Carter, and I got screwed."

I left Canarsie during the summer of 1977. It has been a little more than two years since I have spent much time in the neighborhood. I have made only brief visits, and now, a week before the presidential election, I feel a sense of strangeness. Back in a community I spent much time in, but never was of, I am reminded of all the self-denial and prohibitions that are the lot of the ethnographer. Gradually that feeling fades as I greet old friends and confidants. I begin to detect an odd dynamic at work, as I hear wives interrupt their husbands' digressions with "Jon doesn't need to hear about that. He only has a little time now, he has to finish his research." Some Canarsians in a small way have made the research their own.

Canarsie looks pretty much the same, but there are some minor changes: a Russian Jewish restaurant, sign of the growing population of recent Jewish emigrés from the Soviet Union; more taxicabs parked on the street, apparently owned by new Israeli residents; and a few storefront-type synagogues, patronized by the increasing numbers of black-coated, full-bearded ultra-Orthodox Jews. An elected official describes the changing character of the residents. "When I first came here twenty years ago, there were lots of dentists, podiatrists, and teachers. But they've all moved. And we've had a decline in the number of lawyers in the Jefferson Club. The new people are different. They are more right-wing, in part because of crime inside of Canarsie, but also because they are the kinds of people who tend to be more right-wing."

The most striking change is the rising number of black home owners and tenants in the blocks of Canarsie across from the Breukelen Houses. In spite of the efforts to regulate or halt the pace of this change, the predominant attitude among white Canarsians is one of resigned acceptance. An Italian PTA leader puts it like this.

"The race issue is way down in Canarsie. People just aren't panicking like before. You were here when if a black bought a house in some areas, they would have been bombed." A Jewish official seconds her thoughts. "A black bought a house in the Venus Diner area. Seven years ago a black buying there would have been threatened. But the money market has prevented a stampede. If there was a place to go, the people wouldn't accept it, but they can't move laterally." It is a perverse irony that the ferocious interest rates have had one benign result: the conditions for an integrated Canarsie. Maybe, just maybe, Canarsians will put aside their panic and discover the possibility of a stable, integrated community.

The absence of any strong rightist challenge to the Jefferson Club symbolizes this era of outward racial calm, as does the change in outlook of a once ardent right-wing activist. Still a conservative, he has marked his move to the suburbs with a shift to the Republican party, but his talk has a different tone now:

Back in Canarsie, I would have seen the black man as "The blacks are taking over," but here I look at him with more compassion. My perspective has changed. Never having lived out of Brooklyn, I was never exposed to the wonderful black people I know out here. It was like Jews and Southerners. But now I understand that the important thing is class, not race. It's definitely a class thing. In Brooklyn we were dealing with people who were invading, but here, if a black man can buy, then he's on my socioeconomic level. The odds of panic are less out here. It's very basic. Most Canarsians don't have the security of money or the security of safety. So you think to yourself, am I safe in the streets? Do I have the dollars to leave?

The political mood of the community is different from the uncertainty that was evident just before the 1976 election. Now the mood is one of anger, sharply focused on President Carter. A Canarsie rabbi tells me, "There's even more anti-Carter sentiment out there than there was anti-McGovern sentiment in 1972." He is speaking mainly of Jews, but the Italians feel much the same. In 1976 many Canarsians gambled on Carter's pious rhetoric, his invitation to trust, but now, four years later, it is time to settle scores. As one Italian puts it, "Carter said in 1976, 'Trust me, trust me, trust me.' So I trusted Carter, and I got screwed."

For months the Italian Republicans have sensed the chance for a big victory. At last, one of them tells me, the conservative revolution of 1972, stalled by Watergate, is coming to fruition. The four-year Carter interregnum has validated only the fears, not the hopes, of Jews and Italians. In the week before the election, all I hear people talking about are the Iranian crisis and the economic situation, which Reagan has skillfully dramatized with his "misery index."

The seizure of the American embassy in Tehran has given form to all the diffuse anxieties Canarsians feel about national decline in the post-Vietnam era. A leader in the Jewish Community Council observes, "As Jews, we know what it means to be hostages. We have been hostages since day one. The Jewish people in Canarsie feel sympathy for the hostages, they feel the United States should have done more for them. It's partly their Holocaust mentality: trust nobody but God. Why the deals? Why the delay? Why no action? The government could have solved this two days into the Iranian crisis."

Carter's failure to liberate the hostages has underscored the dangers of misty-eyed proclamations of universal human rights. Many residents, not bellicose jingoists but patriots concerned about global blackmail and anarchy, have concluded that the risks of nationalist toughness are trifling compared to those of craven equivocation. It is not that they want militaristic adventurism all around the globe, but they will heed more carefully the kind of arguments offered by this Italian Republican in Canarsie:

> I am not an isolationist but a realist. Reagan deals with the world as it is, not as he would like it to be, but Carter lives in a make-believe world. He created the hostage situation in Iran by his vacillation and weakness. The result is that any country seeking redress sees us as a paper tiger. We should never have let the shah fall. We should have sustained him by clandestine methods. The U.S. is naive, we have a puritanical background, we act as if we lived in a great big church. But we need to play by our adversaries' rules. I could care less that the shah was a puppet dictatorship! He may be a son of a bitch, but at least he's *our* son of a bitch. We have to worry about the United States first. It's great to be altruistic and religious, but we're not here for a religious crusade for human rights throughout the world.

Local Reaganites have another reason for confidence in their candidate's victory. Notwithstanding the Camp David agreement between Egypt and Israel, many Canarsie Jews view the Carter years as a string of betrayals of Israel's security: Billy Carter's anti-Zionist pronouncements and flirtation with the Libyans, Andrew Young's seeming to cozy up to the Palestine Liberation Organization, the sale of F-15 jets to Saudi Arabia. The administration's failure to veto the condemnation of Israel in the United Nations in March 1980 was the ultimate insult. For months now, according to an Italian Republican leader, the signs have all been there in the taxi stands, around newsstands, in the delis, in the little and not so little shuls: "Reagan is going to do incredibly well in the Jewish community. He's maybe even going to get a majority this time. That vote in the United Nations was the final straw." Teddy Kennedy's drubbing of Carter in the June primary was hardly an endorsement for a resurrected liberalism: "They were getting even for Israel." The Flatbush-Midwood Board of Rabbis has formally endorsed Reagan. And now, as election day approaches, the rabbis are saying from the pulpits, go out and punish Carter, Reagan will stand firm for Israel.

The local Democrats are as nervous as the Republicans are eager. They bear the burden of a dismal economy, an unpopular president they never fully supported, the humiliation of Tehran. The Jefferson Democrats have to distance themselves from the incumbent. Their literature and oratory, barely mentioning Carter, stress party loyalty and local accomplishments. In a Canarsie synagogue a few days before the election, on Candidates' Night, the Republican and Conservative challenger to Assemblyman Stanley Fink, Peter Tinvervia, lets loose with a rousing stump speech that goes something like this: we have to do something about these animals who kill. If you want to uphold the sanctity of the lives the criminals take, then take the lives of the criminals. There is a rustling of disapproval in the audience when he complains, "The government is telling us who [meaning blacks] we have to live with and work with!"

The unvarnished New Right pitch is all wrong for this respectable crowd. The synagogue is Fink territory, Democratic territory, and above all, the territory of their favorite *mensch,* Councilman Herbert Berman—"That's our Herbie." Berman's task is to give these classical New Deal Democrats a reason to vote for Carter. That will not be easy. A state senator from Flatbush tries the cool, pragmatic approach, reminding them of the benefits that flow into the locale because of the Democratic party. Berman, however, goes for their guts, decrying the fundamentalist Christians and hard-core rightwingers who have flocked to the Reagan candidacy. "The Moral Majority infuriates me; they want to turn this into a country just for

Christians!" He continues in this visceral fashion, taking the congregation on a brief tour of history, emphasing that since Israel's birth the Democrats have been there for Israel, don't forsake the party now, do not fall for Reagan's play for the Jewish vote. His audience may love Berman, but the defensiveness of the Democrats on the dais attests to their vulnerability. The baiting of a young, smartly dressed Jewish Reaganite—"Hey, what are you doing with Reagan? You're not a WASP, but you dress like one. The Republicans aren't our kind of people"—symbolizes the widening chasm in the Jewish community. The Democrats are in trouble.

Election day morning is overcast, full of ominous hints of drizzle. There is a portentous feel to the day, inspired by the possibility of the impossible: the imminent victory, not of a Republican nor even of a conservative Republican, but of a true conservative ideologue who wishes to alter the course of American politics and culture. Of the fifteen people I talk to in the first hour of voting, just three own up to a vote for Carter, and even they have nary a kind word to say about the president. An Italian man summarizes the force of revitalization gone awry that will shape voting across the nation today. "I just don't trust Carter. I voted last time on trust, and look where it got me." He details the shambles of the economy, then turns to foreign policy. "Carter is not aggressive enough. The whole world shits on the United States, and we do nothing about it. We need to get our prestige back."

Dissent from the anti-Carter refrain comes mainly from Jews. Even then, it's a weak and occasional voice. Elderly Jews, New Deal Democrats to the core, will not forsake the party. The liberal Jews preface their comments with a telling adverb—"Unfortunately, I voted for Carter"—and then proceed to name a host of fears about Reagan. "I have no other choice. Reagan is against the right to abortion and the Equal Rights Amendment. But a woman is entitled to control her own body!"

A small number of old-style progressives and younger, educated liberals defect to Anderson as an alternative to a half-hearted endorsement of the incumbent. For one Jewish woman, Carter means vacillation in foreign affairs and unreliable support for Israel, while Reagan means retrograde moralism and militarism. "He's allied with the right-to-life people, and they scare the hell out of me. They would impose censorship on our personal freedom. They would try to spread their 'Thou Shalt Nots' onto the entire citizenry."

These are not dominant tendencies; the Anderson vote will be paltry, the Carter vote uninspired. Indeed, the disaffection with Carter is so great that some Democratic loyalists who resisted Nixon in 1972 are voting for Reagan this time out, like the Jewish schoolteacher who explains, "Reagan has more backbone than Carter. They made a fool out of the United States in Iran. We need to take a firm stance. We are not mice. It's like the Cuba missile crisis. Sometimes you have to say, 'You do this, or else.' "

Anger over Carter's handling of the hostage taking is pervasive. Curiously enough, the last-minute release of the hostages does not redound to his benefit. Now that they are coming home, the suppressed rage, damped down by the need to rally around the president, can be vented. Some residents vowed not to vote, so disgusted were they with the choice between a weak-kneed Carter and a reactionary Reagan. They remain at home on election day, watching the release of the hostages on TV, and their anger mounts. That growing wish to avenge dishonor propels them out of the house to pull the lever for Reagan. Despite the rain, despite the kids crying in the car at curbside, they are so mad they want to stay and talk and berate Carter.

As the polls close, the rain is beating down steadily; it has become a gloomy night. Back at the Jefferson Democratic clubhouse, the mood is equally dark. The regulars have a supreme feel for the electorate, and that street sense, along with the network reporting of exit polls, has been telling them all day that the Democrats will lose. But now the precinct captains are calling in from the polls, relaying the precise count fresh from the machines. Canarsie does not stand apart from the emerging national picture.

In the Italian precincts Reagan is victorious. Although he does not repeat the Republican rout of 1972, he takes between 60 and 65 percent of the vote, midway between the Nixon high of eight years before and the Ford total of the last election. In another sign of the "post-1960s" character of the election, Reagan receives 5 percent of the vote on the Conservative party line, only half of Nixon's 1972 Conservative showing. Meanwhile, subtracting Anderson's showing of 4 percent leaves Carter with a third of the vote, not quite as low as McGovern received in 1972, but a sizable drop from 1976. All in all, Reagan runs about 10 percent more strongly in Italian Old Canarsie than in the nation as a whole.

Reagan does not achieve that landslide in Jewish precincts. The tenants of the heavily Jewish middle-income Bayview Homes project give Carter majorities of between 60 and 66 percent, but that vote is inflated by the sizable number of blacks and Puerto Ricans living there. Elsewhere in Canarsie, Carter wins majorities or pluralities in eight precincts, but four of them lie in the areas of expanding black presence around the Breukelen Houses. In the other four precincts, predominantly Jewish, Carter does not even top the 50 percent mark. Reagan takes between 50 and 60 percent of the vote in the overwhelming majority of Jewish precincts, with Anderson receiving about 6 percent. Despite the decline in the racial and cultural polarization that marked the 1972 presidential election, Reagan does better than Nixon did in 1972.

Even so, the Jews of Canarsie lag behind the Orthodox Jews— fierce Zionists and adversaries of the Soviet Union—of Brooklyn's Borough Park. And as Milton Himmelfarb noted, though most Jews fear the Moral Majority, the Orthodox accept the fundamentalist Christian premise that the Supreme Court's forbidding of school prayer is tantamount to secular humanism. "For Borough Park it is *'avodah zarah,'* paganism." Borough Park Jews give Carter 21 percent, Reagan a whopping 76 percent, and Anderson, who once initiated a constitutional amendment to make America a Christian country, only 3 percent of the vote. In contrast, the affluent Jews of Great Neck, Long Island, give Carter 55 percent, Reagan only 32 percent, and Anderson a hefty 13 percent of the vote.[14] Canarsie Jews fall right between New Right Orthodox and "limousine liberal" Jews.

What are the voters saying on this rainy November day? What will the consequences be? Next to me in the Jefferson Club, wincing as the networks spit out their projections of defeat for senators McGovern, Bayh, and Church, one Democratic stalwart is disconsolate. A restorationist president like Reagan is one thing. A vigilant Democratic congress will hem him in. But the Senate is now utterly changed, he observes, and mad-dog reactionaries like Hatch, Garn, and Helms give the Republican majority its exultant edge. Envisioning an era of nuclear saber rattling and religious crusading, the Jewish Democrat groans.

An Italian conservative foresees a different future. The election fulfills his hope for an end to his exile in the America he loves so much; as he has barked many times, those who do not love it should leave it. Drinking coffee with him in his kitchen a few days after the election, I am struck by his optimism. For most of the years I have known him, he has been afflicted with a grumpy, often bitter sense of betrayal, most of it generated by the racial crisis. Today he describes a wondrous vision of possibilities. "I see a bright future for America. I see sixteen years ahead, not of right-wing extremism but of a moderate ideology that will bring the country flowing. Jobs will be created. In the next year or two, unemployment will be down to 5 percent. Look at the stock market! It's thriving. And we will have a lot more respect as our defense builds up. We will get the respect we had years ago. Let's wake up the sleeping giant."

Canarsians may have disagreed about the meaning of the Reagan victory, but its national significance soon became clear. Jeff Greenfield convincingly argued that beneath the usual hype of the media, the tendency to reduce political argument to the spectacle of a horse race, the 1980 election was a contest of ideas. But what ideas were clashing for supremacy? Reagan offered an articulate conservatism, yet Carter did not parry with an equally articulate progressivism. Little in the national polls confirmed the idea of a mandate, and the midterm congressional elections dispelled any parallels with 1934, further undercutting the claim of realignment. Kevin Phillips glimpsed the free-floating populist streak in the Reagan victory, obscured somewhat by the overtones of conventional business conservatism. If Reaganism fails, he wrote, it might be succeeded by something potentially sinister, an "apple-pie authoritarianism" of the lower middle classes. His analogy between contemporary America and Weimar Germany seems a bit strained; still, Phillips captured the diverse and ambiguous impulses contained within the Reagan victory.[15] The disappointed New Right shock troops of the Reagan revolution have been left to plead "Let Reagan be Reagan" and to talk of forming a Populist Party.

In Canarsie, virtually all the voters squawked loudly about Carter's drawbacks; few voiced enthusiasm for the abstract Reagan agenda. At most, they were making ideologically diffuse demands for leadership, for economic renewal, for resolve in foreign policy, none of which is tantamount to global adventurism or social Darwinism. The Jewish vote was even less a mandate for pure conservatism. As their own words so eloquently testify, dislike of Carter was uppermost in their minds on election day, and that animosity was grounded in distinct ethnic preoccupations. Reflecting on the question "Are Jews Becoming Republican," Milton Himmelfarb concluded, "More than anything else, foreign and military affairs determined Jewish voting in 1980." The decline in Carter's Jewish support between 1976 and 1980 provides ample evidence of his "Jewish problem." Nationwide Reagan received 6.4 percent more votes than Ford had; in Canarsie Jewish precincts the Democratic vote declined by 20 to 36 percent. In only fourteen congressional districts did the Democratic vote decline by more than 15 percent between 1976 and 1980. Almost all of those districts, as Walter Dean Burnham pointed out, had exceptional grievances against Carter: South Floridans swamped by the Cuban refugees, Sagebrush rebels in the Rocky Mountain states upset about MX missiles in their back yards, midwestern farmers angry over the impact on farm exports of the post-Afghanistan boycott of the USSR, and Jews in New York and Pennsylvania furious over the UN's condemnation of Israel.[16] The "aberrant" quality of Jewish Republicanism was also evident in the great majorities that Canarsie Jews gave the liberal candidate for the Senate, Elizabeth Holtzman.

Were the people of Canarsie inevitably lost to the Democrats in those recent presidential elections? Given the culture and the character of Canarsians and the opposed interests of blacks and whites, perhaps a liberal majority was never a real possibility there. No matter what reformers did, white Brooklyn might never have enlisted in their cause. That verdict highlights the undeniable constraints on reform, but it glides too quickly over the contribution liberals made to their own political demise. At a certain point in recent decades, the forces of conscience no longer claimed as their own those famous average Americans who helped form the New Deal coalition. For a variety of reasons, liberals did not sympathize with the suffering of people like those who live in Canarsie: white discontent was morally less compelling than the black plight; a significant portion of white resistance stemmed from ugly racism; and some liberals held stereotypes that denied the progressive strains in Middle America. As a result, left-liberals, and to an important extent the Democratic party, yielded up the center of the political spectrum and the social pyramid. Brooklyn Jews and Italians did not simply bolt from the Democratic party, they were also driven out of it.

Canarsians rallied to conservatives and Republicans in part became liberals and Democrats did not address their immediate practical and spiritual concerns. Left-liberals could have appropriated themes like the debilities of welfare dependency, the need for law and order, and the danger of appeasement in foreign affairs and placed them in a larger framework of analysis and ideology. Instead, left-liberalism hardened into an orthodoxy of the privileged classes.

Was it surprising that many Brooklyn Jews and Italians looked elsewhere for champions?

As with other forms of reaction, Canarsians' political reactions depended as much on external circumstances as on their internal psychological or cultural needs. The partisan swings of the Italian vote over the decades remind us that the Italians of Canarsie were not ordained to move toward the right. Similarly, the lament of a Jewish civic leader after the 1980 election, "We Jews too can become hard like conservatives," underscores the fact that nothing obliges Jews to feel kindly toward the less fortunate. Ultimately, whether communities like Canarsie realize their capacities for avarice or for generosity will turn significantly on the acts of the leaders who either court them or mock them.

Notes

Introduction: Danger and Dispossession

1. *New York Times,* Oct. 25, 1972, p. 46; Nov. 4, 1972, p. 32.
2. Wilfred Cartey, *Red Rain* (New York: Emerson Hall, 1977), p. 41.
3. *New York Post,* Nov. 2, 1972, p. 12.
4. Garry Wills offers a variant of the embourgeoisement thesis in *Nixon Agonistes: The Crisis of the Self-Made Man* (Boston: Houghton Mifflin, 1970). See especially pp. 216–231. Seymour Martin Lipset and Earl Raab apply the concept of status preservatism to the most extreme forms of white backlash in *The Politics of Unreason: Right-Wing Extremism in America, 1790–1977,* 2nd ed. (Chicago: University of Chicago Press, 1978), chaps. 9–13. David Apter provides a general model of the "technically obsolescent" middle strata in advanced capitalist societies in *Choice and the Politics of Allocation* (New Haven: Yale University Press, 1971). Walter Dean Burnham's analysis of right-wing working-class populism in *Critical Elections and the Mainsprings of American Politics* (New York: W.W. Norton, 1970), fuses Apter's tripartite stratification schema and Lipset's appraisal of middle-class "extremism of the center" in *Political Man: The Social Bases of Politics,* 2nd ed. (Baltimore: Johns Hopkins University Press, 1981), chap. 5. Edna Bonacich grounds black and white rivalry in labor market conflicts. See her "Advanced Capitalism and Black-White Relations in the United States: A Split Labor Market Interpretation," *American Sociological Review* 41 (February 1976): 34–51. William Julius Wilson emphasizes the increasing centrality of racial conflicts that originate in the sphere of consumption rather than of production in *The Declining Significance of Race* (Chicago: University of Chicago Press, 1978).
5. Godfrey Hodgson, *America in Our Time* (Garden City, N.Y.: Doubleday, 1976), p. 363.
6. Jonathan Schell, *The Time of Illusion* (New York: Random House, 1975), p. 124.
7. Marshall Frady, *Wallace* (New York: New American Library, 1968), p. 11; Vachel Lindsay, "Bryan," quoted in Peter Viereck, "The Revolt Against the Elite," in *The Radical Right,* ed. Daniel Bell (New York: Doubleday, 1963), p. 162.

1. The Fenced Land

1. See William Wallace Tooker, *Indian Names of Places in the Borough of Brooklyn* (New York: Francis P. Harper, 1901).

2. Federal Writers' Project of the Works Progress Administration in New York City, *New York City Guide* (New York: Random House, 1939), p. 501.

3. *New York Herald Tribune,* Oct. 20, 1963.

4. Alfred Kazin, *A Walker in the City* (New York: Harcourt, Brace & World, 1951), p. 10.

5. William Phillips, "A French Lady on the Dark Continent," *Commentary* (July 1953), p. 26. I thank Dennis Wrong and William Phillips for calling my attention to the reference.

6. *New York Herald Tribune,* Oct. 20, 1963.

7. Samuel Lubell, *The Future of American Politics,* 2nd ed. (Garden City, New York: Doubleday, 1956), pp. 71, 74–75.

8. Julian Pitt-Rivers, *The Fate of Schechem, or the Politics of Sex: Essays in the Anthropology of the Mediterranean* (Cambridge: Cambridge University Press, 1977), p. 117.

9. Jimmy Breslin, *New York Times,* Aug. 20, 1975, p. 37.

10. Frances Fox Piven, "The Urban Crisis: Who Got What and Why," in Richard A. Cloward and Frances Fox Piven, *The Politics of Turmoil: Poverty, Race, and the Urban Crisis* (New York: Vintage Books, 1975), p. 318.

11. Kazin, *Walker in the City,* pp. 139–140.

12. Barry Gottehrer, *The Mayor's Man* (Garden City, N.Y.: Doubleday, 1975), pp. 26–27.

13. Kazin, *Walker in the City,* pp. 34–35.

2. Ethnic Traditions

1. The accounts in this chapter of Jewish and Italian culture are quite generalized, offering ideal types that underscore prominent features of each group. Yet even provincial cultures are not perfectly integrated unities. They encompass and generate the most varied and dissonant sentiments. What we deem a people's essential nature is a construction imposed by our capacity to synthesize, to selectively highlight, and to suppress aberrations. Such ideal types fill our need for an indisputable identity in ourselves and in others, but this gain in parsimony comes at the expense of attention to a culture's diversity. The depth and breadth of a group's cultural repertoire will vary with the complexity of its environment and the heterogeneity of the people it encounters. Both the Jewish and the Italian culture had other, less dominant tendencies, shadow traditions, and sources of counterpoint.

2. Richard Hamilton observes, in *Class and Politics in the United States* (New York: John Wiley & Sons, 1972), p. 406: "There are distinctive patterns of training that are independent of class and that are shared across the class lines but within the major socioreligious communities."

3. John Higham, *Strangers in the Land: Patterns of American Nativ-*

ism, 1860–1925 (New Brunswick, N.J.: Rutgers University Press, 1955), p. 169.

4. Nathan Glazer and Daniel P. Moynihan, *Beyond the Melting Pot: The Negroes, Puerto Ricans, Jews, Italians, and Irish of New York City* (Cambridge, Mass.: MIT Press, 1963), p. 187.

5. For astute discussions of Italian-American personalism, see Herbert Gans, *The Urban Villagers* (Glencoe, Ill.: Free Press, 1962), pp. 174–203; and Gerald Suttles, *The Social Order of the Slum: Ethnicity and Territory in the Inner City* (Chicago: University of Chicago Press, 1968), chap. 6.

6. The lack of cohesiveness in the Italian community parallels the failure of Italian nationalism or a centralized state to restrain the fractiousness of southern Italian life. As John S. MacDonald and Leatrice D. MacDonald observed, "The social structure of this section of Italy is still extremely individualistic and familistic. Bonds outside the nuclear family household were almost exclusively along a dyadic patron-client axis. Corporate organizations are still inconceivable in most of Southern Italy." "Chain Migration, Ethnic Neighborhood Formation, and Social Networks," in *An Urban World,* ed. Charles Tilly (Boston: Little, Brown, 1974), p. 231.

7. Luigi Barzini, *The Italians* (New York: Atheneum, 1964), pp. 190, 192.

8. Richard Gambino, *Blood of My Blood: The Dilemma of the Italian-Americans* (Garden City, N.Y.: Doubleday, 1974), p. 20; Glazer and Moynihan, *Beyond the Melting Pot,* p. 197.

9. See Suttles's analysis of the ethos of "the natural man" in *Social Order of the Slum,* pp. 103–105, and Gambino's analysis of the decidedly nonpuritanical nature of southern Italian views of sexuality in *Blood of My Blood,* pp. 167–193.

10. Joseph Lopreato, *Italian Americans* (New York: Random House, 1970), p. 56.

11. Virginia Yans-McLaughlin, *Family and Community: Italian Immigrants in Buffalo* (Ithica, N.Y.: Cornell University Press, 1977), p. 134. Rudolf Vecoli, countering a more traditional emphasis on the fatalism and resignation of southern Italians, noted, "The contadini were ambitious to advance the material and social position of their families . . . The south Italians viewed a sojourn in America as a means to acquire capital with which to purchase land, provide dowries for their daughters, and assist their sons to enter business or the professions." "*Contadini* in Chicago: A Critique of *The Uprooted," Journal of American History* 51 (December 1964): 407.

12. Gambino, *Blood of My Blood,* p. 225. The lower educational aspirations of Italian Americans do not show that tradition *caused* the diminished attainments of Italians. They reflect the intricate collusion of class, schooling, and culture in reproducing low social position.

13. The sources of that mistake are twofold. On the one hand, overly idealistic discussions of ethnicity fail to properly control for the operation of other variables. On the other hand, analysts fail to ground observable ethnic differences in the environmental contexts in which they are formed. See Jane Schneider's analysis of Mediterranean familism as a response to fea-

tures of ecology, the mode of production, and the formation of state institutions. "Of Vigilance and Virgins: Honor, Shame, and Access to Resources in
Mediterranean Societies," *Ethnology* 10 (1971): 1–24.

14. For an analysis of class culture that transcends the subjectivism
characteristic of many discussions of "values," see Randall Collins, *Conflict
Sociology: Toward an Explanatory Science* (New York: Academic Press,
1975), pp. 61–90.

15. Gambino, *Blood of My Blood,* pp. 293–295; and Andrew Greeley,
Ethnicity in the United States: A Preliminary Reconnaissance (New York:
John Wiley & Sons, 1974), pp. 121–156.

16. For a social organizational model that goes beyond the cultural analysis of literature in the "civic culture" vein, see William Gamson's analysis
of the situational factors that shape trust orientations. *Power and Discontent* (Homewood, Ill.: Dorsey Press, 1968), chaps. 3, 8.

17. Gambino, *Blood of My Blood,* p. 7.

18. Glazer and Moynihan, *Beyond the Melting Pot,* pp. 214–215.

19. Samuel Lubell, *The Future of American Politics,* 2nd ed. (Garden
City, N.Y.: Doubleday, 1956). p. 78. A brief word about my estimates of ethnic voting and registration is in order at this juncture. I have derived my
descriptions of Italian partisanship from the 1920 Kings County enrollment
lists. The twenty-sixth and twenty-seventh election precincts were predominantly Italian; moreover, the distinctiveness of the last names of Italian
voters makes it possible to differentiate their registration from that of other
groups. In reporting ethnic voting patterns in later elections, I do not give
the precincts and assembly districts because over the years the identifying
numbers and boundaries changed dramatically. Despite the changes, many
precincts retained a distinct ethnic character, so that it is possible to talk
about the Jewish or the Italian vote.

20. Alvin W. Gouldner, "The Norm of Reciprocity: A Preliminary Statement," *American Sociological Review* 25 (1960): 161–179.

21. Glazer and Moynihan, *Beyond the Melting Pot,* p. 214.

22. Kevin Phillips, *The Emerging Republican Majority* (New York:
Doubleday, 1970), p. 155; Seymour Martin Lipset, "Three Decades of the
Radical Right: Coughlinites, McCarthyites, and Birchers," in *The Radical
Right,* ed. Daniel Bell (New York: Doubleday, 1962), p. 406.

23. The vision of McCarthyism as a form of "lunatic populist revenge"
achieves its most classical statement in Peter Viereck, "The Revolt Against
the Elite," in Bell, *Radical Right.* The argument that popular McCarthyism was essentially a less restrained form of anticommunism is put forth by
Michael Paul Rogin in *The Intellectuals and McCarthy: The Radical Specter* (Cambridge, Mass.: MIT Press, 1967), p. 244: "Lack of sophistication on
matters of civil liberties can have as dangerous consequences as the political
mobilization of status anxieties and anti-industrial hostilities."

24. Phillips, *Emerging Republican Majority,* p. 164.

25. Leo Baeck, *The Essence of Judaism* (New York: Schocken Books,
1948), p. 214; Walter Kaufmann, *Nietzsche: Philosopher, Psychologist, An-
tichrist* (New York: Random House, 1968), pp. 372, 371.

26. Glazer and Moynihan, *Beyond the Melting Pot,* p. 197; Irving Howe, *World of Our Fathers* (New York: Harcourt, Brace Jovanovich, 1976), p. 12.

27. Howe, *World of Our Fathers,* p. 251.

28. Howe, *World of Our Fathers,* chap. 7; Glazer and Moynihan, *Beyond the Melting Pot,* pp. 155-159; Compare the Jewish quest for education with the picture of Italian educational attitudes in *Blood of My Blood,* pp. 223-234; and Thomas Kessner, *The Golden Door: Italian and Jewish Immigrant Mobility in New York City, 1880-1915* (New York: Oxford University Press, 1977), pp. 93-99.

29. Arthur Liebman notes the tendency to confound ethnic and other factors in explaining "Jewish" traits or behavior. "The relatively few Jews in the United States generally means that studies not purposely generating a sizable Jewish sample wind up with a very small absolute number of Jews. The size factor, then, precludes virtually any form of multivariate analysis or the introduction of sociological 'controls.' " *Jews and the Left* (New York: John Wiley & Sons, 1979), p. 616 n16.

30. Quoted in Howe, *World of Our Fathers,* p. 182. "Suspicion of the physical, fear of hurt, anxiety over the sheer 'pointlessness' of play," notes Howe, "went deep into the recesses of the Jewish psyche."

31. Baeck, *Essence of Judaism,* pp. 197-198.

32. Milton Himmelfarb, "Jewish Class Conflict," in *Overcoming Middle-Class Rage,* ed. Murray Friedman (Philadelphia: Westminster Press, 1970), p. 209.

33. Terry Nicholas Clark, "The Irish Ethic and the Spirit of Patronage," *Ethnicity* 4 (December 1975): 305-359.

34. The importance of networks of transmission suggests the limits of overly cultural explanations of Jewish radicalism. Arthur Liebman demonstrates that Jewish radicalism was the historical and organizational expression of a class-based subculture born of the response of Jewish workers to specific economic experiences. See Liebman, *Jews and the Left.*

35. Lipset, "Three Decades of the Radical Right," p. 406.

36. The literature on Jewish liberalism is too vast to summarize here, but see Richard Hamilton, *Class and Politics in the United States* (New York: John Wiley & Sons, 1972), pp. 406-408; and Greeley, *Ethnicity in the United States,* chaps. 9-10.

37. For a good discussion of the factors that account for fluctuations in the strength of the Jewish Democratic vote in any particular election, see William Schneider, Michael D. Berman, and Mark Schultz, "Bloc Voting Reconsidered: 'Is There a Jewish Vote?' " *Ethnicity* 1 (1974): 345-392.

3. Vulnerable Places

1. The fear of living close to minorities epitomizes the power of "potential concepts," or the family of "variables defined in such a way that influence of an area is a declining function of distance and an increasing function

of a spatially distributed variable. The exact form of the functions, of course, depends on how one thinks the causal force in fact operates." Arthur L. Stinchcombe, *Constructing Social Theories* (New York: Harcourt, Brace & World, 1968), p. 230.

2. Julian Pitt-Rivers, *The People of the Sierra,* 2nd ed. (Chicago, University of Chicago Press, 1971), p. 30.

3. Ibid., pp. 29–30.

4. To put the dynamic somewhat more formally, the greater the differentiation of the black population by class, the greater should be the white tendency to distinguish among "elements," or categories, of blacks, especially during the transition to a more differentiated population of blacks. In this sense the detail and elaboration of classificatory schemes are responses to features of environment and social organization. If there has been a growth in the tendency of Canarsians to make such distinctions, and the ethnographic approach does not produce the kind of data necessary to test that claim with rigor, then to some extent Canarsians' social constructions may be "signs" of the underlying class differentiation of the black population described by William Julius Wilson in *The Declining Significance of Race* (Chicago: University of Chicago Press, 1978).

5. Mark Zborowski and Elizabeth Herzog, *Life Is with People: The Jewish Little-Town of Eastern Europe* (New York: International Universities Press, 1952), p. 148.

6. Of course, support for this version of ghetto culture was not unanimous. Of a sample of New York City's Jewish population in the late 1960s, 43 percent believed that blacks had less ambition than did whites; while 51 percent of Brooklyn Jews agreed with that invidious opinion, only 23 percent of Manhattan Jews harbored such an opinion. Louis Harris and Bert Swanson, *Black-Jewish Relations in New York City* (New York: Praeger, 1970), p. 103.

7. Kai Erikson, *Wayward Puritans: A Study in the Sociology of Deviance* (New York: John Wiley & Sons, 1966), p. 13.

8. Rosabeth Moss Kanter discusses the cognitive effects of numbers and proportions in *Men and Women of the Corporation* (New York: Basic Books, 1977), chap. 8.

9. Richard Gambino, *Blood of My Blood: The Dilemma of the Italian-Americans* (Garden City, N.Y.: Doubleday, 1974), p. 148.

10. Ibid., p. 31.

11. Canarsians grasped some of the essentials of immigrant history. Virginia Yans-McLaughlin observes that the Italian migrants to Buffalo "made a relatively smooth transition from the Old World to the New. Strain and conflict occurred certainly, but not disorganization." Furthermore, she contends, "The nuclear family pattern proved extraordinarily resilient; unstable male employment, for example, rarely resulted in desertion or diminished male control . . . The extended family not only survived but actually aided the adjustment to the New World." *Family and Community: Italian Immigrants in Buffalo, 1880–1930* (Ithaca, N.Y.: Cornell University Press, 1977), p. 18.

12.   Perhaps the ordinary epithets of "pigs" and "animals" that were sometimes applied to ghetto blacks embodied this opposition between society and nature. Animals are unrestrained by the rules that in humans surround natural processes with a thicket of rituals and taboos, that embody their capacity to master nature. "Nor like the coyote," wrote Robert Zingg, "does the Tarahumara avail himself of meat torn from a scarcely dead animal and eaten raw. The Tarahumara interposes between his meat and his hunger a cultural system of cooking." The irony in this vision of ghetto blacks as "uncooked" escaped Canarsians' most resentful residents. It could be said that whites who hurled nasty epithets were indecorous like pigs; those whose feelings toward blacks were tinged with their own violence and sexuality were raw and needed cooking. See Robert M. Zingg, "The Genuine and the Spurious Values in Tarahumara Culture," *American Anthropologist* 44, no. 1 (1942): 82.

13.   Garry Wills, *Nixon Agonistes: The Crisis of the Self-Made Man* (Boston: Houghton Mifflin, 1970), pp. 51-52.

14.   James Q. Wilson observed of the increase in criminality that began in the early 1960s, "Crime soared. It did not just increase a little; it rose at a faster rate and to higher levels than at any time since the 1930s and, in some categories, to higher levels than any experienced in this century." *Thinking about Crime* (New York: Basic Books, 1975), p. 4.

15.   David W. Abbott, Louis H. Gold, and Edward T. Rogowsky, *Police, Politics, and Race: The New York City Referendum on Civilian Review* (Cambridge, Mass.: American Jewish Committee and the Joint Center for Urban Studies of the Massachusetts Institute of Technology and Harvard University, 1969), p. 36; Harris and Swanson, *Black-Jewish Relations,* p. 47.

16.   See the social organizational analysis of the factors that prevent or elicit racial conflict in Gerald Suttles, *The Social Order of the Slum: Ethnicity and Territory in the Inner City* (Chicago: University of Chicago Press, 1968), and *The Social Construction of Communities* (Chicago: University of Chicago Press, 1972).

17.   Andrew Greeley delineates the independent contributions of exposure to threat and of social contact to negative white feelings about blacks in *Ethnicity in the United States* (New York: John Wiley & Sons, 1974), chap. 10.

18.   Greil Marcus, *Mystery Train: Images of America in Rock 'n' Roll Music* (New York: E. P. Dutton, 1976), p. 76.

19.   Erving Goffman, *Relations in Public* (New York: Basic Books, 1971), p. 284.

20.   Abbott, Gold, and Rogowsky, *Police, Politics, and Race,* p. 16.

21.   Ibid., p. 33.

22.   Andrew Hacker, *New Yorkers: A Profile of an American Metropolis* (New York: Mason/Charter, 1975), pp. 53-54.

23.   Milton Himmelfarb, "Jewish Class Conflict," in *Overcoming Middle-Class Rage,* ed. Murray Friedman (Philadelphia: Westminster Press, 1971), p. 205.

24. The struggle to preserve the stability of ethnic neighborhoods is to some extent a form of class conflict, if we take our lead from Max Weber's definition of class struggle as rivalries that arise from conflicts of interest, actual or potential, generated by any market situation, including markets of credit, labor, and consumption. John Rex developed the Weberian analysis in his study of race relations in Britain, noting "the differential distribution of housing opportunity which leads to the emergence of what I have called a system of housing class conflict." Like the divisions of the job market, the divisions of the housing market are not simple. Markets may be closed, open, or segmented. "Significant divisions [are] opened up within the various classes, as a result of the conflicting interests which arise from their different housing situations." *Race, Colonialism, and the City* (London: Routledge and Kegan Paul, 1973), pp. 3–4.

25. See Andrew Greeley's summary of the data on Catholic prejudice in *The American Catholic: A Social Portrait* (New York: Basic Books, 1977), chap. 6; and Richard Hamilton, *Class and Politics in the United States* (New York: John Wiley & Sons, 1972), chap. 11.

26. " 'Free from strangers' is again the motif," writes Nathan Glazer. "Even today in Italian neighborhoods strangers are conspicuous. A non-Italian newcomer encounters a tight net of friendship and blood relation that binds the community and excludes outsiders until they are found to be 'all right.' " Nathan Glazer and Daniel Patrick Moynihan, *Beyond the Melting Pot: The Negroes, Puerto Ricans, Jews, Italians, and Irish of New York City* (Cambridge, Mass.: MIT Press, 1963), p. 189.

27. Harris and Swanson, *Black-Jewish Relations,* pp. 94; 55.

28. *New York Post,* Nov. 7, 1972, p. 44.

29. Kai Erikson describes a more extreme form of the same dynamic in *Everything in Its Path* (New York: Simon and Schuster, 1976).

30. See Mark Granovetter, "Threshold Models of Collective Behavior," *American Journal of Sociology* 83, no. 6 (1978): 1420–1443.

31. Erving Goffman, *Relations in Public,* p. 283.

32. Unknown buyers belong to the larger category of strangers about whom perfect information is not available. "Ignorance, incompetence, and variations in expectations mean that social relations are perilous and have judgmental consequence. It would seem essential that people have some way of reading each other's likely responses so as to estimate the risks they are taking." Suttles, *Social Construction of Communities,* p. 157.

33. Marc Fried, "Grieving for a Lost Home," in *The Urban Condition,* ed. Leonard Duhl (New York: Basic Books, 1963), p. 151.

34. Morris Janowitz, *The Community Press in an Urban Setting: The Social Elements of Urbanism,* 2nd ed. (Chicago: University of Chicago Press, 1952); Albert J. Hunter and Gerald D. Suttles, "The Expanding Community of Limited Liability," in Suttles, *Social Construction of Communities,* pp. 44–82.

35. Gaston Bachelard, *The Poetics of Space* (New York: Orion Press, 1964), p. 56.

36. Ibid., pp. 4–5.

4. The Lost People

1. Garry Wills, *Nixon Agonistes: The Crisis of the Self-Made Man* (Boston: Houghton Mifflin, 1970), p. 310.

2. Quoted in Richard Hofstadter, *The American Political Tradition* (New York: Alfred Knopf, 1948), p. 190.

3. Seymour Martin Lipset and Earl Raab, *The Politics of Unreason: Right-Wing Extremism in America, 1790–1977,* 2nd ed. (Chicago: University of Chicago Press, 1978), chaps. 9–13; Nathan Glazer and Daniel Patrick Moynihan, *Beyond the Melting Pot: The Negroes, Puerto Ricans, Jews, Italians, and Irish of New York City,* 2nd ed. (Cambridge, Mass.: MIT Press, 1970), pp. vii–lxxvi.

4. Threats to social and to physical place have much in common. In both cases the magnitude of threat, the resilience of the threatened, and the availability of techniques of fending off threat all determine susceptibility. As with threats to personal safety or housing capital, information affects the estimate of social threat. Risk-aversive people tend to calculate personal danger in terms of best guesses about the future and the lessons of the past. They reckon imaginary and potential threats as well as actual ones. The distribution of knowledge, both truth and distortion, depends on a person's social contacts and experience, the reach and robustness of their social networks, and the historical frames that guide attention and perception. Yet no simple calibration between a person's objective level of resources and their subjective feeling of risk may be found. Suffering is a relative state that varies with the headiness of aspirations, the social groups one considers worthy of emulation or avoidance, and the expectations one uses to determine a benchmark of entitlement.

5. The perception and the actuality of fiscal privation vary a good deal from nation to nation and also, within nations, from region to region. Harold Wilensky describes the intensity of the welfare backlash in New York and California in *The Welfare State and Equality: Structural and Ideological Roots of Public Expenditures* (Berkeley: University of California Press, 1975), pp. 32–34.

6. Some social theorists argue that racial antagonism provides a distraction, urged on by corporate leaders, from genuine conflicts of interest between workers and owners. Racist passion appears in that telling as a charade, a surrogate for "real" grievances. A number of things are wrong with this analysis. First, it underplays the reality of authentic conflicts of interest between white and black workers. Second, it suggests a zero-sum vision of workers' discontents, as if anger at minorities and at the privileged crowd each other out. In contrast, many studies show that sensitivity to black threat often flourishes among those with a pungent feeling of working-class consciousness. Third, while pragmatic self-defense is often a product of ethnic rivalry, protectionism is not equivalent to racism. Ethnic competition does not always erode norms of fair play, even among the unemployed; some workers show both fear for their jobs and a commitment to hiring on the basis of merit. A particular structure of antagonistic interests does not

produce a specific subjective meaning. Fourth, the role played by government in Philadelphia plans and affirmative action suggests the importance of the state in creating antagonism rather than of a simple dynamic of market competition. Fifth, racial fear in Canarsie stemmed more from conflict in the sphere of consumption, whether private or public, than in the sphere of production, a point that is elaborated throughout this chapter. The true meaning of the struggle over work lay elsewhere than in the primacy of labor conflict in framing race relations. It dramatized the relationship between susceptibility to threat and racial tension in the social sphere that was similar to the relationship between security and resentment in the physical sphere.

7. Michael Paul Rogin, *The Intellectuals and McCarthy: The Radical Specter* (Cambridge: MIT Press, 1967), p. 47; Seymour Martin Lipset, *Political Man: The Social Basis of Politics,* expanded ed. (Baltimore: Johns Hopkins University Press, 1981), pp. 127–183. For a more recent application of the concept of center extremism to Ronald Reagan's 1980 coalition, see Kevin Phillips, *Post-Conservative America: People, Politics, and Ideology in a Time of Crisis* (New York: Random House, 1982).

8. Frustration-aggression theory is predicated on a simple hydraulic logic that suggests a more mechanistic conception of human behavior than is warranted. A number of conditions must be fulfilled before frustration is translated into right-wing reaction. Above all, political entrepreneurs must exploit those feelings of deprivation, and their ability to do so depends on the larger constellation of political forces and opportunities in the polity at large.

9. William J. Wilson, *The Declining Significance of Race: Blacks and Changing American Institutions* (Chicago: University of Chicago Press, 1979), especially chaps. 1, 6, and 7. The figures on the proportion of families on welfare are drawn from Egon Mayer, *From Suburb to Shtetl: The Jews of Boro Park* (Philadelphia: Temple University Press, 1979). Charles Morris observes, "During Lindsay's first term the welfare caseload more than doubled and spending jumped from $400 million to $1 billion, with about a third of the total coming from city resources; and because welfare clients were also eligible for the new Medicaid program, total welfare and welfare-related health costs rose to more than $2 billion." *The Cost of Good Intentions: New York City and the Liberal Experiment, 1960–1975* (New York: W.W. Norton, 1980), p. 71.

10. Morris, *Cost of Good Intentions,* pp. 70, 71. The militance of minority demands naturally drew attention to the pressures emanating from the poor. They formed a vivid figure against the ground of timeless privileges exercised by the powerful, to which Canarsians reconciled themselves with resignation as much as with any ideological enthusiasm. The invisibility of organized producer groups protects them from public scrutiny. See Frances Fox Piven, "The Urban Crisis: Who Got What and Why," in Richard A. Cloward and Frances Fox Piven, *The Politics of Turmoil: Poverty, Race, and the Urban Crisis* (New York: Vintage Books, 1975), p. 324.

11. Alan Erlichman, "Chairman's Message," *Citizens News,* Fall 1975, p. 4.

12. In James O'Connor's words, "The fiscal crisis will continue to divide all those groups and strata that today fight in dismal isolation for a greater share of the budget or for a smaller share of the tax burden." *The Fiscal Crisis of the State* (New York: St. Martin's Press, 1973), p. 255.

13. See Seymour Martin Lipset and Earl Raab, "The Message of Proposition 13," *Commentary* 66 (September 1978).

14. Among the many New York City Jews who favored cuts in welfare levels in the late 1960s, the two statements endorsed most often were "get them off welfare, should be working" and "create jobs for people on welfare." Louis Harris and Bert Swanson, *Black-Jewish Relations in New York City* (New York: Praeger, 1970), p. 169.

15. Wills, *Nixon Agonistes,* p. 537; Marcel Mauss, *The Gift: Forms and Functions of Exchange in Archaic Societies* (New York: Norton, 1967), p. 40; Virginia Yans-McLaughlin, *Family and Community: Italian Immigrants in Buffalo, 1880-1930* (Ithaca, N.Y.: Cornell University Press, 1977), p. 134.

16. Alan Erlichman, "Chairman's Column," *Citizens News,* Fall 1975, p. 4.

17. James Scott, *The Moral Economy of the Peasant: Rebellion and Subsistance in Southeast Asia* (New Haven: Yale University Press, 1976), p. 29.

18. Dismay over rioting was not inherently racist or conservative. Richard Hamilton notes, "The adoption of the Black Power rhetoric had the added consequence of frightening large numbers of persons who were either in sympathy or, at minimum, favorably inclined to the goals of integration and improving the conditions of the blacks." *Class and Politics in the United States* (New York: John Wiley & Sons, 1972), p. 551.

19. Wills, *Nixon Agonistes,* p. 519.

20. This analysis of the effects of nonprofit backlash groups fuses insights drawn from J. A. Barnes, "Networks and Political Process," in *Social Networks in Urban Situations: Analyses of Personal Relationships in Central African Towns,* ed. J. Clyde Mitchell (Manchester, Eng.: University of Manchester Press, 1969), chap. 2; Arthur Stinchcombe, "Space-related Concepts and the Ecological Analysis of Activities," in *Constructing Social Theories* (New York: Harcourt, Brace & World, 1968), pp. 265-293; and Mark Granovetter, *Getting a Job: A Study of Contacts and Careers* (Cambridge, Mass.: Harvard University Press, 1974).

21. Glazer and Moynihan, *Beyond the Melting Pot,* p. lv.

22. Roland Barthes, *Mythologies* (New York: Hill and Wang, 1976), p. 142.

23. David W. Abbott, Louis H. Gold, and Edward T. Rogowsky, *Police, Politics, and Race: The New York City Referendum on Civilian Review* (Cambridge, Mass.: American Jewish Committee and the Joint Center for Urban Studies of the Massachusetts Institute of Technology and Har-

vard University, 1969), p. 40. Both the form—the reach, multiplexity, and density—of social networks and their content—the specific cultural lessons flowing through network channels—shaped definitions of threat, justice, and remedy.

24. Ibid., p. 40.

25. "Fatal Affliction" appeared in *Citizens News* in Spring 1974, "Unjust Justice" in December 1974, "Liberal Crunch" in Fall 1975, and "The Great American Nightmare" in Spring 1976.

26. Richard Hamilton demonstrates the endurance of sympathetic racial sentiment in the white lower middle class even during the more polarized period of the later 1960s in *Class and Politics,* pp. 130–136, 399–421.

27. The attitudinal differentiation follows naturally from the class differentiation described by Wilson in *The Declining Significance of Race,* chaps. 6–7. Lipset and Raab report a sizable black support for Proposition 13 in "Message of Proposition 13." For evidence of black rejection of racial quotas and busing, see Louis Henri Bolce III and Susan H. Gray, "Blacks, Whites, and 'Race Politics,'" *Public Interest* (Winter 1979): 61–76. In *Welfare State and Equality,* p. 34, n5, Wilensky cites a variety of studies that report significant support among lower-class blacks, as well as those in the working and middle classes, for statements like "Negroes who want to work hard can get ahead just as easily as anyone else" and "There are too many people receiving welfare who should be working."

28. The hybrid solution was a pragmatic arrangement that ensured the survival of dependent cultural groups within a plural society whose hosts were seldom joyous at the arrival of successive waves of guests. It suggested a conception of cultural equity according to which no corporate group would be penalized or glorified, at least formally. The informal character fit well with the spontaneity of interest-group liberalism, for it did not oblige the state to make rules of ethnic ranking explicit. Of course, the model departed from reality in many ways. Like informal systems of all kinds, it presumed a good deal of deference by the weak, the acceptance of substantive inequalities, and the ability of domination to mask itself as spontaneous comparative advantage. Moreover, the order that emerged from the system often came from the savvy decisions of ethnic groups to huddle together and to avoid testing the official claims of democracy. Finally, racial domination, ethnic monopoly, and nepotism belied the translation of the norm into reality. See the discussion of the ambiguous American ethnic regime in Nathan Glazer, *Affirmative Discriminations: Ethnic Inequality and Public Policy* (New York: Basic Books, 1975).

29. Erving Goffman, "On Face Work," in *Interaction Ritual: Essays on Face-to-Face Behavior* (Garden City, N.Y.: Doubleday, 1967), pp. 16–17.

30. Frank Parkin, *Class Inequality and Political Order: Social Stratification in Capitalist and Communist Societies* (New York: Praeger, 1971), p. 90. Donald Horowitz concludes, "Ascriptive identity is heavily contextual. It embraces multiple levels or tiers, and it changes with the environment." "Ethnic Identity," in *Ethnicity,* ed. Nathan Glazer and Daniel

Patrick Moynihan (Cambridge, Mass.: Harvard University Press, 1975), p. 118.

31. Harris and Swanson, *Black-Jewish Relations,* pp. 122-130, 231; William Schneider, Michael D. Berman, and Mark Schultz, "Bloc Voting Reconsidered: 'Is There a Jewish Vote?' " *Ethnicity* 1 (1974): 363-365, 373; Richard Reeves, "Splitting the Jewish Vote," *New York Magazine* (June 18, 1973), pp. 57-63.

32. From the report by the Personnel Committee of the Ocean Hill-Brownsville Governing Board, reported in Diane Ravitch, *The Great School Wars: New York City, 1805-1973* (New York: Basic Books, 1974), p. 353.

33. Quoted in Ravitch, *Great School Wars,* p. 358.

34. Many vernacular and scholarly treatments of racism neglect the importance of the cultural, rather than the psychological, reproduction of racist statements. See the brief critique of such strain imagery of discontent in Jonathan Rieder, "The Social Organization of Vengeance," in *Toward a General Theory of Social Control,* vol. 1: *Fundamentals,* ed. Donald Black (New York: Academic Press, 1984).

35. Jean-Paul Sartre, *Saint Genet: Actor and Martyr* (New York: George Braziller, 1963), pp. 17-48.

36. The emphasis on the negotiated, socially constructed nature of ethnic identity poses the danger of subjectivism. But social constructions are often adaptive responses to concrete dilemmas in the environment or to specific features of social organization. For a non-idealized vision of the construction process, see Fredrik Barth, ed., *Ethnic Groups and Boundaries: The Social Organization of Culture Difference* (Boston: Little, Brown, 1969).

37. Milton Himmelfarb, "Jewish Class Conflict," in *Overcoming Middle-Class Rage,* ed. Murray Friedman (Philadelphia: Westminster Press, 1971), p. 210.

38. Ibid., p. 208.

39. Luigi Barzini, *The Italians* (New York: Atheneum, 1964), pp. 164, 165.

40. Martin Luther King, Jr., "Letter From Birmingham Jail," April 16, 1963, reprinted as chap. 5 in *Why We Can't Wait* (New York: Harper & Row, 1963), p. 78.

5. The Reverence Is Gone

1. James Sundquist, *Dynamics of the Party System: Alignment and Realignment of Political Parties in the United States* (Washington, D.C.: Brookings Institute, 1973), p. 324; Clifford Geertz, *The Interpretation of Cultures* (New York: Basic Books, 1973), p. 312.

2. Seymour Martin Lipset and Earl Raab, *The Politics of Unreason: Right-Wing Extremism in America, 1790-1977,* 2nd ed. (Chicago: University of Chicago Press, 1978), p. 118.

3. George Marsden refutes one tendency in liberal scholarship to brand Protestant fundamentalism as a paranoid recoil from modernity. "[Ernest] Sandeen showed that the roots of fundamentalism lay much deeper than the social upheavals of the 1920's ... Therefore it was possible to regard fundamentalism as 'an authentic conservative tradition,' rather than the temporary aberration or 'pseudo-conservative' departure that Hofstadter and other historians had seen." *Fundamentalism and American Culture: The Shaping of Twentieth-Century Evangelicalism 1870–1925* (New York: Oxford University Press, 1980), p. 200. R. Stephen Warner analyzes many of the flaws in conventional treatments of so-called "antimodern" movements in "Theoretical Barriers to the Understanding of Evangelical Christianity," *Sociological Analysis* 40 (1979): 1–9.

4. Guy Swanson, *Religion and Regime: A Sociological Account of the Reformation* (Ann Arbor: University of Michigan Press, 1967), pp. 12, 261.

5. The allegory of the grid resembles Mary Douglas's portrait of "grid societies" in which "the public system of rights and duties equips each man with a full identity ... In this society piety is the order of the day." *Natural Symbols: Explorations in Cosmology* (New York: Vintage Books, 1973), pp. 86–87.

6. Clifford Geertz developed the theoretical stance that informs this analysis. See "Ritual and Social Change: A Javanese Example," in Geertz, *Interpretation of Cultures,* pp. 142–170.

7. See Randall Collin's conceptualization of the provincialism of working-class culture in *Conflict Sociology: Toward an Explanatory Science* (New York: Academic Press, 1975), pp. 75–79.

8. The Levi quote appears in Richard Gambino, *Blood of My Blood: The Dilemma of the Italian-Americans* (Garden City, N.Y.: Doubleday, 1974), p. 9; Irving Howe, *World of Our Fathers* (New York: Harcourt, Brace Jovanovich, 1976), p. 13.

9. Nathan Glazer and Daniel P. Moynihan, *Beyond the Melting Pot: The Negroes, Puerto Ricans, Jews, Italians, and Irish of New York City* (Cambridge, Mass.: MIT Press, 1963), p. 197.

10. M. Kent Jennings, *The Student-Parent Socialization Study* (Ann Arbor: University of Michigan Inter-University Consortium for Political Research, 1971).

11. The traditionalist lament is firmly grounded in the insight offered by sociologist Alvin Gouldner: "With declining paternal authority and growing maternal influence, the autonomy strivings of children are now more difficult to repress; hostility and rebellion against paternal authority can become more overt. There is, correspondingly, increasing difficulty experienced by paternal authority in imposing and reproducing its social values and political ideologies in their children." Moreover, as the education system separates from the family system, teachers, experts, and therapists, committed to quite different moral and speech codes, become "an important source of values among students divergent from those of their families." *The Future of Intellectuals and the Rise of the New Class* (New York: Seabury Press, 1979), pp. 2–3.

12. Mary Douglas, *Purity and Danger: An Analysis of Pollution and Taboo* (New York: Frederick Praeger, 1966), p. 53.

13. The women of Canarsie had many grievances in need of redress, both in the marketplace and at home. Ministering to their needs would have obliged a shift in feminist rhetoric and demeanor and, above all, the acceptance of the authenticity of ethnic values of family life. Such a change would have helped reduce injustice in private and public life, solve the practical problems of less affluent women, and validate the pluralism of American culture. Feminists, however, often saw the equivocations of Middle American women as "false consciousness," as the slavish internalization of the aggressor's identity, or as a flight into reassuring obedience. Misogynist and right-wing propaganda has encouraged a distortive focus on the extreme fringes of the women's movement in order to discredit it. And the sensationalist framing of the movement by the mass media has undoubtedly reinforced the same perceptual narrowing. But it is also true that organized and not-so-organized feminism, in its radical feminist, gay, and liberal upper-middle-class incarnations, failed to develop an opening to millions of women who were sympathetic to many of its concerns. The cues of dress and rhetoric emanating from the leadership hardened the intuition that the women's movement embodied values alien to average Americans. For Canarsie women to have embraced feminism would have meant the slavish internalization of a pedagogy that equally did violence to their prized values.

14. Ironically, this man did not perceive how closely the modern family he criticized conforms to one common pattern of sexual division of labor among Eastern European Jews: the wife active in the marketplace supporting her husband's religious studies.

15. On the importance of familistic ideology in differentiating participants and nonparticipants in rightist moral crusades, see the summary of the literature in Clarence Y. H. Lo, "Countermovements and Conservative Movements in the Contemporary U.S.," in *Annual Review of Sociology,* vol. 8, ed. Ralph Turner and James F. Short, Jr. (Palo Alto, Calif.: Annual Reviews, 1982).

16. The principles that explain the mobilization of participants in class-based social movements also explain the mobilization of the culturally aggrieved. The reach of the networks of moral organizations and exposure to the moral suasion and ideological viewpoints disseminated through those channels enhance susceptibility to recruitment by social movements.

17. Andrew Greeley, "Catholics and Coalition: Where Should They Go?" in *Emerging Coalitions in American Politics,* ed. Seymour Martin Lipset (San Francisco: Institute for Contemporary Studies, 1978), p. 288.

18. Quoted in Jonathan Schell, *The Time of Illusion* (New York: Random House, 1975), p. 37.

19. Andrew Greeley, *The American Catholic: A Social Portrait* (New York: Basic Books, 1977), chap. 5; *New York Post,* Sept. 16, 1970.

20. The effect of the popular lore was to restrict the breadth of discourse about the legitimate means and ends of the state in the global arena and to undermine rational criticism of authority. The tolerance of the antidemo-

cratic acts of national leaders does not mean that authority no longer required legitimation. Rather, it points to the existence of an ethnic system of justification at odds with concepts of constitutional legitimacy. When provincial Italians glided from the realm of the family to that of the country and back again, they provided openings to national leaders who manipulated and personified the homier virtues of honor in order to recoup legitimacy for policies carried out in an illegitimate manner.

21. The conceptions of legitimacy held by Jewish leaders came from three sources. First, the more educated backgrounds of the Jefferson Democratic leaders, their circle of friends and neighbors, and the most active part of their constituency opened them to learning that diverged from that circulating in Italian leadership circles. Second, Jewish traditions of tolerance, fear of mass binges, and reverence for rights contributed to antipathy toward bellicose nationalism. Third, partisan traditions opened Jewish leaders to liberal internationalist versions of anticommunism and progressive sympathy for movements of national self-determination.

22. *Canarsie Courier,* undated, unpaginated clipping from early 1970s.

23. *Canarsie Courier,* May 1971, undated clipping.

24. *Canarsie Courier,* May 1971, undated clipping.

25. *Canarsie Courier,* Oct. 18, 1973.

26. Edward Shils, *The Torment of Secrecy* (Glencoe, Ill.: Free Press, 1956), pp. 12–13.

27. Lionel Trilling, *Sincerity and Authenticity* (Cambridge, Mass.: Harvard University Press, 1972), p. 161.

6. Striking Back

1. My general approach to reaction has been influenced by resource mobilization theory, especially as formulated in the work of William Gamson. See his *The Strategy of Social Protest* (Homewood, Ill.: Dorsey Press, 1975). Gamson underlines the impact of situational factors that elicit or thwart a particular method of influence, but he does not stress the culturally learned, sanctioned, and transmitted status of those influence orientations. Combat-readiness, however, is shaped by normative dispositions as well as by organizational resources.

2. Alan Erlichman, "Chairman's Message," *Citizens News,* Spring 1974, pp. 6–7.

3. Albert O. Hirschman, *Exit, Voice and Loyalty: Responses to Decline in Firms, Organizations, and States* (Cambridge, Mass.: Harvard University Press, 1970), p. 30.

4. Seymour Martin Lipset and Earl Raab offer an excellent discussion of the irrational responses to ethnic dispossession in *The Politics of Unreason: Right-Wing Extremism in America, 1790–1977,* 2nd ed. (Chicago: University of Chicago Press, 1978).

5. These items come from the scale of political vengeance devised by William Gamson and James McEvoy. The scale does not adequately sepa-

rate the dynamic of *ressentiment* from vengeance, and the authors do not attempt to distinguish various sentiments in the family of hostility and revenge. Moreover, the strictly psychological interpretation of the Wallace vote fails as a general model. See James McEvoy, *Radicals or Conservatives: The Contemporary American Right* (Chicago: Rand-McNally, 1971), pp. 136–138.

6. Quoted in E. Adamson Hoebel, "Song Duels among the Eskimo," in *Law and Warfare: Studies in the Anthropology of Conflict,* ed. Paul Bohannan (New York: Natural History Press, 1967), p. 256.

7. Max Scheler, *Ressentiment* (New York: Free Press, 1961), p. 50.

8. Gerald Suttles describes the early warning systems of "para-linguistic modes of communication which help us sort people according to our own concerns with safety and success" in *The Social Construction of Communities* (Chicago: University of Chicago Press, 1972), p. 158. The employer faced with a queue of job-seekers who screens applicants using racial or sexual stereotypes based on past experience or folk knowledge offers an analogous example of the way stereotypes reduce uncertainty. If two sexes or races differ statistically in talent or experience, then even if the origins of the disparities lie in a brutal history of exploitation, it is still the case that exclusion of the less endowed sexual or racial pool may serve as an economic device for decision making. The gain in efficiency may be perceived as outweighing the cost of all the missed virtuosos inevitably neglected by such rough-hewn classifications. Pedestrians, like employers, have incentives to make those predictions, for they do not face accountability for their actions except in the most abstract, deferred manner. Above all, they do not pay for the injury to the pride and opportunity of the excluded.

9. Erving Goffman, *Relations in Public* (New York: Basic Books, 1971), pp. 239–240.

10. Suttles, in *Social Construction of Communities,* chaps. 5–8, provides a social organizational explanation of informal police systems.

11. Michel Foucault, *Discipline and Punish* (New York: Random House, 1979), p. 74.

12. David W. Abbott, Louis H. Gold, and Edward T. Rogowsky, *Police, Politics, and Race: The New York City Referendum on Civilian Review* (Cambridge, Mass.: The American Jewish Committee and the Joint Center for Urban Studies of the Massachusetts Institute of Technology and Harvard University, 1969), p. 33.

13. Ibid., p. 29.

14. Albert J. Reiss, *The Police and the Public* (New Haven: Yale University Press, 1971), p. 140.

15. Pyschological measures of authoritarianism do "not seem to be a very important discriminating variable in the sample from which these data were collected." McEvoy, *Radicals or Conservatives,* p. 140.

16. Malcolm X, *The Autobiography of Malcolm X* (New York: Grove Press, 1966), p. 366.

17. Gerald Suttles pinpoints the impact of social schedules and traffic patterns on racial discord in *The Social Order of the Slum: Ethnicity and*

Territory in the Inner City (Chicago: University of Chicago Press, 1968); in my more general analysis of the impact of the social environment on disputing, I have drawn insights from Howard E. Aldrich, *Organizations and Environments* (Englewood Cliffs, N.J.: Prentice-Hall, 1979).

18. Alter F. Landesman, *Brownsville: The Birth, Development and Passing of a Jewish Community in New York* (New York: Bloch, 1971), p. 59.

19. Confusion over the scope of responsibility and level of liability characterizes disputes in primitive societies. As Sally Falk Moore has written, the ambiguity of conflict situations involving disputants from two different collectivities permits the larger collectivities to negotiate the outcome. They may interpret the dyadic fight as expressive of larger cleavages between the two groups, thereby collectivizing liability, or they may seek to insulate the two groups from any reverberations of the fight, thereby individualizing liability. Sally Falk Moore, "Legal Liability and Evolutionary Interpretation," in *The Allocation of Responsibility,* ed. Max Gluckman (Manchester, Eng.: Manchester University Press, 1972).

20. The process through which bridges were built between working-class youths and adult champions parallels the dynamic involved in using contacts to find an "in" in the job market. Mark Granovetter has noted that the people most motivated to help a job seeker, like family members, are often the least well placed to do so, compared to helpers more removed in social distance. Intimates tend to share the same pool of contacts. As a result, overlap comes at the expense of an expansive reach to a rich and diverse group of ties. See *Getting a Job: A Study of Contacts and Careers* (Cambridge, Mass.: Harvard University Press, 1974), chaps. 2–3, 5, and 7. Plebeian brokers in the local community lacked the connections enjoyed by respectable elites in the Jefferson Democratic Club, whose tentacles of influence stretched to far-away places and institutions. But conservative activists in Canarsie were more motivated to help the youngsters settle their disputes in the physical fashion the youths wanted to vindicate their honor. As compensation for their lack of access to influentials, the rightist patrons imposed fewer restraints on the mode of settling the dispute.

21. Rafael Karsten, *Blood Revenge, War, and Victory Feasts among the Jibaro Indians of Eastern Equador,* Bureau of American Ethnology, bulletin no. 79. (Washington, D.C.: Government Printing Office, 1923), p. 11.

22. Quoted in Gaia Servadio, *Mafioso: A History of the Mafia from Its Origins to the Present* (New York: Stein and Day, 1976), p. 69.

23. Max Weber, *Economy and Society: An Outline of Interpretive Sociology* (1922; Eng. trans., New York: Bedminster Press, 1968), pp. 205–206.

24. Harvey Molotch describes a similar dynamic in Chicago. Classical human ecology theory, he writes, attributes competition among land users to "reasons relating to topography, centrality, or proximity to another strategic element. But the South Shore case suggests that there is a second system of competition—a competition among already situated land users to attract to their area a kind of land user who is seen as one who will enhance the condition of the shared territory." The result of the pressures of human

ecology and social prejudice is that "the scarce commodities in the competitive process are middle-class whites." *Managed Integration: Dilemmas of Doing Good in the City* (Berkeley: University of California Press, 1972), p. 215.

25. *Canarsie Courier,* Sept. 11, 1980, p. 21. The ability of the Jewish community to pyramid resources of influence was critical. Because the Jews had organizational rather than network ties, all they needed to patch into the system was a point man at an organizational node who could bridge two organizational systems. The linkage expanded the degrees of freedom with which they acted on the environment.

26. For a more elaborate analysis of the resort to vengeance, see Jonathan Rieder, "The Social Organization of Vengeance," in *Toward a General Theory of Social Control,* vol. 1: *Fundamentals,* ed. Donald Black (New York: Academic Press, 1984).

27. William Gamson, *The Strategy of Social Protest* (Homewood, Ill.: Dorsey Press, 1975), pp. 87–88.

28. Weber, *Economy and Society,* p. 363.

7. Canarsie Schools for Canarsie Children

1. This mimetic process offers a cultural version of the economic advantages reaped by latecomers in the product cycle. All the start-up costs, the slow evolution of recipes for action, the tortuous process of testing and modifying prescribed ways of acting on the world can be skipped.

2. I did not arrive in Canarsie until two years after the busing crisis. The interviews are retrospective accounts of the key participants. In addition, I have relied heavily on the accounts in the *New York Times, New York Daily News, Long Island Press, New York Post,* and *Village Voice.*

3. Iver Peterson, "Canarsie: The Anatomy of a School Crisis," *Race Relations Reporter,* January 1973, p. 9.

4. Quoted in Lois Tendler, "The Canarsie Integration Crisis," unpublished paper, Harvard College, 1976.

5. *New Yorker,* Nov. 11, 1972, p. 169.

6. *New York Daily News,* Oct. 27, 1972, p. 2.

7. *New York Times,* Oct. 30, 1972, p. 25; *New York Daily News,* Oct. 30, 1972, p. 57.

8. *New York Times,* Oct. 31, 1972, p. 33.

9. Wilfred Cartey, *Red Rain* (New York: Emerson Hall, 1977), p. 41.

10. *Long Island Press,* Nov. 2, 1972, p. 12.

11. *New York Post,* Nov. 2, 1972, p. 3.

12. Ibid.

13. *Canarsie Courier,* Nov. 9, 1972, p. 1.

14. *New York Daily News,* Dec. 12, 1972, unpaginated clipping.

15. *Village Voice,* Mar. 8, 1973, pp. 20, 34.

16. A deflationary spiral characterized much of the participatory efforts of social activists during the 1960s. Low trust and high fate control led to

284 Notes to Pages 213-232

vigorous attempts to influence authorities, which were followed by disenchantment and withdrawal. See the summary of the causes and effects of participation in Sidney Verba and Norman H. Nie, *Participation in America: Political Democracy and Social Equality* (New York: Harper & Row, 1972).

17. William Gamson, *Power and Discontent* (Homewood, Ill.: Dorsey Press, 1968), p. 169.

18. Marvin Harris, *Cows, Pigs, Wars and Witches: The Riddles of Culture* (New York: Random House, 1974), pp. 172-173.

19. *New York Times,* Oct. 30, 1972, p. 25.

20. *Citizens News,* Fall 1973, p. 1.

21. I am following the general perspective developed by Mayer Zald and Roberta Ash. "Social Movement Organizations: Growth, Decay and Change," *Social Forces* (March 1966): 327-341.

22. Vacant niches do not automatically generate an appropriate organizational solution. The impediments faced by the Italian-American Civil Rights League in securing a mandate underline the limits of a notion of group formation as natural selection. Factors of cultural and political selection proved equally important.

23. *New York Times,* Nov. 5, 1972, p. 31.

24. Clifford Geertz, *The Interpretation of Cultures* (New York: Basic Books, 1973), p. 432.

25. Peterson, "Canarsie," p. 12; *New York Times,* Nov. 5, 1972, p. E9.

26. *New York Times,* Oct. 25, 1972, p. 46; Nov. 4, p. 32.

27. William Gamson, *The Strategy of Social Protest* (Homewood, Ill.: Dorsey Press, 1975), p. 139.

28. The dependence of protest acts on the larger historical milieu is described in Gamson, *Strategy of Social Protest,* pp. 110-129.

29. The broker role assumed by the Italian-American Civil Rights League betrayed an affinity with southern Italian institutions. Anton Blok writes, "As elsewhere in Sicily's interior, the control over the means of production was closely related to control over the means of violence. People were dependent upon kinsmen, friends, and powerful protectors for sheer physical survival. To right wrongs, to settle conflicts, and to solve problems of various sorts, they could hardly rely on the police and law courts ... Others less skilled in the realm of violence turned to them for mediation and protection." *The Mafia of a Sicilian Village, 1860-1960: A Study of Violent Entrepreneurs* (New York: Harper & Row, 1975), pp. 210-211.

30. Dislike of busing, like opposition to the Civilian Review Board, cut across ideological lines. More than 60 percent of a New York City Jewish sample supported "boycotts to prevent busing of black children into Canarsie schools," and the percentage of Brooklyn supporters of boycotts was undoubtedly higher. Richard Reeves, "Splitting the Jewish Vote," *New York Magazine,* June 18, 1973, p. 61.

31. Max Weber, *Economy and Society: An Outline of Interpretive Sociology* (1922; Eng. trans., New York: Bedminster Press, 1968), p. 362.

8. The Trials of Liberalism

1. Nathan Glazer and Daniel Patrick Moynihan, *Beyond the Melting Pot: The Negroes, Puerto Ricans, Jews, Italians, and Irish of New York City* (Cambridge, Mass.: MIT Press, 1963), p. 214.

2. Richard Gambino, *Blood of My Blood: The Dilemma of the Italian Americans* (Garden City, N.Y.: Doubleday, 1974), pp. 121, 122, 128.

3. Irving Howe, *World of Our Fathers* (New York: Harcourt, Brace Jovanovich, 1976), pp. 632–633.

4. *New York Times,* June 3, 1977, B2.

5. Ibid.

6. Alan Erlichman, "Chairman's Message," *Citizens News,* Fall 1975, p. 4.

7. Everett Carl Ladd, *Transformations of the American Party System: Political Coalitions from the New Deal to the 1970's* (New York: W. W. Norton, 1975).

8. Garry Wills, *Nixon Agonistes: The Crisis of the Self-Made Man* (Boston: Houghton Mifflin, 1970), pp. 34, 37.

9. Richard Scammon and Ben J. Wattenberg, *The Real Majority* (New York; Coward-McCann, 1970), p. 100.

10. For an incisive discussion of the distinctly Jewish element in Jewish voting patterns, see William Schneider, Michael D. Berman, and Mark Schultz, "Bloc Voting Reconsidered: 'Is There a Jewish Vote?' " *Ethnicity* 1 (1974): 345–392.

11. Samuel Lubell, *The Future While It Happened* (New York: W. W. Norton, 1973), pp. 59–60.

12. Seymour Martin Lipset, ed., *Emerging Coalitions in American Politics* (San Francisco: Institute for Contemporary Studies, 1978), pp. 271–325.

13. Gary R. Orren, "Candidate Style and Voter Alignment in 1976," in Lipset, *Emerging Coalitions,* p. 173.

14. Milton Himmelfarb, "Are Jews Becoming Republican," *Commentary* 72 (Aug. 1981), p. 30.

15. Jeff Greenfield, *The Real Campaign: How the Media Missed the Story of the 1980 Campaign* (New York: Summit Books, 1972); Kevin P. Phillips, *Post-Conservative America: People, Politics, and Ideology in a Time of Crisis* (New York: Random House, 1982).

16. Himmelfarb, "Are Jews Becoming Republican," p. 28; Walter Dean Burnham, *The Current Crisis in American Politics* (New York: Oxford University Press, 1982), pp. 302–303.

Index

tism, 47–48, 122–124, 154, 244–245; and Israel, 47, 163–164, 248, 256–258; and commitment to civil liberties, 48–51, 81, 153–154, 160–161; political universalism of, 48–49; radical political traditions of, 49–50; and loyalty to Democratic party, 49–51, 53–54; and New Deal, 50; and view of Soviet Union, 50, 163; and moral traditionalism, 139–140; and Vietnam war, 155, 161–164; Russian, 194–195. *See also* Liberalism: Jewish; White backlash: Jewish

Kaufmann, Walter, 43
Kazin, Alfred, 14, 22–23, 25
King, Martin Luther, Jr., 130

Law and order, 67, 138, 144, 147, 167, 180–182
Levi, Carlo, 142
Liability, 63, 68–69, 91, 109–110, 120, 191–192
Liberalism: crisis of, 2–6, 9, 233–263; meanings of, 5–6, 72–73, 78–79, 107–109, 136; Jewish, 43, 53–54, 76–79, 111–112, 124–125, 129–131, 248–249
Liebman, Arthur, 269nn29, 34
Lindsay, John V., 128–129
Lindsay, Vachel, 4
Lipset, Seymour Martin, 100, 133
Lorenzoni, Giovanni, 192
Lubell, Samuel, 18, 248

Malcolm X, 182–183
Marcus, Greil, 74
Mauss, Marcel, 106
McGovern, George, 158, 241–242, 246–249
Middle class: ideology of, 1, 27–28, 35, 37, 95–100, 105, 113–114; vulnerability of, 36–37, 46–47, 96–100, 107–108, 250–252; and protectionism, 114–119, 125, 204–207, 240–241. *See also* Busing crisis; White backlash
Molotch, Harvey, 282n24
Moral breakdown, fears of, 132–167
Moral Majority, 154
Moynihan, Daniel P., 164

Nationalism, 154–166. *See also* Italians: nationalism of
Networks, social, 28, 31, 33, 46–47, 63–64, 68–69, 86–88, 110–111, 152–153, 157–158, 181, 189–190, 213–215; and information flow, 68–69, 111, 275n23, 283n25; and race riot, 183–188, 282nn19, 20
Nixon, Richard, 42, 95, 154–155, 158–159, 241–243, 246–249

Ocean Hill-Brownsville school crisis, 123–124
Orren, Gary, 253

Parkin, Frank, 122
Patriotism, 154–166
Permissiveness, attitudes toward, 132–141
Phillips, Kevin, 42, 261
Pluralism, 119–120
Politics, local, 51–54, 161–162, 233–241; New York mayoral election (1969), 128–129; state assembly Democratic primary (1976), 229–232, 237–241. *See also* Busing crisis; Civilian Review Board; Esposito, Meade; Fink, Stanley; Thomas Jefferson Democratic Club
Politics, national, 5, 241–263. *See also* Presidential elections
Predictive cues. *See* Environment, signs of danger in
Presidential elections: (1968), 242–246; (1972), 246–249; (1976), 249–254; (1980), 255–262
Procaccino, Maro, 128–129
Protest, 171–173, 203–207, 213–215. *See also* Busing crisis; White Backlash

Quondam complex, 133–134

Raab, Earl, 133
Race riot, high school, 183–193
Racial displacement, 21–26, 83–85; Canarsians' memories of, 90–94. *See also* Integration, residential
Racial dispossession, 119–128
Racism, 58–59, 63–67, 125–126
Reagan, Ronald, 5, 256–262